Atlas of the Mysterious in North America

Atlas of the Mysterious
in North America

❖ ❖ ❖ ❖ ❖ ❖ ❖ ❖ ❖ ❖ ❖

Rosemary Ellen Guiley

Atlas of the Mysterious in North America

Copyright © 1995 by Rosemary Ellen Guiley

Facts On File, Inc.
460 Park Avenue South
New York NY 10016

Library of Congress Cataloging-in-Publication Data
Guiley, Rosemary.
Atlas of the mysterious in North America / Rosemary Ellen Guiley.
p. cm.
Includes bibliographical references and index.
Contents: Power points and sacred places—Earthworks and mounds—
Stoneworks—Haunted places—Phantom and haunted ships—
Ghost lights—Water monsters—Mysterious creatures.
ISBN 0-8160-2876-1.—ISBN 0-8160-2882-6 (pbk.)
1. Folklore—North America—Maps.   2. Folklore—United States—
Maps.   I. Title
G1106.E627G8   1994   <G & M>
398.2'097'022—dc22   93-41985

Facts On File books are available at special discounts when purchased in bulk quantities for businesses, associations, institutions or sales promotions. Please call our Special Sales Department in New York at 212/683-2244 or 800/322-8755.

Printed in the United States of America

VB VC 10 9 8 7 6 5 4 3 2 1

This book is printed on acid-free paper.

For Linda Lee
soror mystica

CONTENTS

ACKNOWLEDGMENTS

This book required a great deal of compilation work, and without the help of several persons, the project would not have been possible. James G. Matlock, parapsychologist and anthropologist, was indispensable in the pulling together of the most complicated sections of the book, Power Points and Sacred Places, Earthworks and Mounds, and Stoneworks. Ron Rosenblatt, a cryptozoologist and Fortean of formidable knowledge, provided tremendous help on the Haunted Places and Mysterious Creatures sections. Likewise, tremendous help was provided by Joanne P. Austin on petroglyphs (in Stoneworks), Bigfoot (in Mysterious Creatures) and Ghost Lights, and by Doreen M. Beauregard on Water Monsters. I would also like to thank in particular Robert Michael Place for his original artwork on Bigfoot; Anastasia Wiertrzychowski for her unusual photograph inside a stone chamber at Magnetic Mine Road, New York; and Gary S. Mangiacopra, cryptozoologist, for sharing information from his files.

Finally, I would like to thank John A. Keel, Forteana's most stellar light, for his foreword. John's business card puckishly reads, "Not an authority on Anything." It invariably gets a good laugh, for John probably knows more Forteana than the rest of Forteans combined. His years of investigative research, and his wonderful books and articles, have fueled much interest in the unknown. Thanks, John, for all your help.

AUTHOR'S NOTE

North America is a land of amazing contrasts. It boasts two of the most industrialized, high-tech countries in the world—yet it also contains vast reaches of wilderness seldom penetrated by human beings. It's easy to think that the spread of civilization pushes back the darkness of the unknown, and that mysterious places and mysterious creatures are confined to the wild, remote areas. But, as numerous entries in this book show, the mysterious often can be found as close as one's own backyard. Even the continent's greatest cities—such as New York, Houston, Chicago, Toronto and Vancouver—are home to the unexplained. Despite our advances in civilization, we still live close to our primitive psychic roots. Just beyond the city or suburbs—or even within them—lie numerous portals to the Unknown. Here the rules of the mundane world are suspended, and if conditions are right, we might have an unusual encounter or experience.

In compiling this book, I have attempted to provide a survey of some of the most intriguing mysteries of North America. Much of mysterious North America is derived from the mythology, legends, folklore and sacred rites of the indigenous cultures that were here long before Europeans arrived on the scene. Native Americans gave us the continent's sacred places and power points, as well as folklore that supports the existences of mysterious creatures. Immigrants to these shores have imparted to the mix their own homeland traditions as well.

The contents are divided into eight sections. The sites within each section are numbered consecutively; sites that are in close proximity have the same number. These numbers correspond with the numbers on the map illustrations. Because of the limitations of space and a need to be as even geographically as possible, the listings in each section are not exhaustive but are selective. Nonetheless, they are more comprehensive than most guidebooks to the mysterious in North America. Readers will find a wealth of sites all around the continent.

The first three sections, Power Points and Sacred Places, Earthworks and Mounds, and Stoneworks, have to do with power of place, and concern both natural and artificial sites. According to native traditions, many of these sites are associated with supernatural phenomena, or are the abodes of spirits and gods.

With the section called Haunted Places, the book moves more into the realm of the supernatural and paranormal. Haunted Places provides a selection of sites from around the continent that reputedly are haunted by spirits, beings or ghosts. Ghost Lights discusses mysterious lights that haunt certain areas. Phantom and Mystery Ships concerns ghostly vessels that ply North American coasts and waterways.

The last two sections, Water Monsters and Mysterious Creatures, are devoted to sightings of odd, mythological, fantastical and phantom beings. Readers may be surprised to learn that North America is home to sea serpents and water monsters far more exotic than the famous Loch Ness monster of Scotland. The range of mysterious creatures that pop up regularly on the North American landscape is astonishing—winged humanoids, werewolves, cat monsters, bizarre birds, demons and more. Mysterious Creatures also includes some sightings of known but strangely displaced animals, such as kangaroos and various wild cats. A large section is devoted to Bigfoot.

In closing, I hope that this book contributes to an honored tradition established by Charles Fort (1874–1932), an American journalist who spent the latter part of his life cataloging anomalies and unexplained events and phenomena. Forteana, as such things are called by enthusiasts, has attracted a dedicated worldwide following. I hope that both Forteans and the casual reader will find this book a useful guide to uncharted territories.

—ROSEMARY ELLEN GUILEY

FOREWORD

Our little blue planet is pockmarked with areas where time and space are convoluted, where strange things seem to happen just beyond our reality and where our fallible human senses often go askew. Some of these places have baffled us for thousands of years. We speak of them with almost hushed reverence: Stonehenge, Giza, Delphi, Fatima, the Bermuda Triangle. In another era, seamen carefully marked their maps, noting, "Here there be monsters," and primitive tribes made wide circles around sacred mountains and eerily haunted deserts. Today, when an apparition appears to a fortunate (or sometimes unfortunate) human, we build a church on the spot. Or, if the apparition is in the UFO category, we might erect a hot dog stand.

In today's rank commercial world, many of these mysterious places have become tourist traps and archaeological Disneylands. Stonehenge is roped off because too many visitors were trying to carry off too many stones. The Great Pyramid is a victim of graffiti artists through the ages. When a hairy monster terrified a few people in Michigan back in the 1960s, the local Dairy Queen started selling "Monster Burgers." Roswell, New Mexico, now proudly calls itself "the flying saucer capital of the world" because a mass of paper, plastic, tinfoil and balsa wood fell on a ranch 70 miles away back in 1947. Thousands of people brave the chill mists of Scotland annually to sit on the banks of Loch Ness and wait for the sea serpent called Nessie to appear. Camera crews from tabloid television shows (they call themselves "reality shows") sit up all night in haunted houses, hoping some blob of ectoplasm will materialize and pose.

To run down and investigate these myriad mysterious places is an awesome task. Few would dare to undertake it. Even fewer would have the necessary stamina and courage. There have been many individuals who have become enthralled with a single site or a solitary mystery, however. They have formed clubs and cults and devoted all their spare time to chasing monsters or UFOs, or tediously measuring ancient stoneworks while they openly sneered at their peers who were engaged in similar activities. Thus the sea serpent hunters frowned upon the pyramidologists who, in turn, laughed at the folks who studied haunted houses. One sad result of this mayhem has been the dearth of books which try to objectively examine all the facets of all these myster-

ies. This is one of those rare books. It has been compiled by Rosemary Ellen Guiley, who is just as remarkable as any of the things outlined in these pages.

When you first meet Ms. Guiley you might easily mistake her for a fugitive from a Madison Avenue advertising agency. She hardly looks the type who would sit up all night in a haunted cemetery or wade through the mud of an English pasture looking at mysterious crop circles. But Ms. Guiley does not just write about mysterious places. She has been to many of them and she has talked to all the experts, both genuine and self-acclaimed. This is no armchair investigator. She is constantly on the move, lecturing widely, interviewing all kinds of people ranging from those who claim to be vampires to those who claim to have visited another planet. And, yes, she is very familiar with the Madison Avenue scene, too.

After graduating from the University of Washington (she grew up in Seattle), Rosemary embarked on a journalistic career, serving as a reporter and later as an editor. It was while she was punching a typewriter for United Press International in Dallas, Texas, that she honed her considerable investigating skills. Later she became a senior editor of *Adweek* in New York City. She is a trained, experienced, objective reporter immune to all those messages that one encounters when studing mysterious places.

Humans have always attached special meanings to the sacred sites. (Why else would they be sacred?) When a black stone appeared suddenly on the desert, men hauled it laboriously to Mecca and erected a silken tent around it. It now serves as the all-important centerpiece for the religion of Islam. A garbage dump in Lourdes, France, has been a sacred site ever since a girl named Bernadette had an encounter with a luminous being there in 1858. There are scores of sites around the world where bright lights appear night after night, generation after generation. People flock to these sites to find support for their personal belief systems. Some regard the lights as religious manifestations. Some speak respectfully of the little fairy folk. Others say that they are space ships from some distant planet. Still others mumble cynically of scientific explanations and reflections of far-off automobile headlights.

Over one hundred lakes around the world harbor giant, slinky, serpentlike monsters that are rarely photographed and have never been caught. A multitude of myths, legends and primitive beliefs have been generated by their appearances. Many writers get caught up in the belief systems and lose sight of the actual facts. The temptation to do this is great and the cult literature that evolves is usually worthless, even intellectually catastrophic. Ms. Guiley has successfully managed to weave her way through these labyrinths of belief, and this book is a demonstration of her unique talents. It will guide you to places . . . and ideas . . . where few writers have dared to go before.

—JOHN A. KEEL
New York, N.Y.

POWER POINTS AND SACRED PLACES

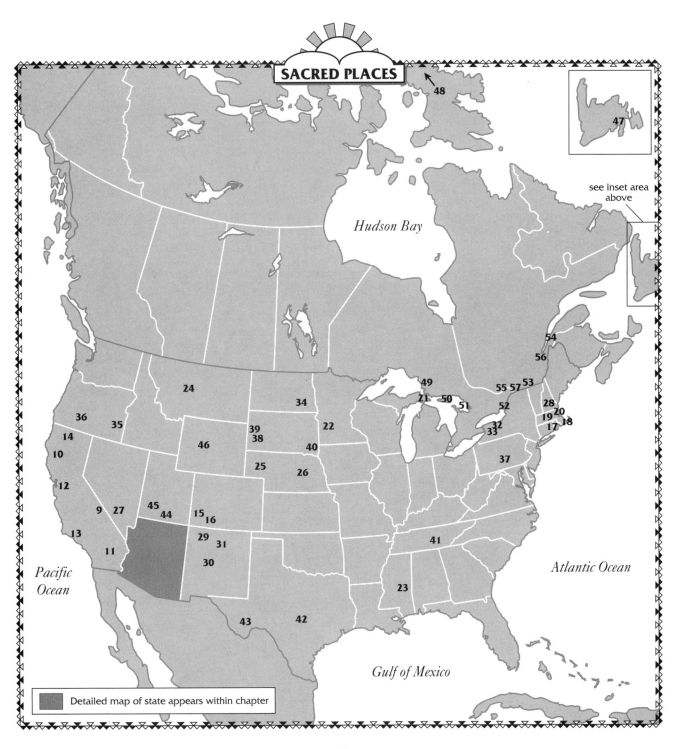

SACRED PLACES

48

47

see inset area above

Hudson Bay

54

56

49

21 50

51

55 57 53

52

28

19 20

17 18

24

34

36

35

22

14

39

38

10

46

40

25

26

37

12

9 27

45

44

15

16

13

29 31

30

11

41

Pacific Ocean

23

Atlantic Ocean

43

42

Gulf of Mexico

Detailed map of state appears within chapter

SACRED PLACES

Perhaps all of us have a special place that we consider sacred, a place where we can go for spiritual rejuvenation and renewal. It might be a green meadow, a nearby hill, the church down the block. These personal sacred sites have qualities in common with the sacred sites listed in this book, except that the ones here are public, culturally validated, and therefore likely to have an even more profound influence on the psyche.

Almost all of the sacred places described here are natural sites or human-made structures situated to take advantage of natural sites. This is probably no accident. Whether or not we believe in ley lines (earth energy lines), psychic vortexes, the Gaia hypothesis (the earth as self-regulating organism) or the like, the potential of certain parts of the landscape and heavens to transport us into reveries and other altered states of consciousness is indisputable.

The vast majority of places listed were considered sacred by early American Indians, who, like all peoples who traditionally lived without modern contrivances, were particularly close to the earth. For Native Americans, not only was the earth a living entity, it was populated by a host of supernatural beings and forces, some benign, others helpful, and still others malevolent. For many groups, the earth was also the womb from which the tribe was born in the distant past, and it was to secluded places of special power that adolescents and mature shamans alike went in quest of visions and supernatural helpmates. Many American Indians keep this world view alive today, and continue to honor ancient sacred sites.

This chapter is organized so that the most generalized sacred sites appear first. Many of these sites involve human manipulation of the environment. They are followed by sacred mountains, then sacred lakes and springs and finally vision quest sites. Although there are many sites listed, it is important to realize that these are only the more significant or better known ones, those considered particularly powerful or especially endowed with mystery. Almost every natural feature had some spiritual significance for the native peoples who lived near it, and it would be impossible to have included all of them.

The sites that American Indians held (and continue to hold) sacred vary greatly in type. Some are impressive, broad expanses of land like the Badlands of South

Badlands, South Dakota (photograph by Richard Frear, courtesy National Park Service)

Not only American Indians, but many of the persons who came to these shores in later centuries have sacred places, and a few of these have been included. In the 19th century, Shaker villages were instructed by elders to select sacred hills for worship sites. Many of those chosen were in fact places held sacred by native peoples.

The use of a sacred place by people of more than one cultural tradition occurs particularly in the case of Sedona. Many of the natural features of the Sedona area in Arizona were held sacred by American Indians, and legends abound. Sedona has also become a New Age Mecca, drawing spiritual seekers of all walks of life. The following are some of the outstanding power places and sacred places in North America.

UNITED STATES

Arizona ✛

Crystal Cave (1) Cave Creek, near Arizona's southeastern border with New Mexico, runs near this fantastic cave. This is one of only three quartz crystal caves in the United States.

Arizona: Sacred Places

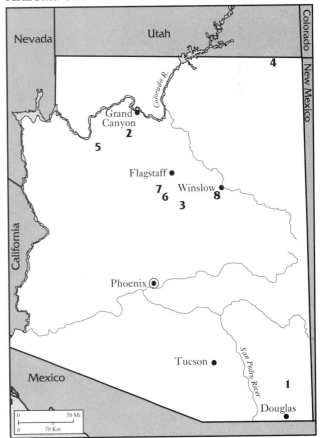

Ruins of Pueblo Bonito, Chaco Canyon, New Mexico (photograph by Fred E. Mang Jr., courtesy National Park Service)

Dakota. The whole of this brutal land is a place of incredible spiritual power for the Lakota Sioux. The Lakota also consider the Black Hills to be part of their spiritual landscape, although parts of these hills are considered more sacred than others.

Other sacred sites are more narrowly defined in character. In Wyoming stands a curious natural tower that fires the imagination of the many visitors who come every year to see it—Devil's Tower is the stuff legends are made of, and local peoples have several to tell. Rainbow Bridge in Utah and the Sunset Crater in Arizona are other natural sites that have a special spiritual significance.

Not all sites were formed by the hand of Mother Nature. Ruins of cities where ancient peoples once lived contain structures whose function as houses of ritual and worship was similar in some respects to that of churches, temples and mosques. These round structures, called kivas, are discussed in the entries about Chaco Canyon in New Mexico and Mesa Verde in Colorado.

Montezuma's Castle cliff dwelling (photograph by Fred E. Mang Jr., courtesy National Park Service)

Mat Taav Tiivjundva (2) The Havasupai consider this area, located near the Grand Canyon, to be the abdomen of the Great Mother who gave birth to the Havasupai.

Montezuma's Well (3) This 400-foot-wide sink near Montezuma's Castle, a 700-year-old cliff dwelling, is fed by an underground spring that produces up to a million gallons of water a day. The Sinagua consider the water to be holy and the well to be the gate through which they came into this world.

Monument Valley (4) This land of fantastic wind-carved buttes is called Land of Room Enough and Time Enough by the Navajo. Each butte is occupied by its own spirit and the valley as a whole is considered sacred. The Navajo still live in Monument Valley and protect it, many working as park rangers and guides, but they were not the first residents. The Anasazi and pre-Anasazi left dozens of petroglyphs in the area to attest to their prior occupancy.

Red Butte (5) This sacred Havasupai site is related to Mat Taav Tiivjundva, being the navel of the Great Mother.

Bell Rock, Sedona (photograph by Bob Clemenz, courtesy Sedona-Oak Creek Canyon Chamber of Commerce)

Charcoal kilns in Death Valley   (photograph by Richard Frear, courtesy National Park Service)

Sedona and Oak Creek Canyon   (6) Known for its powerful energy, the Sedona area has become a New Age Mecca. People who are interested in New Age practices find Sedona to be very conducive to the enhancement of these ideas and abilities, due, in part, to the strong energy vibrations there and the support of others with similar feelings. Many medicine wheels have been constructed in the area, by both visitors and native peoples.

Tuzigoot National Monument   (7) The name for these pre-Columbian village ruins near Clarkdale, Tuzigoot, is an Apache word that means "Crooked Water," referring to the nearby snakelike Verde River. This ruin is near Clarkdale, about 20 miles from the intense power spot of Sedona and has some of its energy.

Window Rock   (8) Window Rock is a stone formation with a natural hole in its center called Tseghahodzani, or "Perforated Rock," by the Navajo. The spring below the rock was one of the four sources of water used in a traditional ceremony to guarantee plentiful rain. The Navajo considered the area around Window Rock as

sacred ground, calling it by the name Ni"alnii'gi, which means "Earth's Center."

California ✛

Death Valley   (9) Paiute legend has it that a city they call Shin-Au-av lies beneath the valley in Death Valley National Monument. The people who live in the city dress in leather and speak an unknown language. Several first-person reports from individuals who claim to have been in the city have been recorded.

Doctor Rock   (10) Despite Native American opposition, a logging road was built in Six Rivers National Forest next to this sacred site. The case was taken all the way to the U.S. Supreme Court, who decided with a five-to-three majority vote to allow the road to be built.

Joshua Tree National Monument   (11) Like Sedona, this park near Twenty-nine Palms is an important modern sacred site, known for its power to convey serenity and a feeling of peace.

Stark landscape at Joshua Tree National Monument, California (photograph by Richard Frear, courtesy National Park Service)

The Joshua Tree that gave the Joshua Tree National Monument park its name is part of its sacred charm. The Mormons who came to the area saw the unusual tree with its shaggy branches stretched upward and thought that it looked like Joshua with his arms raised up to God in prayer. American Indians have other ideas about the tree. Deep in the night all of the animals and birds of the desert come out and the spirit of the Joshua Tree begins to dance, more and more furiously as the night wears on. At the first light of morning, the tree's branches are frozen in place, arms still lifting up to the sky.

Muir Woods (12) Said to be one of the most notable sacred sites in the United States.

Point Conception (13) For the Chumash peoples, Point Conception in the Santa Barbara vicinity is their sacred Western Gate. It is through this gate that souls enter and exit from this earthly plane.

Trinidad (14) Known to the Yurok as Tsurai-wa, this sacred site is a training ground for modern native shamans.

Colorado ✤

Hovenweep National Monument (15) The people who built the six groups of ruins in Hovenweep National Monument in the Pleasant View vicinity were innovative builders who respected their surroundings and constructed their homes in accommodation with the terrain. Hovenweep is Ute for "Deserted Valley." Archaeological evidence suggests that the inhabitants of Hovenweep were observers of the night sky.

Mesa Verde National Park (16) Abandoned by the Anasazi in the 1300s, the Mesa Verde ruins near Cortez are some of the most impressive in the United States. The Cliff Palace ruin is the largest Anasazi cliff dwelling in the country. Mesa Verde National Park was created in 1906 by President Theodore Roosevelt to protect the site's ancient artifacts, but not before hundreds of well-preserved artifacts were looted from Cliff Palace and other dwellings. The Sun Temple, a surface site that is directly across from Cliff Palace, is thought to have had a religious function. A curiously carved sandstone block, named the Sun Shrine, is located at this site.

Connecticut ✣

Devil's Footprint   (17) Near an Indian church constructed by a missionary in Montville lies a granite boulder with a crevice cut into its surface. This crevice is said to have been caused by the Devil when he stepped on the stone on his way out of the area.

Massachusetts ✣

Devil's Bridge   (18) According to American Indian legend, this rocky reef that lies off Gay Head, Martha's Vineyard, is a remnant of a great bridge. Before its destruction this legendary bridge was believed to connect Gay Head to the Elizabeth Island of Cuttyhunk.

Holy Hill of Zion   (19) In 1842 the Shakers claimed this former American Indian sacred site in Harvard as their own. They leveled the top of the hill, moving the earth down to the northern slope. Sacred rituals were held on this hilltop for a while during the time that is commonly known as the second appearing of Mother Ann, the founder of the Shaker religion.

Nashoba Praying Village   (20) This 17th-century village was founded by missionary John Elliot for American Indians who had begun to follow Christian ways. The village was located near several sites held sacred to the Native Americans, including the Boxborough Esker Stoneworks and the Oak Hill Ridge Stone Chambers.

Michigan ✣

Arch Rock   (21) The American Indians of the Mackinac County area thought that this natural arch was sacred because it was built by the Great Spirit himself, as a symbol of his strength.

Hovenweep Castle ruins, Hovenweep National Monument, Colorado-Utah   (courtesy National Park Service)

Minnesota ✛

Pipestone National Monument (22) It was here at Pipestone that Plains peoples mined the material for their ceremonial pipes. Their legends tell that this is the site of the center of creation. Smoke from pipes made of the stone carry messages to the Great Spirit.

Mississippi ✛

Nanih Waiya Cave Mound (23) This large natural mound in the Philadelphia vicinity is thought by the Mississippi Choctaw to be the Mother Mound spoken of in Choctaw creation mythology.

Montana ✛

Badger-Two Medicine (24) Within the Lewis and Clark National Forest is an area known to the Blackfoot as Badger-Two Medicine. Blackfoot tradition holds the whole area as sacred and worthy of great respect. Many Blackfoot legends refer to Badger-Two Medicine, making clear how very important this land is to the Blackfoot people and their religion.

Nebraska ✛

Chimney Rock (25) This unusual rock formation in the vicinity of Bayard lies along what used to be the Oregon Trail. These types of unique formations were usually believed to have been of divine origin by local Indian peoples. Chimney Rock marks the end of the Plains and the beginning of the Rocky Mountains.

Dark Island (26) One of the four sites sacred to the Pawnee, Dark Island is near Central City. The Pawnee called the site Lalawakohtito, which means "Dark Island."

Nevada ✛

Devil's Hole (27) Charles Manson, convicted ring-leader of the Manson family, who were accused of the

Ruins at Pipestone National Monument, Minnesota (photograph by Richard Frear, courtesy National Park Service)

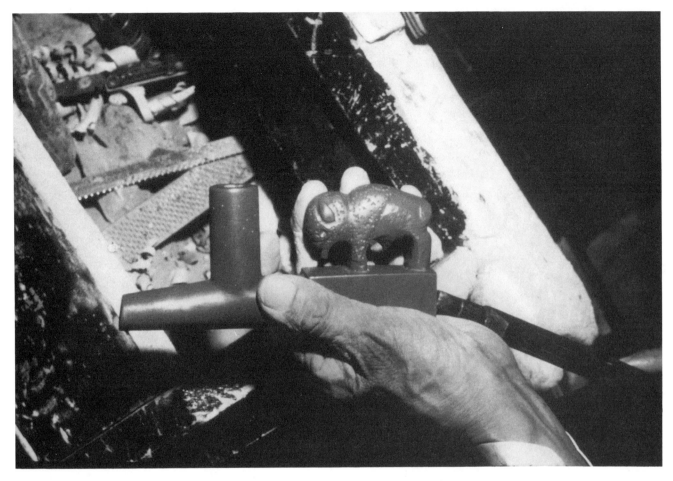

Native American craftsmen keep alive the art of making ceremonial pipes from materials mined at Pipestone (photograph by Richard Frear, courtesy National Park Service)

brutal Tate-LaBianca murders, believed that Devil's Hole in Death Valley National Monument was the entrance to another level of existence. Manson planned to lead his family through it when the war he foretold between the whites and the blacks began.

New Hampshire ✤

Chosen Vale (28) This site at Enfield was one of the many Shaker sacred places that was in use during the mid-1800s. It is unusual for a Shaker site because the grounds were laid out in orientation to cardinal direction. It is thought that the site shows American Indian architectural influence.

New Mexico ✤

Chaco Canyon National Park (29) This large city-complex of ruins near Bloomfield is believed to have been a huge trade center for Anasazi who inhabited the site for hundreds of years. The abundance of kivas—

special ceremonial rooms where rituals take place—at the Chaco Canyon ruins indicate that religion was very important to the Anasazi who lived there. The considerable ruin of Pueblo Bonito alone has 32 kivas. Casa Riconada, across from Pueblo Bonito, is a large, circular, ceremonial kiva that is almost 66 feet in diameter and around 14 feet deep. It is thought that this huge, astronomically aligned kiva may have been a type of sky-watching station because of the 28 niches in its walls that follow a lunar pattern. Evidence of the interest the Anasazi had in charting the seasons and the sky can be found at Fajada Butte, where spiral petroglyphs are cut into the rock. During certain times of the year, most notably the summer and winter solstices, a shaft of light in the shape of a dagger shines through three strategically placed slabs of sandstone onto the petroglyphs.

A ghostly vision of a tall, naked man has been seen in the area, both by visitors and park officials. The native peoples in the area say that this vision is the *genus loci*, replenishing itself from the Mother Earth womb. It is also said that there is a witch who haunts the region.

Kiva ruins, Pueblo Bonito, Chaco Canyon, New Mexico (photograph by Fred E. Mang Jr., courtesy National Park Service)

Her name when translated from the Navajo means "She Who Makes Men Thin By Starving Them."

Some UFO researchers believe the Chaco Canyon area is a major contact site for visiting extraterrestrials. There are numerous anecdotes of sightings.

El Mapais National Monument (30) This recently created national monument at Grants includes a 13,000-acre tract of land that is sacred to the Acoma peoples. They objected to the opening of the park for fear that tourists would treat their ceremonial sites with disrespect. They also feared the destructive effects of looters searching for priceless American Indian artifacts. In spite of this protest, in June 1987 the documents were signed that made this area a national park.

El Sanctuario de Chimayo (31) Built in 1816 by a well-to-do family, this little church at Chimayo has a reputation as a healing site. Even the soil itself is said to have miraculous powers, and many who visit take home samples of it. Because of this curative power, Chimayo is also known as the Lourdes of America. The

Tewa considered the site sacred even before the whites built a church on it.

New York ✚

Ganondagan State Historic Site (32) This site near Rochester, sacred to the Iroquois, was once a town inhabited by Jikonsaseh. This Iroquois woman was central in the formation of the great League of Five (later six) Nations. Jikonsaseh was also known as the Mother of Nations or the Peace Queen. More than just Jikonsaseh's hometown, Ganondagan is also sacred because it is a symbol of the League of Five Nations.

Goat Island (33) Although this island below Niagara Falls is better known today as Goat Island, the Iroquois named it Turtle Island, corresponding with their idea that the world is supported by a turtle. Goat Island was used as a burial site for Iroquois warriors. At its western edge are three small islands named The Three Sisters, the furthest of the three only 300 yards from Horseshoe

Falls. Iroquois shamans prayed on this island, sacrificing food and other items to the Great Spirit of the Thunder Waters.

North Dakota ✚

Standing Rock Historic Site (34) This standing rock, located in the Fort Ransom area in the midst of ancient woodland burial mounds, has in historic times been considered sacred by the Sioux.

Oregon ✚

Balancing Rocks (35) These unusual rock formations are comprised of a conical stone spike with a large flat stone balanced on top, resulting in what looks to be a forest of giant fossilized mushrooms. They are found in a small canyon in east-central Oregon.

Wizard Island (36) This relatively young island sits in the middle of Crater Lake. It has a profound but dark beauty that causes some who visit to see it as an Underworld gateway. For more information on Crater Lake, see "Sacred Lakes and Springs."

Pennsylvania ✚

Indian Echo Caverns (37) American Indian traditions suggest that this cave that lies off the banks of the Swatara Creek is home to evil spirits. Several apparitions of a decidedly evil aspect are said to have appeared in the caves before several witnesses.

South Dakota ✚

Badlands National Park (38) To the American Indians who live in this area, this is an area of extraordinary spiritual power. At one time millions of bison roamed this arid, rocky land. Wovoka, the great American Indian prophet, held his spiritual ghost dances in the Badlands at a place called Stronghold Table. These ceremonial dances became very threatening to the non-natives who took steps to stop them. In 1890 the U.S. Cavalry

Wizard Island in Crater Lake, Oregon (photograph by Walter Roth, courtesy National Park Service)

Badlands, South Dakota   (photograph by Richard Frear, courtesy National Park Service)

massacred more than 200 American Indian men, women and children at Wounded Knee, resulting in the extinction of the Ghost Dance religion. Some claim that this is the reason for the fierce energy that permeates the Badlands.

Black Hills   (39) This range of mountains is sacred to the Sioux peoples, who look at this land as a place of vision and renewal. Several sacred sites discussed in "Sacred Mountains" are in the Black Hills, including Bear Butte and Devil's Tower.

Spirit Mound (Paka Wakan)   (40) The Omaha and other American Indian groups in the Vermillion vicinity believe this naturally occurring mound is the residence of spirits.

Tennessee ✤

Old Stone Fort Archeological Park   (41) Located in the fork of the Big and Little Duck rivers near Manches-

ter, this enclosure functioned as a ceremonial site for 2,000 years. The American Indians who constructed the site are thought to have practiced rites associated with the sun. The entrance way to the site faces the sunrise of the winter solstice. The site was named Old Stone Fort by the first white settlers who mistakenly thought that the remains of the enclosure walls were those of a fort.

Texas ✤

Enchanted Rock   (42) This 500-foot-high, billion-year-old dome batholith of pink granite in the Fredericksburg vicinity has been a holy site for thousands of years. American Indians believe it to be a doorway to the spirit world. The spirit guardians of the rock are said to move around mostly at night. Legends tell that the rock was feared because it groaned at night and glistened when the moon was full. Today the rock is still considered sacred and church services are held on its summit. It is also a place for vision questing.

Ranger Canyon (43) This beautiful canyon near Alpine is the spiritual home of a mythic silver wolf.

Utah ✤

Rainbow Bridge National Monument (44) At 270 feet across and 290 feet high, this natural bridge at Lake Powell is the largest in the world. Unlike many other sites sacred to Indians, the name of this sacred place was simply translated from Navajo to English, rather than being changed altogether. For the Navajo, it is the home of the Rainbow God and the Rainbow People, who are significant due to their role as rain-bringers.

Zion National Park (45) The contrasts between the high cliffs, mesas and deep canyons make this park breathtakingly beautiful. Although it is a national park, American Indians consider it to be a very holy site. Many feel upset that non-natives come to the park to camp and do not show the respect that Zion is due.

Wyoming ✤

Dinwoody Canyon (46) This canyon, located within the Wind River Reservation, is the site of hundreds of pictographs. Local Indians consider it to be a very sacred place.

CANADA

Newfoundland ✤

Bay du Nord River (47) The Micmac consider the Land of the Stone Cross to be a powerful healing center. The site is located inland and over the cliffs of Devil's Dancing Table. There one can find a diamond-shaped open cross, about 30 feet long, ringed by white boulders and stones. The Micmac say that each stone has healing properties, and can be removed as long as each one is replaced. Two basins are nearby, one for holy water (probably dry) and one for offerings.

Northwest Territories ✤

North Pole (48) According to the *Veda*, ancient sacred texts of India, the North Pole is the site of Mount Meru, the world mountain or center of the world. It is said to be made of gold. It is linked to the Pole Star, through which all things temporal and spatial must pass on their way out of the material plane.

Ontario ✤

Cape Gargantua (49) A small community on Lake Superior's eastern shore, said to be one of the most sacred places on that shore due to its enchanted atmosphere. The Ojibwa considered it a most important spiritual center, and the abode of Nanabozho, the trickster god who governed the moods of the lake and granted peaceful journeys upon it to those who paid him homage. Nearby is the Devil's Chair, a lozenge-shaped rock 50 to 60 feet high, which rises out of the water. The rock appears to be in the form of a man or a woman, depending on perspective.

Dreamer's Rock (50) Quartzite rock rising 1,650 feet above Lake Ontario, located on the White Fish Indian Reserve on Manitoulin Island. Here the Anishabec worshipped the Michi Manitou, the Great Spirit. See "Vision Quest Sites" for more on Dreamer's Rock.

Martyrs' Shrine (51) One of Canada's most famous healing springs and sites of miraculous cures. The Midland shrine was built beside Fort Ste.-Marie. It was the first outpost of Christianity in the area, originally called Huronia. There were martyrs in the wars with the Iroqouis, whose relics are interred here. Besides the spring, there is a grotto, a church and the Stations of the Cross.

Marysburgh Vortex (52) A funnel-shaped area of Lake Ontario that includes Wolfe Island, where the lake narrows into the St. Lawrence River, that compares to the Bermuda Triangle. An unusually high number of shipping accidents have occurred here for more than 100 years.

Québec ✤

Kahnawake (53) Miraculous cures have been reported on the Kahnawake (also Caughnawaga) Indian Reserve. The power of the place is credited to Kateri Tekawitha (1656–1680), a native woman who was so pure she was called the Lily of the Mohawks. She lived a life of chastity and sanctity, and suffered illness just prior to her death. Legend has it that her body remained incorrupt for many days. Her relics are in the Mission Church of St. François-Xavier. Pope Paul II beatified her on June 22, 1980.

Owl's Head Mountain (54) At this Saint-Benoit-du-Lac site, Masonic rituals are held.

Rigaud Mountain (55) The Shrine of Our Lady of Lourdes and the Devil's Garden are located here at Rigaud. The Devil's Garden, formed some 50 million years ago by a glacier, is a field of stones that, according to legend, once was a potato farm. Baptiste Laronde ploughed his potato field here on a Sunday, despite warnings not to do so from a pastor. As he ploughed, he sank deeper and deeper into the earth, until he vanished. The field became a field of stones. It is said to be haunted by wisps of smoke and crackling sounds, which manifest at dawn on Sundays.

The Shrine was founded in 1870 to foster devotion to the Blessed Virgin Mary, who had appeared at Lourdes, France, in 1856. A grotto was created in 1886. The site is visited by pilgrims. Interestingly, the Stations of the Cross were built with stones from the Devil's Garden.

Sainte-Anne-de-Beaupré (56) The shrine of Sainte-Anne-de-Beaupré, located northwest of Québec City, is the largest Roman Catholic shrine in North America, and the site of numerous miraculous cures. It is built on the spot where three shipwrecked Breton sailors were washed ashore in 1638. They built a chapel in gratitude. The first recorded cure was in 1658. A stonemason, Louis Guimond, was crippled with rheumatism and unable to work on the chapel. To show his devotion, he placed three pebbles on the chapel's foundation, and was instantly cured.

St. Joseph's Oratory (57) This basilica, located on Mount Royal in Montreal, is famous for the faith healing done by Brother André (1845–1937), né Alfred Bessette, who joined the Congregation of the Holy Cross as a lay brother. He was functionally illiterate and in poor health most of his life. Tens of thousands of pilgrims came to be healed by him, a miracle that the faithful believed was accomplished through his intervention on their behalf with his patron saint. His preserved heart was once displayed in the Oratory.

Ville-Marie (57) A giant, illuminated cross stands atop the 764-foot Mount Royal, an extinct volcano and the tallest peak on the island of Montreal. The cross commemorates the saving of a missionary community, Ville-Marie, which was established at the base of Mount Royal in 1642 to work with the Iroquois. The same year, it was threatened with flood waters of the St. Lawrence River. Paul de Chomedey de Maisonneuve, who founded the colony, vowed that if Ville-Marie would be spared, he would carry a cross to the top of the mountain and plant it there. The waters receded immediately, and Maisonneuve made good on his promise.

SACRED MOUNTAINS

There is something about a mountain that inspires awe in people, and makes them feel as if they were in the presence of a towering sacred power. Some say it is the gigantic size of the mountain, others say that the wildlife and beauty inspire these feelings. Possibly, according to some research, there may be real physical power flowing through some of these peaks. These sacred mountains of great power, of majestic beauty, of poetic inspiration have shaped many peoples' lives, both modern and ancient. At the foot of Mount Shasta, California, at least 20 religious communities find spiritual inspiration. Shasta's snow-covered peak silences many people in awe of its beauty.

American Indians say that many North American mountains are sacred. Legends and myths of many groups say that the Creator of all made these peaks, they are the Creator's own sacred altar. The Papago tell that the Creator used the very soil of the sacred mountain Baboquiver to create humankind. Within some Indian groups, shamans climb these peaks to communicate with the Creator or their ancestors, coming to pray for guidance or blessings. Places like Bear Butte and Harney Peak in South Dakota have left powerful marks on the history of native people. Visions that were inspired on these peaks brought forth the great leaders of the people, Black Elk and Crazy Horse. Mountains are the dream places, the vision quest sites, the boundaries of the American Indian's world.

Some of these peaks, like Shiprock in New Mexico, are so holy, so precious, that American Indians themselves do not climb their slopes. Some native groups feel that the power on these sacred mountains is too great to approach lightly. On great holy mountains like Shasta, the Creator is too near and most people are not pure enough to approach. Groups with these beliefs do not think it is proper to hike up a sacred mountain without a very powerful reason and a very pure heart.

These towering peaks have reached into the souls of many people, stirring their creative forces and bringing forth immortal legends, myths and art. Navajo sand paintings often depict their four sacred mountains, the boundaries of the known safe world for a Navajo. Hopi tell stories of how the sacred San Francisco peaks came to life and how all of creation was born on these peaks. The sacred songs of creation came to them while they sat in prayer on the seats worn into the ledges of the Siskiyou Mountains by generations of their ancestors. The writings of the great naturalist John Muir were inspired by Mount Shasta and Mount Ritter, where he was mysteriously saved from sure death.

A geological study of San Francisco peaks suggest that the peaks may have a measurable energy flowing through them that could have enhanced the Indians' notion that the peaks are sacred: a strong electrical "telluric" current that flows in response to the earth's magnetic field. It is unknown what effects these currents have on life forms, but one geological report suggests that these currents could increase geological activity in the area, such as a higher incidence of lightning strikes and, during dry weather, electrical discharges of a glowing light. Here are some of the major sacred mountains in North America.

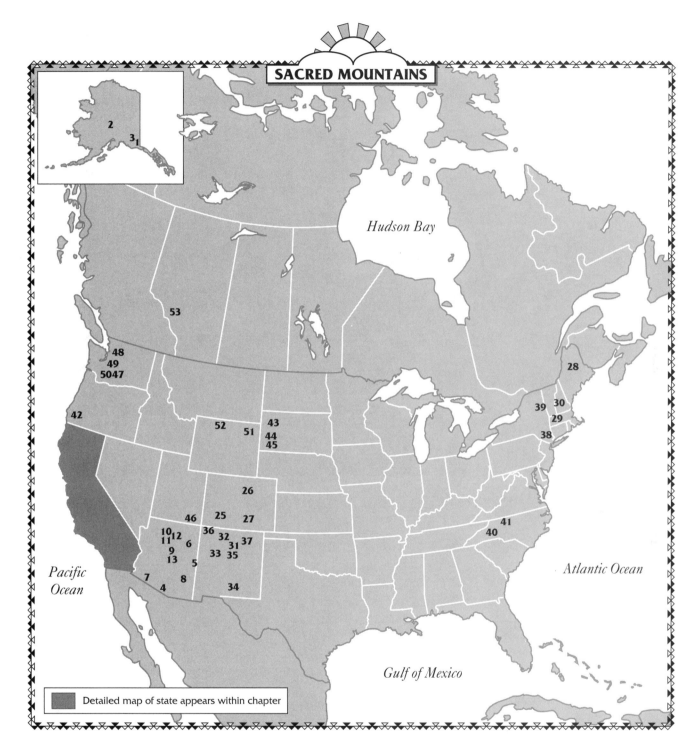

UNITED STATES

Alaska ✤

Mount Fairweather (1) The Yakutat Tlingit believe Mount Fairweather to be the estranged wife of Mount Saint Elias. Bickering broke up the marriage, which had been unstable from the beginning. After the split,

Mount Saint Elias moved 100 miles west, while Mount Fairweather and her children, the peaks to the east of her, stayed right where they had always been.

Mount McKinley (2) At 20,320 feet, this is the highest mountain in North America. The majestic height of this mountain engenders a feeling of awe and respect in the people who live in its shadow. The Koyukon named

Mount McKinley, Alaska   (photograph by Elizabeth Joy, courtesy National Park Service)

the peak Denali, meaning the "High One." Possessing powerful energies, this sacred mountain is said to help people achieve a more harmonious state of mind. It fosters a feeling of unity with all of life within those who visit it.

Mount Saint Elias   (3) This mountain is one of the highest in North America, second only to Mount McKinley. The Yakutat Tlingit regard Mount Saint Elias as the alienated husband of Mount Fairweather. In spite of the peaks' unhappy marital history, they considered this spot to be one of their most sacred peaks. According to legend, the whole world was once flooded and the only safe havens during this time were the high peaks of Mount Saint Elias and two other nearby mountains. These mountains saved humankind from a sure death of drowning in the high flood waters.

Saint Elias is a powerful mountain that is seen as having an aggressive masculine personality. Yakutat shamans climb up toward the soaring peak in order to obtain their supernatural powers. Powerful spirits live on this and other nearby sacred mountains, and the

Tlingit are careful to avoid offending them. If the spirits perceive that they are not being treated with the proper respect, they could create clouds and cause bad weather.

Arizona ✤

Baboquivri Mountains   (4) In Papago legend this is the location where humankind was first created. E'etoi, the elder brother, took the mud of Baboquivri and began his attempt to create the perfect people. On his first attempt he let the people on the slopes of Baboquivre bake in the sun too long. The intense heat of the day blackened their skin; these people have come to be known as the blacks. E'etoi did not bake the second batch of people long enough, their underdone skin was left white, creating the whites. The last batch of people were baked to perfection. These beautiful golden-skinned people were the American Indians.

Big Mountain   (5) Sacred to both the Hopi and Navajo, this land was turned over to the Hopi in the 1974 Navajo-Hopi Settlement Act. The result of this controversial decision was that several hundred Navajo families living there were given orders to leave their homes and relocate. The area is still considered sacred.

Black Mesa   (6) To the Hopi, Black Mesa is their sacred homeland and the center of the universe. God told the Hopi to look all over the world for this universal center and once they found it they were to live there until this Fourth World ends.

Cabezon Peak   (7) This peak is the core of a volcano that erupted 10 million years ago, during the Cenozoic Age. Navajo legend has it that this peak is the head of a monster killed by Navajo hero twins who purged the land between the mountains of evil.

Mount Graham   (8) Three Southwest groups and many non-American Indians who are interested in Indian religious beliefs consider this mountain to be a power place.

Mount Humphrey   (9) The Navajo call Mount Humphrey Dook'o'ooliid, or "Light Shines From It." This mountain in the San Francisco peaks is one of the Four Sacred Mountains of the Navajo created by First Man and First Woman. Mount Humphrey was set down in the western part of the San Francisco peaks, north of present-day Flagstaff, Arizona.

Mount Superstition   (10) More of a hilly group of volcanic extrusions than a set of mountains, the Superstition Mountains have a bad local reputation. Many Indian tribes such as the Pima and Maricopa avoid the area, seeing it as the lodgings of the supreme evil forces of the Southwest. Apache avoid this evil place, also.

Many legends and tall tales surround the Superstitions, some told by local Native Americans and some by the whites who have visited and seen strange sights. The Apache, who believe the area to be sacred, tell that there is a cave in the hills that leads to the interior of the earth. This cave is guarded against human entry by a huge nine-headed snake. Winds from the Underworld can blow up through this cave to the land above, causing severe dust storms.

Red Butte   (11) This sacred site on the southern rim of the Grand Canyon is in danger of being exploited by mining companies in search of uranium ore.

San Francisco Mountains   (12) When a mountain has very powerful energies it is often seen as sacred by more than one group living in the vicinity. This is the case with the San Francisco Peaks, considered sacred by both the Navajo and the Hopi.

According to Navajo legends, Mount Humphrey within the San Francisco peaks was formed by First Man and First Woman along with three other peaks

(Sierra Blanca Peak, Mount Taylor and Mount Hesperus), and these mountains became the Sacred Mountains of the four cardinal directions.

The Hopi call the peaks Nuvatukya'ovi, which means "Snow Mountain Higher Than Everything Else." Hopi ceremonies involving the peak tend to be calendrical, reflecting the agricultural character of the people.

For the Hopi, these mountains are one of the major dwelling places of the kachinas, supernatural beings whose goodwill is critical for Hopi survival. Kachinas can take many physical forms and act as messengers to communicate with the ancestors and other sacred deities who live in the peaks. The Hopi are very careful not to displease the kachinas in any way. A major offense could cause a serious upset in the individual's life or, worse yet, it could affect the whole group, for example, in the form of a drought.

Sunset Crater National Monument   (13) Not truly a mountain in the geological sense, this extinct volcano last erupted in A.D. 1064. No matter what the time of

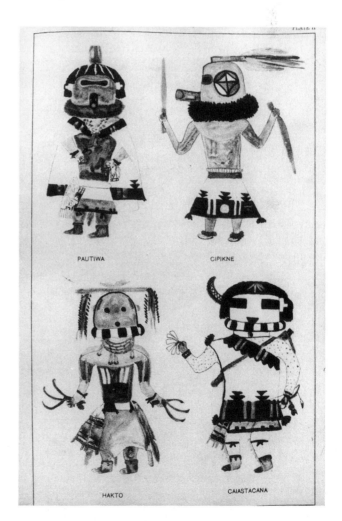

Kachinas, 19th century, by Jesse Walter Fewkes

day, sunlight strikes the 1,000-foot cone in a strange way, making the volcano appear as though it is in the setting sun. The Hopi Kana-a kachinas live in the crater along with the Wind God, Yaponcha, who sends cold winds blowing up through the crater. The Kana-a kachinas, who are more friendly toward people than Yaponcha, are known for their kindness and the special magic they do for those who live nearby or come to visit.

California ✤

Birch Mountain (14) Sometimes a mountain has a powerful personal effect on people, an effect so dynamic that it seems to have a supernatural ability to intervene in individuals' lives. One such story is told of Birch Mountain.

A Paiute named Hoavadunaki had a dream in which the mountain appeared to him and foretold that he would always be well and strong; nothing could hurt him. Not long after, while walking through the desert, he fell ill. Sure that he had been poisoned by an evil witch doctor, he crept under a bush to die. But then he remembered the words that Birch Mountain had spoken

California: Sacred Mountains

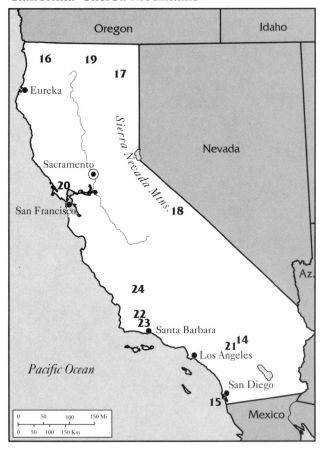

in his dream. Determined not to die, he revived enough to walk to the village where a medicine man healed him. Forever after this experience, Hoavadunaki felt that he and Birch Mountain had a special bond.

Coronado Island (15) These partly submerged mountain peaks are one of the four sacred places of the Diegueno of San Diego County. This was more than likely a place where initiation ceremonies were staged.

Marble Mountains (16) Said to be among the more notable sacred sites in the United States.

Mount Lassen (17) This peak is the remnant of what was once the largest volcanic peak in its area. Part of the Cascade Range, it is in the company of some better-known peaks, including Mount St. Helens, Mount Shasta and Mount Rainier. On the northeast slope of Lassen is a small stream that used to be the traditional summer camp site for American Indians. Ishi, the Indian immortalized in *Ishi in Two Worlds* by Theodora Kroeber, came from the area around Mount Lassen.

Mount Ritter (18) John Muir, the naturalist, felt a close bond with this peak after a remarkable experience he had while climbing it. On a cliff close to the top of the mountain, Muir ran out of holds. He clung to the face of the cliff, filled with the knowledge that he was surely to die. Suddenly something took over, some instinct or guardian angel led him up to the top of the peak and safety. At last secure, Muir, looking down from the summit, was struck by the transcendent glow that bathed Mount Ritter.

Mount Shasta (19) The Indians who once occupied most of the Siskiyou County area named this sacred mountain Wyeka, or "Great White." Large mountains like Shasta were not climbed by native peoples because the power of the Great Spirit was too strong there. The Great Spirit temporarily resides on peaks like Shasta and he demands respect. Only those of very pure heart can walk up the slopes of the mountain and not be harmed.

Shasta is reported to be the home of many different spirits and beings, including extraterrestrials, who are said to use the peak as a landing area and refueling station. One belief, popularized by the Rosicrucian order, is that a group of Lemurians, who escaped the destruction of the mythical Pacific continent of Lemuria, live underground near the summit of the mountain. One other group of mysterious beings that inhabit the peak are the Yaktayvians, who use magic bells to keep humans away. Shasta is only one of their homes. These beings inhabit several secret cities across the planet.

Over the years American Indian interest in Shasta has been revived, caused in part by the attention given to the peak by contemporary groups. There are now annual summer gatherings to practice Indian ceremonies led by native medicine women and men.

Mount Tamalpais (20) This peak in Marin County is just north of San Francisco's Golden Gate Bridge. The summit is easy to reach; you can drive to within a few hundred feet of the top. This accessible location has made Tamalpais one of the most visited sacred mountains in the world.

San Bernardino Mountain (21) Along with three other sites, San Bernardino Mountain is a sacred place to Dieguaeno. Initiation rites may have taken place here.

San Rafael Mountain (22) See SIERRA MADRE.

Santa Ynez Mountains (23) See SIERRA MADRE.

Sierra Madre (24) There are thousands of wind-carved caves in these coastal mountains between Santa Barbara and Los Angeles decorated with colorful Chumash pictographs. It is thought that these pictographs depict dream images of Chumash who came to these mountain caves to seek guidance from the spirits.

Colorado ✛

Hesperus Peak (25) Known as Dibenitsaa, "Mountain Sheep," by the Navajo. The Navajo First Man and First Woman created four sacred mountains, one in each of the four cardinal directions. Hesperus Peak was the mountain created in the north. After its creation, First Man and First Woman attached the peak to the earth with a rainbow. They ornamented it with beads of black jet and placed blackbird eggs on its slopes to hatch. Pollen Boy and Grasshopper Girl were sent to the peak to live high on the summit.

Old Man Mountain (26) American Indians came to Old Man Mountain to fast in order to obtain healing powers, success in battle and communication with spirit guides. This peak is littered with artifacts—bits of obsidian pottery flakes, sandstone tools for grinding paint and so forth—that give silent testimony to its history as a great vision quest site. See OLD MAN MOUNTAIN under "Vision Quest Sites" for more information.

Sierra Blanca Peak (27) Located near Alamosa, this peak, known as Sisnaajini, "Black-Belted One," by the Navajo, is part of the Sangre de Cristo Range. One of the four sacred mountains created by First Man and First Woman, this peak was fastened to the earth with a lightning bolt after its creation. The creators decorated the peak with white shells, white corn and white lightning. They also gave it the black clouds that bring the hard male rain. To guard Sierra Blanca, First Man and

First Woman sent Rock Crystal Boy and Rock Crystal Girl to reside there. This peak is also called Mount Blanco or "White Shell Mountain" by some.

Maine ✛

Mount Katahdin (28) An imposing 5,267-foot granite peak, Katahdin stands near the northern end of the Appalachians. The Penobscot and Passamaquoddy peoples of the area saw this peak as the home of a wide variety of deities, in particular Pomola, a spirit being with the wings of an eagle, the body of a man and the head of a moose. To the Abenaki, Katahdin was the Greatest Mountain.

White people have also felt the power of Katahdin. Thoreau took a trip to the mountain in 1846 and climbed it alone. He was profoundly struck by the experience, by the transcendent sense of otherness that the peak exudes.

Massachusetts ✛

Mount Sinai (29) In 1842 the membership of all Shaker communities were requested by Shaker leaders to worship twice a year on the highest point of land near to them. Thereafter, Mount Sinai became a sacred peak to the little Shaker community in Hancock, known as the City of Peace. Remains and artifacts found on Sinai seem to indicate that this peak was sacred to American Indians before it was utilized for Shaker worship. The Shakers had outdoor worship ceremonies on the peak that incorporated some elements of Indian rituals.

New Hampshire ✛

Mount Assurance (30) When Shaker leaders, in 1842, requested that their membership worship on the highest point of land near to them twice a year, Mount Assurance became a sacred peak to the Shaker community in Enfield, known as the Chosen Vale.

New Mexico ✛

Chicoma Mountain (Tsikomo Mountain) (31) Chicoma is called Tsikomo, "Obsidian Covered Mountain," by the Tewa, who consider it one of their four sacred mountains. A body of water, such as a pond or lake, is associated with each of the four. Within these bodies of water live deities who did not walk the earth after it hardened. The Tewa called them "Dry Food Who Never Did Become." These peaks are also sacred because there is a nansipu or earth navel on each summit. This earth navel is an arrangement of stones in the patterns of keyholes with stone-bordered paths, called rain roads, that radiate toward several Tewa villages. Within these nansipu live the Tewa-e who stand watch over the Tewa world.

The summit of Chicoma is often shrouded in clouds, which is an indicator of a special sacredness to the Tewa and other Pueblo peoples because of the constant quest for rainfall. That which brings them closer to the source of rain is sacred, and the spirits must be especially active there. Annual pilgrimages once were made by the Tewa to Chicoma to "go and get the rain."

Mount Conjilon (32) This peak is one of the four sacred peaks of the Tewa, a Pueblo group descended from the Anasazi. Conjilon is known as Tse Shu Pin or "Hazy/Shimmering Mountain" to the Tewa. For more information on Tewa sacred mountains, see CHICOMA MOUNTAIN.

Mount Taylor (33) Known as Tso'dzil or "Tongue Mountain" to the Navajo, this peak is one of their four sacred mountains. First Man and First Woman gave each of the four mountains gifts when they created them. To Taylor, which they fixed to the earth with a great stone knife, they gave turquoise, many kinds of animals, and a soft, gentle female rain. Boy Who Is Bringing Back Turquoise and Girl Who Is Bringing Back Many Ears of Corn were put on the peak to guard it and live on its summit forever.

Sacramento Mountains (34) Home of Apache mountain spirits, these mountains are in the area of Petroglyph State Park and Three Rivers, New Mexico.

Sandia Crest (35) Sandia Crest is the northern peak of the four sacred mountains of the Tewa. To the Tewa, this peak's name is Oku Pin or "Turtle Mountain." For more information on Tewa sacred mountains, see CHICOMA MOUNTAIN.

Shiprock Peak (36) The Navajo know this peak as Tse'bit'a'i or "Rock with Wings." Legend has it that once the Navajo ancestors sought refuge from enemies on top of Shiprock. In answer to a prayer for deliverance, the mountain sprouted wings and flew away, carrying the ancestors to safety.

According to another Navajo legend, Shiprock is where Monster Slayer outwitted and killed two terrible flying dragons. With magic and his clever tricks, he destroyed the adult male and female dragons but spared the two young ones. Instead he flung them into the sky, turning one into an eagle and the other into an owl.

Other legends about this peak suggest that Shiprock was once a monster that was turned to stone or a great bird that was changed into a mountain. Because they consider this peak sacred, the Navajo do not climb it and request that others respect their beliefs.

Truchas Peak (37) One of the four sacred mountains of the Tewa. Truchas is known to the Tewa as "Stone Man Mountain" or Ku Sehn Pin. This peak is to the east and is associated with white. See CHICOMA MOUNTAIN for more information on Tewa sacred mountains.

New York ✤

Holy Mount (38) Peak sacred to the nearby Shaker community of Holy Mount.

Mount Marcy (39) Marcy is the highest peak in New York State's Adirondack Mountains. It was on the peak, sacred to the Iroquois, that well-known philosopher William James had a mystical experience. Marcy seemed to bring James closer to a mystical union with the world in the same way it did for the Iroquois searching for the spiritual powers sought in the vision quest.

North Carolina ✤

Mount Mitchell (40) Mitchell, a 6,684-foot peak in the Appalachian range, is the highest mountain east of the Mississippi River. According to a Cherokee myth, in this peak is a sacred cave from which magically spring forth the game animals that provide food for the people.

Pilot Mountain (41) Sacred to the Cherokee, who once used this peak for initiation rites. A Cherokee spirit guide named Jommeoki resides on this hallowed mountain.

Oregon ✤

Siskiyou Mountains (42) High in these rugged peaks on the California-Oregon border, the Karok, Tolowa and Hoopa people came to pray to the Creator. Sacred songs to be used in ceremonies were created by these people as they sat on ledges in depressions worn into the rock by centuries of ancestors doing the same.

South Dakota ✤

Bear Butte (43) Bear Butte's name is a reflection of its unusual form, which reminds many of a huge sleeping bear. The Sioux named this mountain Mato Pah or "Sleeping Bear Mountain." It was on this peak, known for its power to stimulate visions and dreams, that Crazy Horse had his great vision of the future. He saw that the Indian people had hard times ahead; wars would kill many, but eventually a time of peace would come and the people would have a spiritual awakening.

This peak is also sacred to the Cheyenne, who call it Noahavose or the "Good Mountain." It was in a cave on this peak many generations ago that the Cheyenne leader Sweet Medicine and his wife met Maheo, the

Great Father and Creator of All. Maheo gave Sweet Medicine four arrows that would bless and protect the Cheyenne. Other than one brief period when they were stolen by Pawnee raiders, the arrows have remained in the possession of the Cheyenne, protected by an appointed keeper.

Harney Peak (44) At the age of nine, the Oglala Sioux chief Black Elk had a vision that incorporated Harney Peak. His spiritual guides took him to the top of a mountain that he later identified as Harney Peak and revealed that this was the center of the earth. Later in Black Elk's life he went to Harney Peak to communicate with the Grandfathers. He had lived most of his life at this point and was convinced that he had failed in his sacred mission. Standing on top of the sacred mountain, he begged the Grandfathers to let his people live again.

Thunderhead Mountain (45) This sacred site in the making is a huge memorial to the great Native American chief Crazy Horse, carved in the style of Mount Rushmore's "Shrine to Democracy." Work on the sculpture, started in 1948, is still in progress.

Utah ✛

Navajo Mountain (46) Not far from the Grand Canyon is a 10,388-foot peak that the Navajo compare in appearance to a loaf of blue cornbread. Navajo Mountain was not recognized as a sacred peak by the American Indians until 1836, when a group of Navajo found refuge there from a U.S. Cavalry troop that was hunting them down. While the Navajo were encamped there, the mountain revealed to them that it was the Head of Earth Woman, the site where the heroic warrior Monster Slayer was born and raised in a single day. This sacred peak is a very special pilgrimage place to modern Navajo. They are protective of this holy place and allow no one to climb its sacred slopes.

Washington ✛

Mount Adams (47) Adams is a major volcanic mountain that is now owned by the Yakima. Like most volcanic mountains, it has a history of being sacred to the American Indians who have lived nearby.

Mount Baker (48) Surrounded by the old-growth temperate rain forest of Washington, this seemingly peaceful sacred mountain is part of a growing controversy. Developers and logging industries are demanding access to the towering cedars on and around Baker while Indian groups, led by the Lummis, are fighting to keep their sacred land in its pristine condition.

Mount Rainier (49) This soaring, 14,408-foot, snow-covered dormant volcano is the highest peak in the Cascade Range. Its presence is so majestic and powerful that even today residents of Washington State call Rainier the Mountain. The native peoples of the area called the peak Tacoma, the "Great White Mountain." Like Shiprock and Shasta, Rainier was considered too powerful to climb. To do so would anger the powerful spirits who lived there, thus sealing one's own death warrant.

Indians who lived in this region—Puyallup, Yakima and Nisqually—had many legends about Rainier, most dealing with family strife due to its great size and isolation. One of these myths tells that Rainier once lived on the other side of Puget Sound, married to a peak in the Olympic Mountains, and part of a family. But Rainier grew jealous of the peak's other wives and moved to the far side of the sound. Her bitterness and anger caused her to swell up, explaining her present enormous size.

Mount St. Helens (50) According to some American Indians, the cataclysmic destruction brought about by the eruption of Mount St. Helens in 1980 was meant as a protest. The Great Creator, who at times resides on this sacred mountain, was displeased about the desecration of its sacred slopes by the white man.

Wyoming ✛

Devil's Tower (51) This 1,267-foot rock tower is called Mato Tipila or "Bear Lodge" by the Indians of the area. The tower got its present name from a team of scientists who came to the region in 1875 to confirm reports of gold. Mato Tipila was a sacred area for several different tribes who used it as a vision quest site. Some moviegoers might remember Mato Tipila as the site where the alien starship lands in Steven Spielberg's film *Close Encounters of the Third Kind*.

Medicine Mountain (52) The Bighorn Medicine Wheel (see "Medicine Wheels") is located on this peak. The medicine wheel is still used by American Indians in the area for ceremonies around the summer solstice, and out of respect to them it is recommended that the site not be visited at that time.

CANADA

Alberta ✛

Rocky Mountains (53) The natives who inhabited the foothills of these majestic peaks called them the shining mountains, and considered them the abodes of supernatural beings. Madame H. P. Blavatsky, cofounder of Theosophy, said the Rockies held a hidden sanctuary where ancient adepts lived and preserved the secret doctrine, the wisdom of the ages.

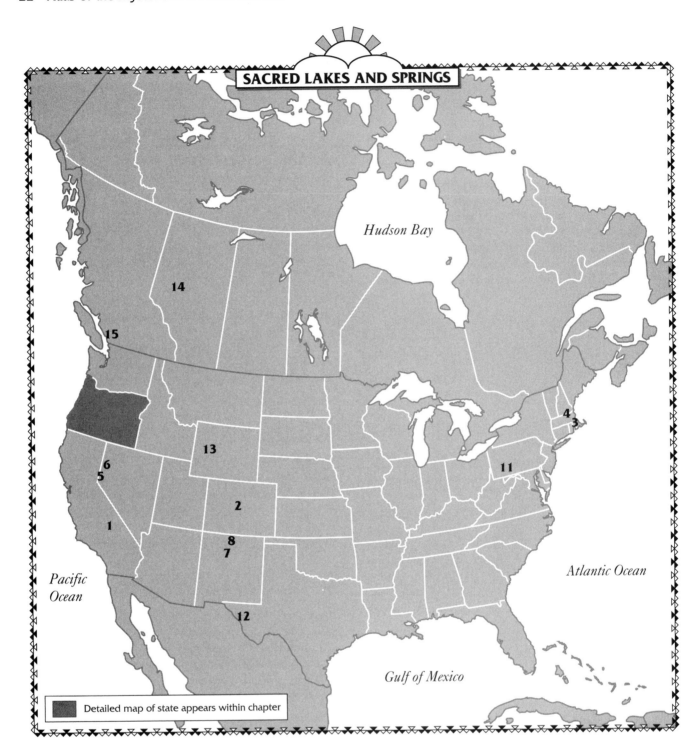

SACRED LAKES AND SPRINGS

SACRED LAKES AND SPRINGS

Not only mountains, but lakes and springs are considered sacred places by many American Indian peoples, for a variety of reasons.

Some sites, like California's Coso Hot Springs, were renowned for their healing powers. Others—the Hobomonk Swamps of Massachusetts, for example—were

believed to be the hangouts of supernatural beings. Blue Lake in New Mexico, believed by the Taos to be the place of their emergence into the earth world, is the site of an annual pilgrimage.

As with other types of places revered by American Indians, sacred lakes and springs have been adopted also by non-natives. El Sanctuario de Chimayo, near Chimayo, New Mexico, has renowned healing springs, whereas Crater Lake, in Oregon, is considered one of the holiest of places in North America by many in the New Age movement.

UNITED STATES

California ✠

Coso Hot Springs (1) These springs sacred to the Shoshone and other tribes are now located in the middle of a government installation, the China Lake Naval Weapons Center. Permits are granted to the Indians, giving them access to the springs that they believe have healing powers.

Colorado ✠

Manitou Springs (2) Located at the foot of Pike's Peak, these springs supply sparkling-pure water known to the local Indians for its healing properties. The Algonquin, Ute, Comanche and others worship these springs (which they called "Medicine Fountains") by leaving gifts such as blankets, robes and knives. The name Manitou comes from an Algonquin word that means "Great Spirit."

Massachusetts ✠

Hobomonk Swamps (3) Legends of East Haven people told of devils coming out of these swamps. In their language Hobomonk is said to mean "Devil."

South End Pond (4) This pond is in the middle of the remains of a series of trenches that form a triangle approximately seven miles in circumference. Inside the triangle are seven hillocks. When the first white settlers moved into the Millis area, the local Indians fought bitter battles to keep the sacred pond from them.

Nevada ✠

Lake Tahoe (5) For the Washoe, Lake Tahoe was one of the principal homes of the feared water babies, small people with long black hair.

Pyramid Lake (6) American Indians tell that this lake is inhabited by a mysterious, giant serpent.

New Mexico ✠

Blue Lake (7) For the Taos peoples, this lake is a place of spiritual renewal. Every year the group makes a journey up the Sangre de Cristo Mountains to conduct ceremonies of remembrance at this lake that, according to legend, is their creation place.

El Sanctuario de Chimayo (8) Near this holy 160-year-old church is a now-dry spring that the Indians held sacred. Pilgrims come from all over the world to rub the healing mud from the spring bed on the afflicted parts of their bodies or to pack the mud into containers to take home. See EL SANCTUARIO DE CHIMAYO under "Sacred Places."

Oregon ✠

Crater Lake (9) The second deepest in North America, this lake is said to contain what is perhaps the cleanest water in the world. The purity of this water is due to the fact that it is fed almost entirely by precipitation. The lake occupies a crater, or caldera, formed when a powerful volcano named Mount Mazama erupted approximately 7,000 years ago.

The Klamath considered Crater Lake so sacred that no one save experienced shamans could approach its shores. In the New Age movement this lake is regarded as one of the ultimate holy places in North America. It is the complement of Mount Shasta, offering dark watery access to the spirit of Goddess. See WIZARD ISLAND in "Sacred Places."

Multnomah Falls (10) This breathtaking waterfall on the south wall of the Columbia Gorge drops 542 feet and is the fourth highest in the United States. Local Indians have a legend about the falls. They say that there was once an evil sickness that came to their people. Nothing anyone did helped those who became ill, until finally an old medicine man had a vision. He told his people that a young maiden must willingly sacrifice herself by jumping from a high cliff. The chief's daughter, determined to save her people, climbed to the top and jumped. In her memory the Great Spirit

Oregon: Sacred Lakes and Springs

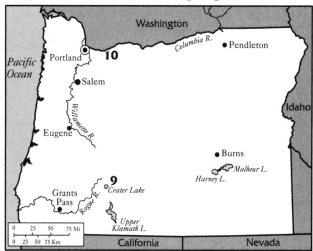

caused glistening water to pour over the cliff at the spot from which she hurled herself, thus creating the falls.

Pennsylvania ✣

Bedford Springs (11) Indian legends described this medicinal spring in Bedford as a kind of fountain of youth. In the 19th century this site became a popular spot to take the water to cleanse one's internal system.

Texas ✣

Indian Hot Springs (12) This group of 22 artesian springs is known for its healing powers. For hundreds of years, folk healers and doctors have made use of the curative powers of the water and the mud of these springs with some dramatic results.

Wyoming ✣

Bull Lake (13) Indian legends tell that this lake is home to a strange, malevolent white water buffalo. It's also said that ghosts periodically meet here.

CANADA

Alberta ✣

Lac Sainte-Anne (14) The lake waters are said to have curative properties, and thousands of American Indians visit the lake and shrine of Sainte-Anne-de-Beaupré each year for healing. A tiny community by the same name rests on the lake, northwest of Edmonton. Pilgrimages here culminate on the saint's feast day, July 26.

British Columbia ✣

Sproat Lake (15) When the first white settlers came to the Vancouver area they were attracted by this beautiful lake. The local Indians warned them to stay away as the lake was possessed by a powerful devil they called Cheeka. The whites, who were stubborn and did not listen, suffered Cheeka's wrath and were driven away. The area around this lake remained almost uninhabited because of Cheeka until after 1910, at which point the lake became a popular tourist site.

VISION QUEST SITES

The vision quest site traditionally is a carefully chosen place that has strong power and welcomes spirits. Not all vision quest sites have been used repeatedly. Many are sites selected by an individual or the elders to suit one person's special needs. Because of this, many vision quest sites have been lost. Only those with a large assemblage of artifacts that identify them as vision quest sites, or those that have been handed down through the generations, remain for us to learn about.

Many early Plains peoples preferred mountains for their vision quest ceremonies. Standing high on the summit of a grand peak, one feels small and insignificant. The world takes on a new perspective. The mountain is majestic in its beauty and brutal in the harshness of its environment. The Bighorn Mountains are a fine example of the summits that are typically used for the vision quest. These mountains are a true challenge to the neophyte. The terrain is wild, rough and isolated. This same type of terrain is found at another famous vision quest site, Bear Butte in the Black Hills of South Dakota. The well-known American Indian chief Crazy Horse had a vision here that told the future of all mankind.

Not all vision quest sites are mountains, and not all are chosen for the roughness of their topography. Enchanted Rock is not a tall mountain, but for the Comanche it was truly sacred. The spirits lived in this granite dome that emitted mysterious crackling noises in the cold, dark Texas night. Vision pits found near Lake Superior and Rock Lake illustrate that Indians also quested for the sacred vision near special bodies of water.

Today traditional American Indians continue to follow their forefathers in the quest for the vision. At sites like Chimney Rock, modern shamans still go through initiation rituals and seek the truth that the sacred vision has to offer.

UNITED STATES

California ✣

Chimney Rock (1) The American Indian name of this sacred mountain is Hey-ah-klau or "Golden Rock." Modern Indians still occasionally make the trek up this mountain to seek visions.

Colorado ✣

Forest Canyon Pass (2) This site in Rocky Mountain National Park is, like the Caribou Lake site, Indian Peaks Wilderness Area, thought to be a vision quest site because of the types of artifacts collected here by

VISION QUEST SITES

Hudson Bay

14

16

15   17

10

13   8 7
5 9

1

11

2 4 3

Pacific
Ocean

6

Atlantic Ocean

12

Gulf of Mexico

archeologists. The two sites have comparable artifact assemblages.

Indian Peaks Wilderness Area   (3) Archeologists infer from artifacts such as obsidian, ocher and large amounts of pottery found here in the Caribou Lake area that it was once used by Indians for vision questing.

Old Man Mountain   (4) Like many American Indian vision quest sites this high place in Estes Park is remote from the secular world. Its wild beauty is imposing and likely to inspire a feeling of awe. This peak is littered with artifacts, suggesting its use as a vision quest site as long as 3,000 years ago.

Connecticut ✤

Montville Prayer Seat (5) A circular stone "prayer seat" is situated by a high-voltage power line constructed in Montville in 1950, implying a recent or contemporary use of the site, probably for vision questing.

Georgia ✤

Fort Mountain Stone Wall (6) The 29 circular pits found at this site in Fort Mountain Park, near Chatsworth, are thought to be related to the vision quest. The pits are small, only large enough to hold one squatting man.

Massachusetts ✤

Beaver Dam Brook Stone Mounds (7) In one of the cairns on this site near New Plymouth, close to a brook, a collection of 19th-century patent medicine bottles were found. Presumably they were left there as memorials or sacrifices during vision quests.

Esker Stoneworks (8) Metal buckets and other ritual objects used in modern vision quests were found here in Boxborough.

Great Point (9) The original name of this sacred site, Natick, means "the place of seeking." Both this site on Chappaquiddick Island and another located at a bend of the Charles River were vision quest sites for American Indians. New England missionaries turned these vision quest sites into praying villages in which American Indians were converted and taught to live like Christians.

Montana ✤

Billings Humanoid Figures (10) A group of cairns found near three ground figures suggest that this may have been a vision quest site. For more on this topic, see "Ground Figures" in Stoneworks.

Nebraska ✤

Blackbird Hill (11) The Omaha used these hills that lie within the reservation for their vision quest rituals. An interesting keyhole-shaped ceremonial altar/fireplace, said to be a prayer symbol, was located on one of these hills. This altar was cut from sod in front of the sacred pole used in Omaha ceremonies to bring blessings to the camp circle or village.

Texas ✤

Enchanted Rock (12) This billion-year-old mass of pink granite near Fredericksburg, a holy site for thousands of years, was used by the Comanche for vision questing.

Wyoming ✤

Bighorn Mountains (13) The Crow emphasized the role that suffering played in the vision quest, leading them to rank sites according to altitude. The most difficult and thus most sacred of all Crow vision quest sites was high in the Bighorn Mountains where the feared Thunderbird lived.

CANADA

Alberta ✤

Valley of the 10 Peaks (14) These peaks sacred to the Stoney or Assiniboine people lie in the Canadian Rockies near Calgary. The Stoney people still maintain their vision quest ceremonies, going up to the mountain periodically after they purify themselves in sweat lodges and smoke peace pipes.

Ontario ✤

Dreamer's Rock (15) A great vision quest site for the Anishabec is on Manitoulin Island, where youth traditionally went to fast and pray to learn their spirit guide.

Lake Superior Vision Pits (16) Rectangular stone structures found at this isolated site have been interpreted by archeologists as vision quest pits. These stone structures, called Puckasaw pits, may date back as much as 3,500 years.

Rock Lake Vision Pits (17) The pits found on this site in Algonquin Provincial Park are similar to those at Lake Superior. One difference between the sites is the existence of rock cairns at Rock Lake. The cairns are thought to represent successful visions.

EARTHWORKS AND MOUNDS

Throughout the eastern half of North America are still to be seen hundreds of earthworks and mounds of varying description, built by Indians, starting about 3,000 years ago and ending with the arrival of the first explorers and colonists in the 1500s.

That American Indians were the creators of these structures is beyond dispute today, but this was not always so. The few mound-building cultures that had survived to the time of contact with Europeans (such as the Natchez of Mississippi) were quickly decimated by disease and routed from their homesites, and mound-building practices passed with them. For later colonists, the earthworks and mounds were a complete mystery. As the number, size and complexity of these works became known, the idea of an ancient European-derived culture of Mound Builders developed. The candidates for the identity of the Mound Builders included many of those groups considered responsible for the works listed in the Stoneworks section below—Vikings, Greeks, Israelites, Persians, Hindus, Phoenicians and emigrants from Atlantis all received a share of the attention.

Not everyone believed that the Mound Builders were Europeans, however. Thomas Jefferson was among those who held that the mounds were built by native peoples, and he undertook what may have been the first truly scientific excavation of a North American mound near his home at Monticello. Finally, in the latter part of the 19th century, major archeological investigations—including one launched by the newly founded Smithsonian Institution—succeeded in proving native provenance.

With the myth of an ancient European culture in the Americas dispelled, public interest in mounds and earthworks rapidly faded. If there is something of a renaissance of interest in them today, it is because these works-have never really lost their mystery. We know now that American Indians were responsible for them, but we don't know which groups—that is, we don't know for sure who their descendants are. We can see that the mound-building culture developed out of previous cultural traditions, but we don't know exactly what caused it to arise, or what caused it to die out (except for the remnants that were made extinct by European contact). Finally, we don't really know what the purpose of the earthworks and mounds were.

Some of the earthworks may have been fortifications, but many others enclose sites that appear to have been religious centers. Many mounds surround burials whereas others were used as terraces for planting or for building structures of various sorts, but whether these were their only functions is uncertain. There is mounting evidence that at least some may have served in part as astronomical observatories, similar to the medicine wheels and other stoneworks described below. A considerable proportion are sited to face east, the direction of the rising sun, and some include features that could have marked solstices and equinoxes. This is true even of some of the so-called effigy mounds—those that have the shapes of animals—and that probably served as totemic designations of the groups that built them.

The separation of earthworks from mounds and the distinction of different types of mounds—burial mounds, platform or temple mounds, effigy mounds—is somewhat artificial, because they are often found as part of the same sites. However, for organizational purposes, this chapter begins with earthworks and then takes up burial mounds, temple mounds and effigy mounds. Mounds that are not known to fall into any of the three latter groups are listed under "Earthworks."

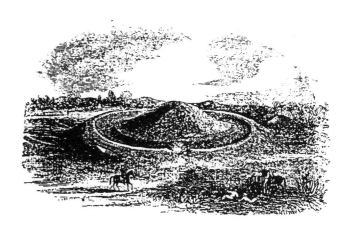

Example of a conical mound with earthworks in Greenup County, Kentucky (Squier & Davis)

EARTHWORKS

Earthworks are piles of earth shaped to form walls, circles, squares, rectangles, octagons and other geometric patterns. Some earthworks surround what seem to have been functional areas such as game yards, public plazas, ceremonial courts, burial grounds or residential areas. However, in most cases their function is not so easily discernible.

Earthworks were constructed by native peoples in what archeologists call the Late Archaic, Woodland and Mississippian periods. The Archaic period ended with the invention of pottery and the advent of horticulture about 3,000 years ago. The Woodland period followed, giving way to the Mississippian period about A.D. 700. The Mississippian period in turn lasted until the first Europeans arrived, in the 16th, 17th and 18th centuries.

Early North American Earthwork-building Cultures

CANADA

Adena-Hopewell heartland
Extent of Hopewell influence
Mississippian cultural regions

Lake Superior
Lake Michigan
Lake Huron
Lake Ontario
Lake Erie

Newark
Athens
Portsmouth
St. Louis ▲ Cahokia
Lexington

Atlantic Ocean

Gulf of Mexico

The most important cultures for the construction of earthworks were the Adena, Hopewell and Mississippian. The Adena people are associated with the Early Woodland period, the Hopewell with the Middle Woodland period, and the Mississippian, of course, with the Mississippian period. The Adena territory extended east to west from southwestern Pennsylvania to southeastern Indiana, and north to south from north-central Ohio to central Kentucky. The Hopewell homeland was less extensive, being largely confined to southwestern Ohio, but its influence was more widely felt. Mississippian cultures were concentrated in the southeastern United States, but also had considerable influence, especially along the Mississippi River. One of the largest Mississippian sites is Cahokia, outside of St. Louis, Missouri.

Each of these three cultures had a distinctive earthwork. Typical of the Adena was a circular enclosure called the sacred circle. Adena sacred circles were from 150 to 200 feet in diameter, with the earth embankment broken in one place to provide an entrance. A ditch, from which the earth was thrown up to form the embankment, ran along the interior wall of the circle except at the entrance, where the surface was left undisturbed to form a sort of causeway. Adena sacred circles appear in groups of two to eight, for example, at the Wolfe's

Plains Group near Athens, Ohio, or the Mt. Horeb Earthworks outside Lexington, Kentucky. Some circles enclose burial mounds. The purpose of others is not known; they may have been places where rituals were held, but they were not habitation sites and were not used for fortifications.

Hopewell earthworks were much larger and more complex than Adena, although there are similarities. In addition to circles, one finds squares, octagons and other regular geometric figures. The Ohio earthworks conform to a set pattern. Apparently all had a square or octagonal forecourt, with four or eight entrances attached to a circle, which could be entered only through a passage from the forecourt. The scale of these structures is immense. The great circle at the Newark, Ohio, earthworks is 1,200 feet in diameter, and the octagon there encloses 50 acres. Others are even larger, enclosing as much as 200 acres in some cases. Some of the Hopewell earthworks complexes stretch for miles; the Newark earthworks covered about four square miles, whereas the Portsmouth earthworks extended for about eight miles in Ohio and Kentucky.

Hopewell geometric earthworks are almost always located in river valleys, where large expanses of flat land were available for building and there was an abundance of easily accessible sediments for use as building materials. The Hopewell also built earthen and stone fortlike enclosures on the tops of isolated hills (e.g., Fort Hill) or other promontories (e.g., Fort Ancient), away from the rivers.

Some researchers believe that the Hopewell used a standard measure equalling about 57 meters and their knowledge of the right triangle to design the enclosures. Others believe that the earthworks served as lunar and solar observatories. Whatever the truth of the matter, it is clear that some of their purpose was ceremonial. Some Hopewell villages were located outside embankments

Hopewell Man

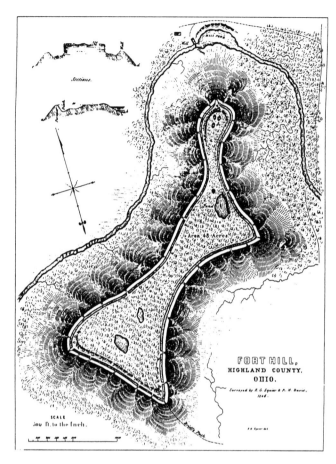

Fort Hill (Squier & Davis, 1848)

near the earthworks, whereas others were at a considerable distance from the earthworks.

Earthworks are most common in the Adena and Hopewell heartlands—there are estimated to have been as many as 1,000 to 1,500 in Ohio alone—but they appear elsewhere in eastern North America as well. Woodland period earthworks are found in Florida, Georgia and South Carolina. Perhaps the most elaborate are the big circle sites of the Lake Okeechobee Basin in Florida. Here, large and diverse earthwork complexes were constructed between 500 B.C. and A.D. 500. Various types of platform mounds (see "Platform and Temple Mounds") occur along with earthworks at these sites.

The Mississippians built primarily platform mounds, but many of their settlements include parallel walls bordering game fields and enclosures surrounding larger ceremonial centers.

Mounds are a special type of earthwork, and are treated more extensively in later sections. However, mounds that are not easily classifiable as burial, platform or effigy mounds are included here. These include mounds built up from sea shells. Shell mounds are

actually refuse piles or middens, but many were shaped like other mounds and may have had similar purposes. The shell mounds listed here are those that are not simply middens, but seem to be something more.

Earthworks resemble in many ways the stone walls and enclosures common in New England (see Stoneworks), and seem to have had some of the same purposes, including being aligned with regular celestial events. Many mounds were also oriented to the east and included structures that assisted in the observation of the heavens. We do not know the precise relationship between the mound-building and stonework cultures, although it is likely that most of the stoneworks were constructed before and during the same period as the earliest mounds. Given the similarities, the difference in building materials may reflect no more than the difference in environment. The following is a list of major earthworks sites in North America.

UNITED STATES

Alabama ✛

Indian Mound Park (1) Six oyster shell mounds in Mobile County, similar to those found in Florida.

Florida ✛

Ancient Canal (2) Runs a mile and a half between Naples Bay and the Gulf of Mexico, 55 feet wide and, in places, 40 feet deep.

Florida: Earthworks

Examples of mounds, located at Mound City National Monument, Ohio (photograph by Richard Frear, courtesy National Park Service)

Big Mound Key (3) A shell mound at Estero Bay, built by the Caloosa.

Chattahoochee Landing (4) Located in Gadsden County on the floodplain immediately east of the Apalachicola River, one of the most important mound complexes along the river in Florida.

Crystal River Mounds (5) Located in the Crystal River State Archaeological Site, Citrus County, these mounds span at least 1,600 years of human activity, with both Hopewellian and Mississippian affiliations.

Mound Key (6) At Fort Myers Beach is one of the largest and most elaborate sites of the Caloosa Indians, with two large oval earth and shell mounds, among others.

Turtle Mound State Archeological Site (7) An oyster shell mound on the Atlantic shoreline in New Smyrna Beach.

Georgia ✛

Rock Eagle Effigy Mound (8) Not a true effigy mound, but a mound topped by a huge open-winged eagle made of milky quartz stones pieced together on the ground in the Eatonton vicinity.

Iowa ✛

Davenport Mound (9) When excavated, this mound was found to contain several stone tablets bearing a wealth of symbols.

Kansas ✛

Hayes Council Circle (10) A mound surrounded by four earthwork ditches, evidently the remains of dugout houses. This mound in Tobias may have functioned as a medicine wheel.

Paint Creek Council Circle (11) A mound surrounded by earthwork ditches in McPherson County, evidently the remains of earth lodges. The mound may have functioned as a medicine wheel.

Paul Thompson Council Circle   (12) A mound surrounded by four earthwork ditches, evidently the remains of dugout houses. This McPherson County mound may have functioned as a medicine wheel.

Swenson Council Circle   (13) A mound in McPherson County surrounded by four earthwork ditches that may have functioned like a medicine wheel.

Tobias Council Circle   (14) Mound, surrounded by earthwork ditches, evidently the remains of earth lodges. The mound at Lyons may have served as a medicine wheel.

Kentucky   ✚

Adena Park   (15) Earthwork enclosure and mound, part of the Mt. Horeb Earthworks, Fayette County.

Catacombs   (16) A complex of tunnels leading to a chamber 300 feet long, 100 feet wide, and 18 feet high, filled with idols, altars and about 2,000 human mummies lying beneath the city of Lexington.

Central Park Mounds   (17) A string of six small mounds, each four to five feet high, are located in the northwest part of the park in Ashland.

Mt. Horeb Earthworks   (18) An extensive earthwork complex in the Lexington vicinity that includes four earthwork formations, one a sacred enclosure, now excavated and restored.

Louisiana   ✚

Poverty Point State Commemorative Area   (19) An Archaic period site in the Epps vicinity with concentric arcs, and with a central avenue that may have been solstice-aligned, leading to an effigy mound in the center.

Massachusetts   ✚

Andover Earthworks   (20) A series of sites with earthen banks and ditches and stone walls in association with a stream, perhaps a sacred place where shamans practiced their art and visions were sought.

South End Pond   (21) This pond in Millis is surrounded by the remains of trenches in the form of a triangle, seven or so miles in circumference, in the middle of which are seven hillocks. The site is believed to have great religious importance.

Mississippi   ✚

Nanih Waiya State Park   (22) There is a mound at this site in the Louisville vicinity where American Indians lived for about 1,500 years before contact with Europeans.

Norman Site   (23) Village site with three mounds in the Lambert vicinity.

Pocahontas Mound B   (24) This site includes a large earthwork containing burials.

Missouri   ✚

Crigler Mound Group   (25) Seven mounds, probably of Woodland affiliation in Florida.

Denton Mound and Archeological Site   (26) Five mound groups with a surrounding village site.

Sharkey Mound Group   (27) A group of 13 mounds in Hannibal.

Sikeston Fortified Village Archeological Site (28) Five of 13 original mounds are visible.

Van Meter State Park   (29) The park in Miami boasts an earthen fort and mounds.

New Hampshire   ✚

Lochmere Indian Stone Fort   (30) Stone and earthworks, with features resembling the earthwork structure at Marietta, Ohio, and probably a sacred enclosure rather than a fortification.

Ohio   ✚

Boyce Fort and Village   (31) An elevated five-acre site, at one time encircled by a horseshoe-shaped wall and ditch in the Wayne vicinity.

Braddock Works   (32) An Adena ceremonial complex in the vicinity of Fredericktown consisting of a circular bank and ditch enclosing a large oval mound, with another smaller mound outside the enclosure.

Burchenal Mound   (33) Hemispherical mound, eight feet high and 75 feet in diameter, built on top of a glacial esker near Woodland.

Cedar-Bank Works   (34) A large, rectangular earthwork near Chillicothe containing an interior wall and a truncated mound, surrounded by a ditch.

Colerain Works   (35) A wide U-shaped earthwork embankment about 416 feet long, in some places six inches high, with an interior area of some 100 acres at Dunlap.

Ohio: Earthworks

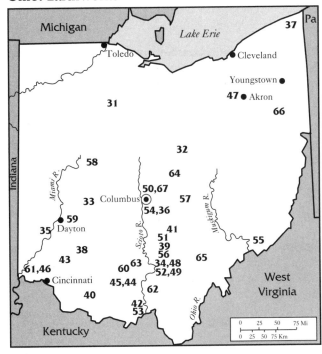

Columbus Country Club Works (36) A low burial mound and ditch surrounded by a circular embankment.

Conneaut Works (37) An earthwork fortification enclosing a village.

Cowan Creek Enclosure (38) Circular earthen wall, about 90 feet in diameter, located in the Wilmington vicinity and closely associated with the Cowan Creek Mound.

Davis Works (39) An oval Hopewellian mound near Laurelville, formerly surrounded by an earthen wall with an interior trench. There are traces of another circular wall and trench immediately to the south.

Eagle Township Works (40) A complex near Fincastle that originally consisted of three circular enclosures, a single-walled enclosure and two mounds, only one of which survives.

Ety Enclosure (41) Circular ridgetop earthen wall enclosure with an exterior ditch and a single gateway, probably a Hopewellian ceremonial center.

Feurt Mounds (42) A four-acre village site with three mounds in the Portsmouth area, associated with the Fort Ancient culture of southern Ohio and northern Kentucky.

Fort Ancient State Memorial (43) Hopewell earthworks near Lebanon that enclosed areas where rituals and funeral services were performed.

Fort Hill State Memorial (44) Around the flat top of a hill stands a wall 40 feet thick at its base, and in places 15 feet high, a well-preserved Hopewell ritual site near Hillsboro.

Fort Hill State Park Works (45) A Hopewellian hilltop ceremonial site in the Sinking Springs area enclosed within a stone and earth wall.

Fortified Hill Works (46) Earthen-walled hilltop enclosure near Hamilton with gateways at cardinal points protected by interior walls of embankments and mounds outside the north, south and west entrances. Although the enclosure is said to be a fort, excavations turned up no signs of habitation.

Fort Island Works (47) An oval-shaped earthen enclosure in Akron with an exterior ditch associated with a Late Woodland occupation site.

Great Seal Park Works (48) An earthwork complex in the Chillicothe vicinity in association with a habitation site and seven Adena mounds.

High Banks Works (49) A Hopewellian ceremonial complex near Chillicothe, consisting of circular and irregular octagonal earthworks, enclosures and mounds.

Holder-Wright Works (50) Three geometric ceremonial earthworks, each consisting of a bank and an interior ditch, in the Dublin area.

Hopetown Earthworks (51) A Hopewellian ceremonial center composed of large conjoined circular and square earthen enclosures, four burial mounds and parallel earthen walls forming a causeway to the Mound City Group.

Hopewell Mound Group (52) A large earthwork enclosure in the shape of a parallelogram enclosing two

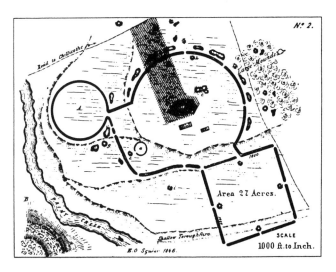

Seip (Squier & Davis)

small earthworks, and an adjacent square enclosure near Chillicothe.

Horseshoe Mound (53) A horseshoe-shaped earth embankment, all that remains of the Portsmouth Group, a once-extensive ceremonial complex that included mounds, circles, parallel walls and many miles of connecting earth embankments.

Jackson Fort (54) An Adena sacred circle near Columbus that once surrounded an earthen mound.

Marietta Earthworks (55) An important earthwork complex with Adena, Hopewell and Mississippian affiliations. (See also MARIETTA MOUND entry under "Burial Mounds.")

Mound City Group National Monument (56) This is a large ceremonial complex located near Chillicothe and consisting of a rectangular earth wall enclosure surrounding 22 burial mounds.

Newark Earthworks (57) A huge geometric enclosure built for rituals 1,800 years ago. This Hopewellian site includes the Octagon Earthworks, Wright Earthworks and Mound Builders State Memorial.

Newlove Works (58) Large Adena ceremonial center near Springfield with two circular enclosures, one containing an elliptical mound.

Pollack Works (Cedarville Earthworks) (59) Hilltop Hopewellian embankment probably constructed as part of a ceremonial center in the Cedarville vicinity.

Rocky Fork Park Works (60) Two concentric circular earthwork enclosures with gateways facing east, built on a hillside near Rainsboro, giving an amphitheater effect.

Ross Trails Adena Circle (61) A circular enclosure about 35 feet in diameter and a foot high, encircling a campsite, dating perhaps as early as 1000 B.C.

Scioto Township Works (62) Geometric Hopewellian earthworks, of which part of a square embankment and several mounds have survived in the Wakefield vicinity.

Seip Mound State Memorial (63) Part of an extensive Hopewell burial complex in the Bainbridge area. An earthwork in the form of a circle surrounds a large oval-shaped mound. There is also a smaller earthen structure and a partly preserved earthen square.

Spruce Run Earthworks (64) A complex of earthworks and mounds, evidently a ceremonial and mortuary center for the Galena area.

Wolfe's Plains Group (65) A large ceremonial center near Athens consisting of numerous burial mounds and circular earthwork enclosures, at least 20 in original condition.

Workman Works (66) Located in Salem Township, these Hopewellian earthworks consist of two conjoined mounds, earthen embankments and a ditch.

Worthington Works (67) Formerly, a large rectangular earth bank enclosure with two interior mounds and two smaller circular bank and ditch enclosures. Only one mound remains.

Tennessee ✚

Indian Town Bluff Mounds (68) A Mississippian village cemetery site with circular mounds on a ridge located in the vicinity of Ashland City.

Texas ✚

Kiomatia Mounds (69) A group of four mounds associated with a prehistoric village site.

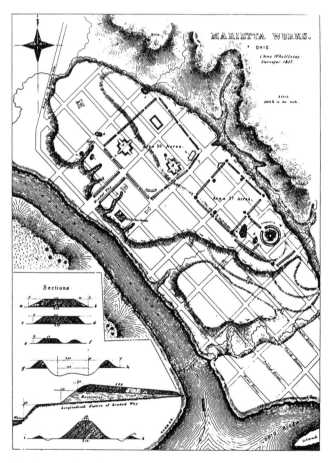

Marietta Earthworks (Squier & Davis)

Mound City   (photograph by Richard Frear, courtesy National Park Service)

Utah ✛

Nephi Mounds   (70) A village site with some 30 mounds.

West Virginia ✛

Criel Mound   (71) A prehistoric mound in Charleston that has been greatly altered by modern use. One hundred years ago its top was taken off to make room for a judges' stand at horse races; later a bandstand was built into its side.

Wisconsin ✛

Aztalan State Park   (72) A major mound site in the Lake Mills area, with Mississippian cultural affiliations.

Medicine Wheel Mound   (73) A prehistoric mound near Fort Atkinson that has been likened in shape to medicine wheels.

Mero Mound Group   (74) Located near Diamond Bluff, a group of over 60 mounds in association with a village.

Roche-a-Cri State Park   (75) This park in the Friendship area sports a mound and rock carvings.

CANADA

Ontario ✛

Royal Ontario Museum Mound   (76) Located in Toronto, this is one of several Rainy River mound sites, radiocarbon dated to A.D. 1200.

BURIAL MOUNDS

Both the Adena and the Hopewell built burial mounds. Adena mounds, in fact, are presumed to be exclusively burial mounds, although since not all have been excavated, this is not known for sure. Burial

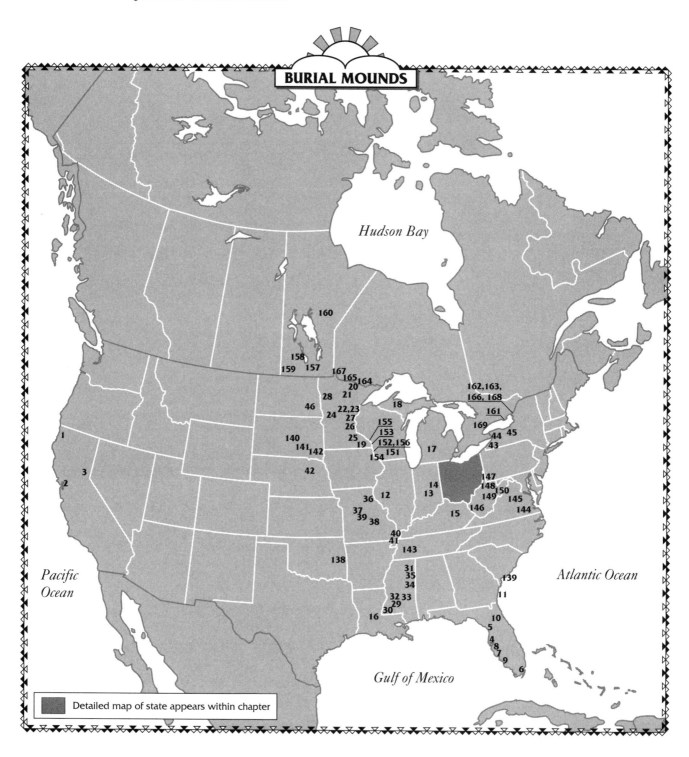

BURIAL MOUNDS

mounds were a major Adena innovation, and set this culture apart from earlier American Indian peoples, who had placed their burials in natural ridges or hills. The Adena began building hills for their dead.

Adena mounds were built up in stages. The first burials were in graves dug in the earth that were then covered over with dirt. Later burials were made on top of the mound, and again covered with earth, so that over the years a sizeable mound was built up. The largest mounds, such as Grave Creek Mound in West Virginia and Miamisburg Mound in Miamisburg, Ohio, were almost 70 feet high.

Adena mortuary practices changed over time. For instance, many early Adena graves were lined with bark, but late Adena graves often had log tombs. Further changes came with the Hopewell complex. Although the Adena mounds were all built as burial mounds, not all Hopewell mounds enclose burials. Moreover, Hopewell burial mounds tend to have fewer burials per mound, and the graves tend to be more finely appointed. Unlike Adena mounds, Hopewell burial mounds were usually built on a single occasion rather than over time, and consequently are not as high. Among existing mounds, Seip Mound in Ohio, at 30 feet, is the highest, and this is less than half the height of the highest Adena mounds.

Hopewell mounds often have irregular shapes. Three fourths of Hopewell burials were cremations, and burial mounds were often built over crematoria and followed the contours of these structures. One of the most interesting of these mounds was the Tremper Mound, in Ohio, which has the appearance of a quadruped animal, something like a bison or buffalo.

The Mississippians employed cemeteries rather than burial mounds. Mississippian mounds are predominantly platform mounds of various types (see "Platform and Temple Mounds"). Here are the major burial mound sites in North America.

UNITED STATES

California ✤

Aikman Mounds (1) These mounds at Bluffton were found to contain huge numbers of crushed human skulls.

Miller Creek School Mound (2) A coastal Miwok burial mound in San Rafael.

Strap Ravine Nisenan Maidu Site (3) Two probable burial mounds close to a grooved petroglyph in Placer County.

Florida ✤

Bay Pines Mound (4) A midden mound in use as a burial place about 4,000 to 2,500 years ago.

Grave Creek Mound (Squier & Davis, 1847)

Crystal River Mounds   (5) Located in Citrus County, at Crystal River State Archaeological Site, this important site, one of the most significant in Florida, includes a conical burial mound.

Culter Burial Mound   (6) In Perrine, a sand mound about 75 feet in diameter and 6.5 feet high.

Historic Spanish Point   (7) Here at Osprey are burial mounds dating from 2150 B.C.

Madira Bickel Mounds State Archeological Site (8) The site in Bradenton includes two burial mounds in addition to a platform mound, and was occupied from about 500 B.C. to A.D. 1600.

Mound Key   (9) This Fort Myers Beach site has a burial mound, among other mounds.

Mount Royal Mound   (10) This Putnam County mound is connected to an artificial pond, created by the sand excavated to build the mound.

Georgia   ✛

Sapelo Mounds   (11) An Archaic period shell mound built in a ring on Sapelo Island.

Illinois   ✛

Dickson Mounds   (12) An excavated, Middle Mississippian burial mound near Lewiston.

Indiana   ✛

Fish Farm Mounds   (13) Located in the New Albin vicinity, about 30 prehistoric Indian mounds representative of the Woodland culture.

Great Circle Mound   (14) This site in Mounds State Park, Madison County, shows both Adena and Hopewell influences.

Kentucky   ✛

Elam Mound   (15) A probable Adena burial mound, seven feet high and 100 feet in diameter, in the Lexington area.

Louisiana   ✛

Marksville Prehistoric Indian Site State Monument (16) This site in Avoyelles Parish is a southern variant of the Ohio Hopewell with burial and temple mounds.

Michigan   ✛

Norton Mounds   (17) A Hopewell site in Grand Rapids with 17 mounds, 13 clearly visible, all that remain of about 40 once standing here.

Sand Point   (18) This site in Baraga County includes four large burial mounds.

Minnesota   ✛

Chatfield Mound   (19) A half-dozen skeletons of enormous size were found in the mound.

Grand Mound Center   (20) The Grand Mound in International Falls is the largest prehistoric burial mound in the northern Midwest.

Laurel Mounds   (21) Five burial mounds and a village site in Koochiching County.

Malmo Mounds   (22) Middle Woodland mounds, associated with village site.

Moose Lake Mound   (23) This mound contained bones of people who must have been eight feet tall.

Morrison Mounds   (24) Series of conical mounds with secondary burials in Otter Tail County.

Mounds Park   (25) The park preserves six burial mounds, all that remain of 18 or more that once stood in the St. Paul area.

Pine City Mounds   (26) Like the Moose Lake Mound, this mound contained bones of people who must have been eight feet tall.

Stumne Mounds   (27) A group of mounds in Pine County consisting of 13 lineal and two conical burial mounds.

Warren Mound   (28) This mound yielded not only 10 gigantic human skeletons, but also skeletons of dogs and horses.

Mississippi   ✛

Berry Mound   (29) A conical mound near an occupation site in Terry, Hinds County.

Boyd Mounds   (30) At milepost 106.9 of the Natchez Trace Parkway is a prehistoric village site with several burial mounds.

Bynum Mounds   (31) A group of burial mounds near Tupelo, in the Hopewellian tradition.

Dupree Mound   (32) A conical burial mound in Edwards, surrounded by a village site.

Mississippi Valley Burial Mounds   (Squier & Davis, 1847)

Mangum Mound   (33) Copper ornaments and other artifacts found in burials have revealed much to archeologists about the people who built the mounds.

Mound Cemetery Site   (34) Located near Amory, a single conical burial mound, 20 feet high and about 125 feet in diameter, possibly Hopewellian.

Pharr Mounds   (35) The largest and most important archeological site in northern Mississippi is in Tupelo and consists of eight large dome-shaped burial mounds, scattered over an area of 90 acres, built and used from about A.D. 1 to A.D. 200.

Missouri   ✤

Boulware Mound Group Archeological Site   (36) A group of 58 burial mounds in Canton, many containing cremated burials.

Harley Park Archeological Site   (37) Four unexcavated conical mounds in Boonville, possibly containing burials.

Mealy Mounds Archeological Site   (38) A total of 14 circular and oval burial mounds in three groups with an associated village site in Mokane.

Mellor Village and Mounds Archeological District (39) A large Hopewell complex in Lamine containing 20 burial mounds.

Sandy Woods Settlement Archeological Site (40) Seven burial mounds and a temple mound with an associated village area in Diehlstadt.

Wardell Mounds   (41) Two large burial mounds near a possible cemetery.

Nebraska ✢

Eagle Creek Mounds (42) Nine burial mounds and an occupation area dated to Woodland times, around A.D. 200 to 1000 in the vicinity of O'Neill.

New York ✢

Cain Mound (43) A nearly circular burial mound, with a diameter of almost 30 feet near Gowanda.

Lewiston Mound (44) An oval burial mound, over 50 percent of which consists of sandstone, overlooking Niagara Gorge.

Rector Mound (45) A relatively small mound, 30 to 40 feet in diameter, situated on Crusoe Creek near Savannah.

North Dakota ✢

Standing Rock State Historic Site (46) A complex of burial mounds near Fort Ransom dating from Woodland times.

Ohio ✢

Aberdeen Mound (47) Unusually large conical burial mound near Aberdeen.

Adena Mound (48) Indian Mound Campground near Athens.

Arledge Mounds (49) Two large conjoined Adena burial mounds near Circleville.

Armco Park Mounds (50) Two conical Adena mounds near Otterbein.

Benham Mound (51) A conical burial mound in Cincinnati, probably Hopewellian.

Bone Mound II (52) Burial mound associated with nearby Bone Stone Graves in the Oregonia vicinity.

Braddock Mound (53) A large oval mound in an earthwork enclosure with a smaller, subconical mound outside the enclosure in the Fredericktown area.

Campbell Mound (Adena) (54) Adena mound in Columbus, administered by the Ohio Historic Preservation Office. Large conical burial mound, probably late Adena.

Campbell Mound (Hopewell) (55) Hopewellian burial mound, largest of a group of seven that formed part of the Trefoil Earthworks, and the only remaining visible manifestation of this ceremonial center near Bainbridge.

Cedar-Bank Mound (56) A truncated Hopewellian mound within an earthwork enclosure near Chillicothe.

Clemmons Mound (57) Large conical Adena burial mound in the Fox area.

Coe Mound (58) One of the largest conical burial mounds in either the Adena or Hopewell culture areas is in Columbus.

Columbus Country Club Mound (59) Low burial mound and ditch surrounded by a circular embankment in Columbus.

Conrad Mound (60) Woodland period mound near Cleves.

Cowan Creek Mound (61) A mound, now inundated, in the Wilmington vicinity. When excavated in 1947, the site revealed 17 log tomb burials. Associated with the Cowan Creek Enclosure (see COWAN CREEK under "Earthworks").

Dayton Power and Light Company Mound (62) Large conical Adena culture mound near Wrightsville.

Deffenbaugh Mound (63) Small conical Adena burial mound near Laurelville.

Dixon Mound (Williams Mound) (64) In Homer, a large Adena mound, unusual for being conical and situated near a river.

Dunns Pond Mound (65) Large subconical Hopewell burial mound near Huntsville.

Eagle Township Works I Mound (66) The single surviving mound of a formerly larger complex near Fincastle.

Edington Mound (67) Large conical burial mound, probably Adena, but possibly Mississippian, near Neville.

Edith Ross Mound (68) A rounded stone and earth burial mound, either Adena or Hopewell, in the Laurelville area.

Elk Lick Road Mound (69) In the Bantam area, conical Adena mound, perhaps containing multiple burials.

Elk Lick Road Mound (69) Located in East Fork State Park, Clermon County, this conical mound, about 50 feet in diameter and five feet high, is probably of Adena affiliation, and stands in the park picnic grounds.

Ellis Mounds (70) Group of three small Hopewell burial mounds near Marysville.

Fairmont Mound (71) Flat-topped conical mound, approximately 15 feet high and with an 80-foot-diameter

Ohio: Burial Mounds

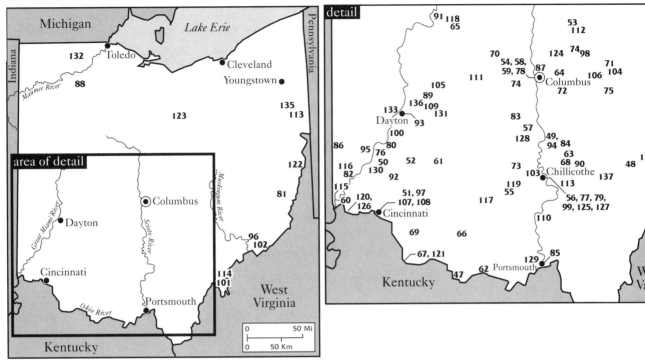

base, on the grounds of the Fairmont Presbyterian Church in Licking County.

Fortner Mounds   (72) Two, paired burial mounds, unusual for the Adena culture, now much reduced by plowing located near Pinkerington.

Frankfort Works Mound   (73) Burial mound that is the last remaining evidence of the Frankfort works, once a large ceremonial complex consisting of one square and two circular earthen embankments and eight burial mounds.

Galbreath Mound   (74) Conical burial mound six feet, six inches high, near Galloway.

Glenford Fort Mound   (75) Conical Hopewellian mound within an earthwork enclosure in the Glenford area.

Great Mound   (76) Second largest Adena burial mound in the Ohio Miami River Valley near Middleton.

Great Seal Park Group   (77) Seven Adena mounds in the vicinity of Chillicothe in association with earthworks and a habitation site.

Hartley Mound   (78) In the Columbus area, a small, subconical burial mound two feet high, its size reduced by cultivation.

High Banks Mound   (79) Hopewellian mounds in association with earthworks near Chillicothe.

Hill-Kinder Mound   (80) Largest Adena mound near Franklin in Warren County, associated with the Miamisburg Mound.

Hodgen's Cemetery Mound   (81) Located in Tiltonsville, this Adena mound is unusual in being located on the Ohio River floodplain rather than in uplands.

Hogan-Borger Mound Group   (82) Large central mound surrounded by a crescent of six smaller mounds on the east near Ross.

Hopeton Works Mounds   (83) Four burial mounds that are part of the Hopeton Works, near Hopetown.

Horn Mound   (84) Large conical Adena burial mound in the Tarlton vicinity.

Horseshoe Mound   (85) In Portsmouth Mound Park, an Ohio Hopewell burial mound.

Hueston Woods Campground Mound   (86) In Hueston Woods State Park, in the vicinity of College Corner, is a partially restored Adena burial mound.

Jeffers Mound   (87) Large truncated mound, the only remaining feature of the Worthington Works (see entry under "Earthworks").

Kinzer Mound   (88) Subconical Adena burial mound.

Knob Prairie Mound (Enon Mound)   (89) A large, remarkably well-preserved conical mound, probably Adena.

Krashner Mound (90) Conical Adena burial mound with slightly truncated top near Laurelville.

Lake Ridge Island Mounds (91) Four low, subconical mounds, probably Hopewellian, in the vicinity of Russells Point.

Landen Mounds (92) Two Adena mounds in the Foster vicinity.

Lichliter Mound (93) Mound in Archaic–Late Woodland context, associated with an extensive village site in the Dayton vicinity.

Luthor List Mound (94) Large Adena burial mound near Circleville.

Mann Mound (Leslie Mound) (95) Large burial mound enclosure with numerous unusual limestone cairns near Jacksonburg.

Marietta Mound (96) In the Marietta cemetery, a large mound, originally part of a complex of mounds and earthworks.

Matthew Mound (97) An Adena or Hopewell mound in Evandale, roughly hemispherical in shape, not associated with any known village site.

Melick Mound (98) Conical mound of the type associated with Adena culture and built to cover house sites, ceremonial grounds or burials near Utica.

Metzger Mound (99) An Adena site in the Chillicothe area consisting of two subconical burial mounds and a semicircular earth embankment enclosing a third small mound.

Miamisburg Mound (100) Located in Miamisburg Mound State Memorial, a cone-shaped Adena mound, 68 feet high; the largest of its kind in Ohio.

Mound Cemetery Mound (101) Unexcavated Adena mound in the Chester vicinity.

Mound Cemetery Mound (Conus Mound) (102) Adena mound and elliptical enclosure, completely surrounded by historic Mound Cemetery in Marietta.

Mound City Group National Monument (103) Near Chillicothe, an earthen rectangle surrounds 23 burial mounds at this, one of the best-preserved Hopewellian sites.

Nashport Mound (104) Large conical Adena burial mound.

Newark Earthworks (105) This important Ohio Hopewell earthwork complex in Mound Builders State Memorial includes a burial mound.

Newlove Mound (106) An elliptical burial mound in an earthwork complex near Springfield.

Norwood Mound (107) An elliptically shaped Adena burial mound.

Odd Fellows' Cemetery Mound (108) In Newtown, a conical burial mound, typical of Adena construction.

Orator's Mound (Glen Helen Mound) (109) Subconical Adena burial mound near Yellow Springs.

Piketon Mounds (110) In the Piketon cemetery, this site was once part of an extensive system of ceremonial and burial mounds, three of which remain. The largest mound has four lobes at each of the cardinal points of its base, probably representing later burials.

Potter Mound (Hodge Mound II) (111) Subconical Adena burial mound near Mechanicsburg.

Raleigh Mound (112) Conical Adena mound, 20 feet high, near Fredericktown.

Ratcliffe Mound (113) Subconical Woodland period mound, probably a burial mound, near Londonderry.

Reeves Mound (114) Adena burial mound near Alfred.

Rennert Mound (115) A Woodland period mound 18.7 feet high and 85 feet in diameter, with an associated village site near Elizabethtown.

Roberts Mound (116) Adena or Hopewell conical mound near Auburn.

Rocky Fork Park Group (117) Group of three Hopewellian burial mounds near Marshall.

Rose Mound (118) Seven-foot-high conical mound with ceremonial associations in Huntsville.

Seip Mound (119) In Seip Mound State Memorial, near Bainbridge, several mounds are still visible at this extensive Hopewell site, the largest an oval 150 feet wide, 250 feet long and 32 feet high, surrounded by a circular earthwork.

Short Woods Park Mound (120) Unexcavated burial mound, assigned to Adena, and perhaps 2,000 years old, located in Sayler Park.

Snead Mound (121) Conical mound, probably an Adena burial mound near Neville.

Speedway Mound (122) A typical Woodland period conical mound, located in Warrenton.

Sprott's Hill Mounds (123) Two mounds in the Ashland vicinity with evidence of typical Adena burial practices.

Spruce Run Mounds (124) A complex of earthworks and mounds, evidently a ceremonial and mortuary center, near Galena.

Stitt Mound (125) A large subconical Adena mound near Chillicothe.

Story Mound (126) Located in Story Mound State Memorial, Chillicothe, this subconical Adena burial mound encloses a circular timber mortuary structure.

Story Mound (127) Large Adena mound with ceremonial and burial functions in Sayler Park.

Tick Ridge Mounds (128) Two conical Adena burial mounds in the Williamsport vicinity.

Tremper Mound (129) An irregularly shaped Hopewellian burial mound near West Portsmouth with the remnants of a surrounding earthen enclosure. The shape results from an addition of rooms to a ceremonial structure that was eventually burned and covered with earth.

Williamson Mound (130) Mound measuring seven feet, six inches in height, and 70 to 75 feet in diameter located near Maud.

Williamson Mound State Memorial (131) Large Adena mound near Cedarville excavated in the 1840s, restored in 1929.

Winameg Mounds (Council Oak) (132) Twelve small mounds constructed by Hopewell peoples in the Delta area between A.D. 300 and A.D. 600 and used in the historical period by the Potowatami as a ceremonial center.

Wolf Creek Mound (133) A conical mound and surrounding ditch, probably Adena, in the Trotwood vicinity.

Wolfe's Plains Group (134) Group of eight burial mounds near Athens, including the Hartman Mound (George Connett Mound), which is the largest of the group. Also on the site are several sacred circles.

Workman Works (135) Two conjoined mounds form part of an earthwork complex in Salem Township.

Wright Brothers Memorial Mound Group (136) A group of six well-preserved mounds, probably Adena, near Fairborn.

Zaleski Mound Group (137) Group of three burial mounds, Markham Mound, Ranger Station Mound and Zaleski Methodist Church Mound.

Oklahoma ✤

Spiro Mound Group (138) Extensive ceremonial complex dominated by nine mounds, some used for burials.

South Carolina ✤

Edisto Island Shell Mound (139) Oyster shell midden that served as a burial mound with a crescent-shaped opening in the northeast.

South Dakota ✤

Fort Thompson Mounds (140) Numerous burial mounds built over an occupation site of an earlier culture.

Mitchell Golf Course Mounds (141) Five burial mounds possibly associated with a habitation site on the grounds of the present municipal golf course.

Sherman Park Indian Burial Mounds (142) In this municipal park are several mounds built by people who followed the Plains lifeway, 1,600 years ago.

Tennessee ✤

Pinson Mounds (143) Located in Pinson Mounds State Archaeological Area, these burial and ceremonial mounds, including Saul's Mound, have Adena and Hopewell affiliations.

Virginia ✤

Hayes Creek Mound (144) Rich burial mound in the territory of Massawomee.

Lewis Creek Mounds (145) A group of 13 accretional earth or earth-stone burial mounds.

West Virginia ✤

Camden Park Mound (146) A conical mound about 20 feet high, probably of Adena affiliation, near the center of the Camden Amusement Park near Huntington.

Cresap Mound (147) In Marshall County, an Adena mound, 15 feet high and 40 feet in diameter, abandoned after a cremation ceremony on its top.

Grave Creek Mound (Mammoth Mound) (148) In Moundsville, the largest mound built by the Adena people.

Hyer Mound (149) Sandy clay mound on top of a ridge near the Elkwater Fork stream in Randolph County.

Romney Indian Mound Cemetery (150) A Late Woodland mound in a cemetery on a bluff overlooking the valley of the south branch of the Potomac River.

Wisconsin ✣

Farwell's Point Mound Group (151) A group of 13 conical mounds, probably burials, along with a group of effigy mounds in the Madison area.

Foley Mound Group (152) A group of 10 burial mounds, seven of them conical, three in effigy shapes, near Lynxville.

LaCrescent Mound (153) Giant skillets and huge bones were excavated from this mound in LaCrosse.

Olson Mound Group (154) Fifty-eight conical mounds and seven linear mounds, possibly representing burials, in Seneca.

Schwert Mound Group (155) Twenty-six Hopewell burial mounds in association with village sites near Trempealeau.

Wall-Smethurst Mound Group (156) A burial mound group near Lynxville that consists of 10 conical mounds, a bird effigy, and a 100-foot linear mound in an irregular row.

CANADA

Manitoba ✣

Pembina Mounds (157) Mounds of varying shapes, most on the edge of a plain.

Souris River Mounds (158) Mounds of varying shapes set on the edge of a plain.

South Antler Mounds Group (159) A group of round or elliptical burial mounds, set well back from the edge of a plain.

Whitemud Mounds (160) Group of four mounds, including two effigy mounds, three of which are set on the crest of a ridge.

Ontario ✣

Bay of Quinte Massassauga Mounds (161) A series of truncated cone mounds.

Cameron's Point Mounds (162) Mounds along the westernmost stretch of the St. Lawrence River.

East Sugar Island Mounds (163) Mounds in the western part of the St. Lawrence River.

Fort Frances Mound (164) A burial mound on Rainy River, near the place where it joins Rainy Lake.

Hungry Hall Mounds (165) Mounds at the western end of Rainy River, near Lake of the Woods.

Le Vesconte Mound (166) Mound on the westernmost stretch of the St. Lawrence River.

Long Sault Rapids Mounds (167) A series of mounds, including the most spectacular prehistoric monument in all of Canada, overlooking the Long Sault Rapids on the Rainy River.

Sea Mound (Tidd's Island Mound) (168) A mound on an island in the St. Lawrence where it joins Lake Ontario.

Serpent Mound (169) Located in Serpent Mounds Provincial Park, near Peterborough, an oval mound containing four burials near the head of a snake-shaped mound.

OTHER BURIAL MOUNDS

State/Province	Site	Culture*
Florida	Fort Center Mound, Lakeport	AH
	Tick Island Mound, Astor	AH
Illinois	Naples Mound, Griggsville vicinity	H
Indiana	Cemetery Mound, Tiltonsville	
	New Castle Mound, New Castle	AH
	Sonotabac Mound, Vincennes	
Kentucky	Portsmouth Mound "C," Greenup	AH
Mississippi	Floyd Mound, Bovina	
	Spanish Fort Mound, Holly Bluff	AH
	Tchula Lake Mound, Tchula	AH
Missouri	Delta Center Mound, Pemiscot County	
Ohio	Bainbridge Mound, Bainbridge	AH
	Brown Mound, Chillicothe vicinity	A

State/Province	Site	Culture*
Ohio	Cannon Mound, Georgesville vicinity	
	Demoret Mound, Ross vicinity	
	Dublin Mound, Dublin	AH
	Graded Way Mound, Piketon	AH
	Highbanks Park Mound II, Delaware County	
	McDaniel Mound, Utica vicinity	A
	Moar Mound, Morrow vicinity	H
	Oldtown, Frankfort	AH
	Seal Mound, Piketon	AH
	Shawnee Lookout Park Mounds, Hamilton County	
	Shorts Woods Park Mound, Cincinnati	
	Stone Work Site, Chillicothe	AH

*Culture: A = Adena;   H = Hopewell;   AH = Adena/Hopewell

PLATFORM AND TEMPLE MOUNDS

Platform mounds have flat tops that serve as surfaces for buildings and various activities, including agriculture. They vary from square to elongated rectangles at the base, and may be of considerable size. Monks Mound at Cahokia, Illinois, the largest platform mound in the United States, measures about 1,000 feet by 800 feet at the base and is 100 feet in height. Platform mounds also occur as truncated cones and other geometric forms.

Perhaps the most common use of platform mounds was to support a ceremonial structure that has come to be called a temple. Temple mounds are characteristic of the Mississippian culture, and are not found in the earlier Adena and Hopewell traditions. The Mississippians, however, were not the only ones to build temple mounds—they were also constructed by the roughly contemporary Caddoans (see SPIRO MOUND GROUP in Oklahoma and CADDOAN MOUNDS STATE HISTORIC SITES in Texas), who may have influenced or been influenced by the Mississippians.

Low platform mounds could have been built all at once, but larger platform mounds were enlarged one or more times. Sometimes burials (probably of deceased leaders) were made in platform mounds, although their usual function was to support a structure of some sort. In many cases, these structures were burned before being piled over with earth. Most platform mounds were built by Mississippian peoples, although some, such as that at Kolomoki in Georgia and Crystal River in Florida, derive from earlier cultures. Here is a list of major platform and temple mounds.

UNITED STATES

Alabama ✛

Bottle Creek Indian Mounds   (1) A Mississippian ceremonial center with six extant temple mounds in Baldwin County.

Florence Indian Mound   (2) One of the largest Mississippian mounds in the Tennessee Valley, built around A.D. 1200. Middle Mississippian temple mound.

Jackson Park   (3) At Fort Toulouse, a platform mound and two forts.

Mound State Monument   (4) Major Eastern mound site where a tourist attraction was removed on protest. Middle Mississippian temple mound near Moundville.

Arizona ✛

Gatlin Site   (5) Hohokam ceremonial center with platform mound in Maricopa County.

Pueblo Grande Museum   (6) Trails with explanatory signs lead to a large platform mound in Phoenix.

Pueblo Grande Ruin   (6) Hohokam village in Phoenix with ball court and platform mounds.

Arkansas ✛

Toltec Mounds (Knapp Mounds)   (7) Now in Toltec Mounds State Park, near North Little Rock, stands a large ceremonial complex and village site with three

PLATFORM AND TEMPLE MOUNDS

mounds and a semicircular embankment occupied for over 1,000 years, beginning about A.D. 400.

Florida ✚

Big Mound City   (8) An extensive Mississippian ceremonial complex in Indiantown, originally consisting of 23 mounds.

Crystal River Indian Mounds   (9) Located in Crystal River State Archaeological Site, Citrus County, this site includes two temple mounds. One of the most significant in Florida, with both Hopewellian and Mississippian affiliations, these mound sites span at least 1,600 years of human activity.

Lake Jackson Mounds   (10) The largest known Mississippian temple mound center in northwestern Florida, located in Tallahassee, Leon County.

Florida: Platform and Temple Mounds

Lake Lafayette Mound (11) A flat-topped pyramidal mound about 15 feet high with Mississippian affiliations in Leon County.

Madira Bickel Mound (Bickel Ceremonial Mound) (12) Part of a complex at Madira Bickel Mound Archeological Site, Bradenton, covering much of the Terra Ceia site, occupied from about 500 B.C. to A.D. 1600.

Mound Key (13) This site in Fort Myers Beach includes a high truncated temple mound, among other mounds.

Safety Harbor Mound (14) A Mississippian temple mound at a village site on Philippe Point, overlooking the west shore of Old Tampa Bay in Pinellas County.

Temple Mound Museum (15) A restored mound, on top of which an Indian temple once stood, in Fort Walton Beach. A temple replica has been built on the top of this Mississippian mound. The site was used by a succession of cultures between about 50 B.C. and A.D. 1650.

Georgia ✢

Etowah Mounds (16) From about A.D. 1000 to A.D. 1500, when it was occupied by Mississippian peoples, this site in Etowah Mounds State Historic Site, Bartow County, was an important political and religious center.

Kolomoki Mounds State Park (17) Seven mounds on a 30-acre site in Early County, with both Late Woodland and Mississippian affiliations.

Nacoochee Mound (Hardman Mound) (18) Elliptical Mississippian platform mound in White County.

Ocmulgee National Monument (19) A Mississippian temple mound with a reconstructed ceremonial lodge in Macon.

Illinois ✢

Cahokia Mounds (20) Cahokia Mounds State Park, in East St. Louis has about 120 Mississippian period mounds, among them the famous Monks Mound, the largest earthen structure in the world.

Indiana ✢

Angel Mounds State Memorial (21) A well-preserved Mississippian temple mound in Evansville.

Restored Earch Lodge (Council Chamber), Ocmulgee, from southeast showing entrance (courtesy National Park Service)

Kentucky ✛

Ancient Buried City (King Mounds) (22) This Wickliffe site was once a large Mississippian community, including temple and burial mounds.

Louisiana ✛

Marksville Prehistoric Indian Park State Monument (23) Southern variant of Ohio Hopewell with temple and burial mounds and defensive earthworks in Avoyelles Parish.

Minnesota ✛

Kathio Mounds (24) Mississippian period temple mound site in Kathio State Park, near Onamia.

Mississippi ✛

Bear Creek Mound (25) At milepost 308.8 of the Natchez Trace Parkway are a ceremonial mound and village site that were occupied as early as 8000 B.C. by hunters.

Emerald Mound (26) The third largest temple mound in the United States, a Natchez site near Tupelo. Each of seven villages had its own mound, but the group as a whole was focused on the Emerald Mound, which was more than 35 feet high.

Holly Bluff Site (27) Two central truncated pyramid mounds surrounded by 20 lesser conical ones.

Owl Creek Indian Mounds (28) Two reconstructed ceremonial mounds that, together with three other mounds, once surrounded a village plaza, now part of Tombigbee National Forest near Old Houlka.

Pocahontas Mound B (29) A Mississippian site, including temple mound and earthwork containing burials.

Rolling Fork Mounds (30) Three Mississippian period mounds in Sharkey County.

Winterville Mounds Historic Site (31) An 800-year-old temple mound site in Washington County.

Missouri ✛

Nanih Waiya Mounds (32) Prehistoric-historic mounds, probably Mississippian with later Choctaw associations, in Winston County.

Sandy Woods Settlement Archeological Site (33) Eight mounds, one probably a temple mound in Diehlstadt, Scott County.

Towosahgy Temple Mound (34) A middle Mississippian temple mound in East Prairie at one of the most strongly fortified sites in pre-Columbian North America.

North Carolina ✛

Nikwasi Mound (35) Representative of a class of relatively small conical platform mounds built by Late Mississippian Indians, evidently ancestors to the Cherokee. The mound in Franklin was later used by the Cherokee and is the subject of mythic tales.

Town Creek Indian Mound State Historic Site (36) Palisade, temples, mortuary and game pole reconstructed at this 500-year-old site, a Mississippian ceremonial center near Mt. Gilead.

Ohio ✛

Fort Ancient (Power Mound) (37) Near Lebanon, in Fort Ancient State Memorial, this important site was built and used by the Hopewell, with the later addition of a Mississippian temple mound.

Keiter Mound (38) An oblong mound with a flat top, situated on high ground above Anderson Fork, near Wilmington, about 2,000 years old.

Oklahoma ✛

Caddoan Mississippian Temple Mound Site (39) Extensive ceremonial village complex dominated by nine mounds, some used for burials, others as bases for temple structures near Spiro.

Spiro Mound Group (39) 15 mounds.

Parris Mound (40) A mound in the Sallisaw area, with a slight ramp on the south slope, dating to about A.D. 1000.

Pine Creek Mound Group (41) Four mounds and a village area, part of a ceremonial center dating to the 14th century A.D., near Bethel.

South Carolina ✛

Blair Mound (42) Late Mississippian mound built on the site of a Late Woodland midden and Archaic site near Winnsboro.

Fort Watson Mound (Santee Mound) (43) A large Mississippian temple mound in Clarendon County occupied by British forces during the American Revolution.

Indian Hill (44) A truncated cone-shaped mound, the summit of which served as a platform for religious or ceremonial building, on St. Helena Island.

Scotts Creek Temple Mound (45) South Appalachian tradition temple mound site.

Tennessee ✛

Duck River Temple Mounds (Link Farm Site) (46) Large Mississippian temple center near Hurricane Mills with at least four large mounds—two flat-topped and two conical—arranged around a plaza, with several smaller mounds scattered around these.

Mound Bottom (47) Mississippian temple mound surrounded by 13 smaller mounds, once a ceremonial center around which several groups were centered in Kingston Springs.

Obion Mounds (Work Farm Site) (48) One of the earliest Mississippian sites in Tennessee, at Paris; seven mounds and a plaza clustered around ceremonial features.

Shiloh Mounds (49) In Pittsburgh Landing, at Shiloh National Military Park, a group of more than 30 mounds, including Mississippian temple mounds.

Texas ✛

Caddoan Mounds State Historic Sites (50) Temple and burial mounds in Alto separate from Mississippian culture, but perhaps influenced or was influenced by Mississippian tradition.

OTHER MISSISSIPPIAN PLATFORM AND TEMPLE MOUNDS

State/Province	Site
Arkansas	Barney Mound, Helena
	Menard Mound, Arkansas Post
	Mineral Springs Mound
	Nodena Site, Mississippi County
	Parkin Mound
	Sherman Mound, Osceola
	Upper Nodena Mounds, Wilson
Florida	Big Tonys, Clewiston
	Long Key, St. Petersburg Beach
	Philip Mound, Marion Haven
	Shields Mound, Jacksonville
	Velda Mound, Leon County
Georgia	Irene Mound, Savannah
Illinois	Kincaid Site, Brockport
Iowa	Fish Farms Mounds, New Albin vicinity
Kentucky	Kincaid Mound, Massac County
Louisiana	Alphenia Mound, Clayton
	Fitzhugh Mound, Mound
	Greenhouse Mound, Marksville
	Jackson Place Site, Floyd
	Jerden Mound, Oak Ridge
	Mott Mound, Lamar
Mississippi	Alligator, Bobo
	Anna Mound, Natchez
	Arcola Mound
	Bowdre Mounds (De Be Voise Mounds; Hollywood Site), Tunica County
	Fatherland Mound, Natchez
	Haynes Bluff Mound, Haynes Bluff Landing
	Kinlock Mound, Tralake
	Lake George Site, Holly Bluff
	Magee Mound, Percy
	Mayersville Mound
	Perkins Mound, Scott
Missouri	Beckwith's Fort Mound, East Prairie
	Lilbourn Mound
	Murphy Mound, Pemiscot County
	St. Louis Mounds, St. Louis
North Carolina	Asheville Mound, Asheville
Tennessee	Chucalissa Mound, Memphis
	Hiwassee Island Mound, Dayton
	Lenoir Mound, Lenoir City
	Lindsley Mound, Lebanon

EFFIGY MOUNDS

An effigy mound is built to resemble something— usually an animal or a person, but sometimes a geometric figure. As with the other types of earthworks, there are—or once were—many more effigy mounds than appear below. Those listed here are only the better known or more interesting of those still existing. Many more have been razed in the name of progress.

Effigy mounds as a type are probably younger than mounds as such. The majority are in Wisconsin or neighboring states, and are attributed by anthropologist Paul Radin to the Winnebago and their ancestors. Unlike other types of mounds, which contemporary native peoples generally say were there when they arrived, Winnebago that Radin spoke with told him that it used to be the custom for different clans to build mounds in the shape of their clan animals near their settlements. They were built on land claimed by the clan, thus serving as property markers. Since the Winnebago were semi-nomadic and moved often, this practice naturally resulted in a fair number of similar mounds spread over the region in which these people lived. Effigy mounds in other areas may have served similar functions, but this is not known for sure.

There is often some uncertainty about what animal an effigy mound is supposed to represent. The Wisconsin mounds include a large number that archeologists have identified as panthers, although for the Winnebago these are water spirits. The water spirit mounds are, appropriately, often associated with water. They were built by the water-spirit clan, who believe that their forefathers were water spirits and that the clans originated in lakes. Other Wisconsin effigy mounds are described as turtles, but the Winnebago did not have a turtle clan. The turtle did, however, figure prominently in their mythology.

The Winnebago had a bird phratry (or group of clans), and the Wisconsin bird mounds are undoubtably attributable to it. Bird mounds in other areas, such as that at Poverty Point, Louisiana, may have had another meaning. For many native Americans, birds were associated with death, because birds were widely believed to help take away the spirit at death. But the Poverty Point bird is in dispute, some modern observers thinking it resembles some sort of monster rather than a bird.

Although the Winnebago effigy mounds probably served exclusively as property markers, these mounds may have served other purposes for other native peoples. Some, like those in the Foley Mound Group near Lynxville, Wisconsin, and the White Mud Mounds in Manitoba, doubled as burial mounds, whereas a few, like the Minton Turtle in Minton, Saskatchawan, may have functioned as observatories.

Effigy shapes were not exclusive to mounds. The Winnebago sometimes dug the same shapes into the earth, producing an intaglio or ground-figure. The production of intaglios is a much more widespread practice than the construction of effigy mounds. The following is a list of major effigy mound sites.

UNITED STATES

Illinois ✛

Bird Effigy Mound (1) A mound 45.5 feet from head to tail in Winnebago County.

Hanover Effigy (2) A mound in the shape of a cow or moose, 216 feet long and 5.5 feet high.

Pecatonica River Mounds (3) A group of mounds, one perhaps in the shape of a panther, in Stephenson County.

Rockford Turtle (4) In Winnebago County, a turtle-shaped mound apparently lacking a head, 184 feet from the tip of the tail to the center of the farther end.

Iowa ✛

Effigy Mounds National Monument (5) Mounds in the shapes of birds and bears are among the 200 or so extant at this site in Allamakee County.

Gitchie Manitou (6) Park in Larchwood composed of the remains of a number of abstract mounds and boulder ground sculptures. Scattered among the mounds are a complex array of circles, ellipses and connecting lines.

Louisiana ✛

Poverty Point State Commemorative Area (7) Concentric ridges and a large effigy mound of a bird that looks to some more like some kind of monster.

Minnesota ✛

Fort Flatmouth Mound Group (8) A group of eight linear mounds in Cottonwood County.

Hay Lake Mound District (9) A group of some 75 parallel linear mounds in Cottonwood County.

Nebraska ✛

Turtle Mound (10) An effigy mound in the shape of a turtle in Murray.

Ohio ✛

Alligator Effigy Mound (11) A Hopewellian mound near Granville supposed to be in the shape of an alligator, and possibly associated with the Newark Earthworks (see "Earthworks" above). If the mound was in fact intended to represent an alligator, which is not native to the area, it would suggest that these people had extensive trade networks.

Serpent Mound (12) Located in Serpent Mound State Memorial, near Peebles. Well-preserved effigy mound. Adena site, used also by Hopewell.

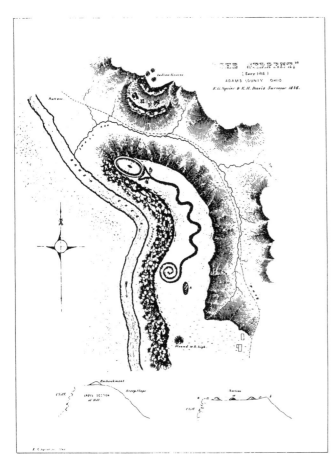

Serpent Mound   (Squier & Davis, 1848)

Tarlton Cross Mound   (13) A large mound in the shape of a Greek cross surrounded by four smaller mounds.

South Dakota ✤

Medicine Knoll   (14) A 360-foot-long snake effigy mound in Blunt.

Wisconsin ✤

Burrows Park Effigy   (15) Effigy mound in the shape of a straight-winged bird in association with a campsite near Madison.

Devil's Lake Effigy Mounds   (16) A mound in the shape of a bear and another in the shape of a lynx are at the north end of the lake in Devil's Lake State Park; a bird-shaped mound is at its south end.

Effigy Mounds   (17) Here, 200 feet above Lake Winnebago, in High Cliff State Park, near Menasha, are 13 effigy mounds, some in the shape of lizards, others in the shape of birds.

Effigy Mounds   (18) Lizard Mound State Park, near West Bend, includes 31 effigy mounds along with Adena-Hopewell style burial mounds. The effigy mounds take the shapes of birds, panthers and lizards, as well as geometric designs.

Farwell's Point Mound Group   (19) A group of mounds in the Madison area that include two panthers, one bird and four linear mounds, along with 13 conical mounds.

Foley Mound Group   (20) A group of 10 burial mounds near Lynxville, three of them in effigy shapes—two fork-tailed birds and one probably a bear.

Forest Hill Cemetery Mound Group   (21) A linear mound, two panthers and a partially destroyed flying goose near Madison.

Green Lake Mound   (22) An oval-shaped mound.

Heller Mound Group   (23) This group includes five mounds in panther shapes and one with a more problematical design.

Kletzien Mound Group   (24) A group of 33 effigy mounds in Sheboygan Mound Park, some resembling deer or panthers, others conical or linear in shape, built between A.D. 500 and A.D. 1000.

Man Mound   (25) Large effigy mound at Baraboo, unusual in resembling a human figure.

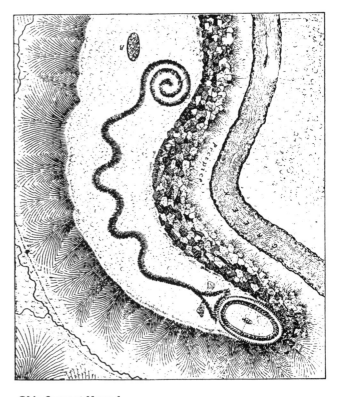

Ohio Serpent Mound

Wisconsin: Effigy mounds

Menasha Mounds (26) An effigy mound, constructed sometime after A.D. 800.

Mendota State Hospital Mound Group (27) Among the mounds on the hospital grounds is a six-foot-high bird whose wingspan stretches 624 feet. Other effigy mounds in this group near Madison include two other birds, two panthers, two bears, a deer, a mound of indeterminate shape and a linear mound.

Muscoda Mounds (28) A group of 50 effigy mounds, on private land and not developed, but visible from the road that passes them.

Nelson Dewey State Park (28) A number of prehistoric effigy mounds in this park near Cassville overlook the Mississippi River.

Utley Mound Group (29) Three mounds, one of them linear, one in the shape of a panther and one in the shape of a bear.

Vilas Circle Bear Effigy (30) A bear-shaped effigy and a linear mound are the only remains of an extensive mound complex, called the Curtis Mounds, near Madison.

Wall-Smethurst Mound Group (31) A bird effigy and a 100-foot linear mound in an irregular row with 10 conical burial mounds.

CANADA

Manitoba ✚

Whitemud Mounds (32) A group of four burial mounds, two of which are effigy mounds.

Ontario ✚

Manitou Mound (33) An effigy mound on Rainy River.

Pelee Island Mounds (34) Effigy mounds on an island in Lake Eire.

Serpent Mound (35) A mound depicting a snake, 80 feet above Rice Lake in Serpent Mounds Provincial Park, near Peterborough. The mound is 189 feet in length, 24 feet in width, and averages five feet in height. Near its head is an oval mound, containing five burials.

Saskatchewan ✚

Minton Turtle (36) Effigy mound whose principal axis, from tail to head, is aligned to Sirius rising at summer solstice. A sunburst rock mosaic is nearby.

STONEWORKS

Was North America colonized by Phoenician traders from Spain, Egyptian miners and Basque sailors, not to speak of Celtic monks and Norse explorers? Do the mysterious prehistoric stoneworks—small stone chambers and meandering walls in New England, rock outlines of men and animals in the West, carvings and drawings on rock faces from Canada to Texas and California—remain as evidence of their presence, or were they created by native American peoples?

The debate over the origins of native North American cultural remains rages today, but it is not new. Columbus's discovery of America created a dilemma for Biblical scholars, because Old Testament accounts described the settlement of only three continents after the Flood. Either the Scriptures were wrong, or the natives were not members of the human race. The delicate problem was resolved in 1512 when Pope Julius II declared that Native Americans were descended from Babylonians who had been banished from their homeland because of their ancestors' sins. Much later, the Puritan Cotton Mather opined that the practice of circumcision, found among certain New England groups, showed that they were descended from the Lost Tribes of Israel.

Today the genetic relation of native American peoples to Asian peoples and their migration across the Bering Strait between 10,000 and 30,000 years ago is undisputed. Those (such as Harvard biochemist Barry Fell) who argue for cultural diffusion from the Old World to the New hold not that the aboriginal peoples brought European culture with them, but rather that the aboriginal peoples were contacted and influenced by European peoples later in their history.

The majority of professional anthropologists and archeologists put little stock in the various diffusionist scenarios. Yes, the Vikings reached North America and may have sailed through the Gulf of St. Lawrence, but the only undisputed Viking site—on the coast of Labrador—was occupied for no more than 10 years around A.D. 1000, and appears to have been used for periodic stopovers during ocean voyages rather than being the site of a permanent colony. Excavations at a stone tower in Newport, Rhode Island, long imagined to be the work of the Norse, turned up nothing predating the colonial era.

Some diffusionists point to supposed similarities between North American and European stoneworks, but these are superficial at best; there is nothing in North America that resembles the megalithic monuments of England. The marks on rocks interpreted as ancient, foreign scripts may be no more than game or astronomical counters or rough maps of the surrounding terrain. The professionals point to indigenous developments and argue that there is no reason why native Americans could not have built up their own cultural traditions; where these parallel those of Europe, they say, is only an example of cultural convergence.

There is debate also over the reason the stoneworks were created, and this debate crosses the lines of the professional and lay communities. The rough stone chambers that dot the New England countryside were once believed to have been built by the English colonials as root cellars. It is only in the last decade, thanks to the work of lay diffusionist groups such as the New England Antiquities Research Association, that the professionals are beginning to admit the possibility that the chambers may have served as astronomical observatories for native shamans. Key rituals—such as those relating to planting and harvesting among agricultural peoples—were tied to annual solar events, so these observatories would have served as a sort of ritual calendar.

Other stoneworks, especially medicine wheels, may also have marked astronomical events, particularly solstices and equinoxes. Not all medicine wheels are aligned in such a way that they could have served as observatories, however; some surround burial sites and may have been constructed as monuments to chiefs or other renowned individuals. Indeed, no stone feature seems to have had the same function or set of functions wherever it is found. This diversity of function lends a certain mystery to these sites that is unlikely ever to be dispelled altogether. If recent research results lend more weight to the arguments of the professionals than the lay diffusionists, it has also shown that no single explanation fits all cases.

The sites covered in this chapter are grouped under four headings—Enclosures, Walls and Cairns; Ground Figures; Medicine Wheels; and Petroglyphs and Pictographs. Many of the sites are points of contention between the diffusionists and those who believe Native Americans were responsible for their construction. All are of human manufacture, or imply human involvement; stone features that did not involve human manip-

Inside stone chamber at Magnetic Mine Road, near Croton Reservoir, New York. Did the camera capture a luminous anomaly? Photograph taken in October 1991 by Anastasia Wietrzychowski, using infrared film and 35-mm single-lens reflex (courtesy Anastasia Wietrzychowski)

ulation are classified as sacred sites and listed in Power Points and Sacred Places. Some important types of stone remain known to archeologists are not covered in this book at all because they lack spiritual or occult significance or have no aura of mystery surrounding them. These include tipi rings—circles of bread-loaf-sized rocks, six to 18 feet in diameter, to which wigwams were anchored—and long rows of stones leading to the edges of cliffs, used in buffalo drives. Both are characteristic of the Great Plains, and are found in profusion from Texas to central Canada.

ENCLOSURES, WALLS AND CAIRNS

Cairns are heaps of stones; they may have been constructed for a variety of purposes. Some prehistoric cairns seem to be no more than boundary markers or trail blazes. Other cairns contain burials and commemorate individuals or events. Still other cairns are found at vision quest sites, where they have been built up over time, each new supplicant adding a stone to the pile.

Cairns of varying function appear throughout North America. Also associated with vision quests among Algonquian peoples in the northern tier of the United States and southern Canada are semicircular rings of stones called prayer seats, in which the vision supplicant sat awaiting the appearance of his supernatural protector, or guardian spirit. Prayer seats are often situated on mountain tops or other remote places.

Walls and enclosures also are typically found in remote places. Although some appear in association with habitation sites and seem to have served as fortifications, the majority probably had some sort of ritual significance. The Fort Mountain Stone Wall near Chatsworth, Georgia, for instance, is at an altitude that makes it an

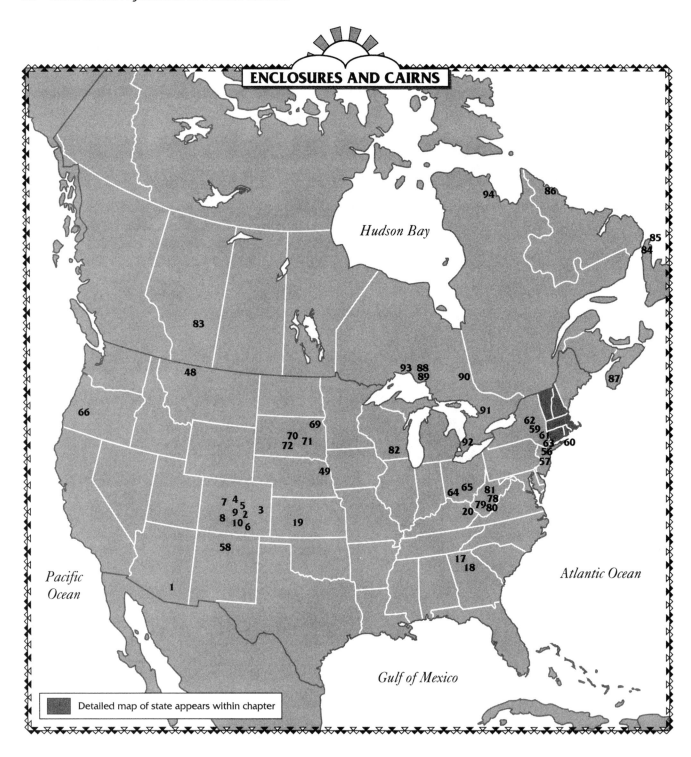

ENCLOSURES AND CAIRNS

Hudson Bay

Pacific Ocean

Atlantic Ocean

Gulf of Mexico

Detailed map of state appears within chapter

unlikely hunting blind, but its base is lined with a series of large pits that may have served as seats for vision supplicants.

The most elaborate enclosures are the stone chambers of New England. Made of unmortared stone, some are freestanding or sunk into the earth, whereas others are reached via tunnels driven into hill- or mountainsides. The chambers typically are associated with networks of walls, tall standing stones and cairns that are aligned with the entrance in such a way that they mark the rising or setting sun or certain stars (such as the Pleiades) on the solstices or equinoxes. Similar alignments are found at many so-called Indian forts, which, far from being fortifications, probably served as ritual sites. Winter solstice alignments are the most frequent in New England stonework, probably because winter solstice was the time of the most important Algonquin festival, the Feast of Dreams.

Perched boulders and balanced rocks are a type of stonework characteristic of New England and the northern tier of the United States, the area covered by glaciers during the last Ice Age. When the ice sheet receded, it left behind many rocks, some of them piled haphazardly, others lying or standing at peculiar angles. Some of these sites, like that at Moodus, Connecticut, are at seismically active places, and the moving earth and associated noises were taken by native peoples even in the historic period to indicate the homes of supernatural beings. In other cases, large boulders have been positioned in such a way that they can rock back and forth, sometimes on a set of four or five smaller stones. These, too, appear to have had some sort of ritual function.

A relatively unusual type of stone complex, rain roads, are found in the Southwest, such as those at Chicoma Mountain in New Mexico. Rain roads run from an "earth navel" in the mountains, the site from which the first ancestors of the people issued, and are designed to direct water down into the arid plateaus and valleys. The following are some of the significant sites of enclosures, walls and cairns.

UNITED STATES

Arizona ✤

Zodiac Ridge Alignment (1) A circle of stones with an east-west alignment of stones near the center, possibly a summer and winter solstice and equinox register near Tucson.

Colorado ✤

Apishapa River Canyon Stone Circles (2) Generally circular arrangements of stones rising about 30 inches above ground level abound in this canyon on the border between Pueblo and Las Animas counties. Most of the enclosures are situated on the tops of cliffs or other promontories and are clustered in sites that appear in pairs, one relatively simple, the other more elaborate, on opposite sides of the Apishapa River. Petroglyphs appear at some sites.

Bent County Stone Circles (3) Stone enclosures similar to those in Pueblo County (see APISHAPA RIVER CANYON STONE CIRCLES).

Canon City Stone Circles (4) Stone enclosures similar to those in Pueblo County (see APISHAPA RIVER CANYON STONE CIRCLES) appear in the Eight Mile Creek Valley near Penrose and on steep mountain peaks along Wilson Creek.

Goodpasture Stone Circles (5) Stone enclosures similar to those in Pueblo County (see APISHAPA RIVER CANYON STONE CIRCLES).

Las Animas County Stone Circles (6) Stone enclosures similar to those at Apishapa River Canyon on the border with Pueblo County are found also in the Purgatorie River Valley and south of the Arkansas River Valley.

Monarch Pass Stone Circles (7) Stone enclosures near Salida similar to those found in Pueblo County (see APISHAPA RIVER COUNTY STONE CIRCLES) meander between two peaks about a quarter mile apart on an 11,000-foot mountain top. The "circles" are made by leaning together slabs of granite, so ancient that they have disintegrated in many places.

Saguache Stone Circles (8) An ancient stone enclosure complex, similar to that at Apishapa River Canyon. The complex consists of 22 circles along the edge of a steep cliff.

Turkey Creek Canyon Stone Circles (9) Stone enclosures resembling those at Apishapa River Canyon. Two large upright boulders at this site on Fort Carson Military Reservation resemble the menhirs (single standing stones) from European megalithic monuments.

Walsenburg Stone Circles (10) Stone enclosures similar to those in Pueblo County (see APISHAPA RIVER CANYON STONE CIRCLES) are located along the Churaras River.

Connecticut ✤

Danbury Stoneworks (11) Stone chamber oriented to winter solstice (midwinter) sunrise.

East Thompson Indian Fort (12) Stone rows, cairns and standing stones aligned to significant points on the horizon suggest that this site served as an observatory.

Gungywamp Indian Fort (13) Situated by the sea, this site includes stone rows, standing stones, perched boulders, cairns, and many marked stones with astronomical alignments.

Gungywamp Prayer Seat (13) One of many New England stone circles, unusual in having a double row.

Montville Hilltop Group (14) A complex of stone structures, including stone chambers, perched boulders and cairns, overlooking a swamp of about 50 acres, with astronomical alignments.

Moodus Stoneworks (15) Unusual stone rows, two stone chambers, many stone piles and mounds of earth and stone in one of the seismically most active places in New England. American Indians believed that the noises and lights emanating from this place indicated that this was the home of the supernatural being called Hobomock, and they gathered here to seek his support.

Shantock Indian Fort (16) An earth and stone structure that probably served as a sacred enclosure rather than a fort, close to the Thames River.

Uncas Fort (14) An ancient stone enclosure on Fort Hill, near Montville, once the site of a Mohegan village.

Georgia ✛

Fort Mountain Stone Wall (17) Near Chatsworth in Fort Mountain State Park is a dry stone wall that zigzags more than 900 feet in a generally east-west direction across one of the highest peaks in southwestern Georgia. See entry under "Vision Quest Sites."

State Botanical Garden of Georgia (18) The Botanical Garden Mounds spread over two acres of a hilltop overlooking the Middle Oconee River in Athens and consist of 30 conical stone mounds, the largest about 10 feet in diameter and 3 feet in height.

Kansas ✛

Pawnee Rock (19) Called Hill that Points the Way by the Pawnee, a rock with a hole in it, within which animals were said to gather.

Kentucky ✛

Stone Serpent Mound (20) Near Catlettsburg, a large snake-shaped stone mound next to a small circular earthen mound with a central depression.

Massachusetts ✛

Acton Waterworks (21) Ancient hydraulic complex of stone and earthworks associated with a swamp and stream.

Acushnet Swamp Site (22) Cairns and stone rows in a swamp are aligned with the winter solstice.

Beaver Dam Brook Stone Mounds (23) Cairns in the New Plymouth vicinity stand along the brook and on a hillside, amidst an array of stone rows connecting larger boulders. See BEAVER DAM BROOK STONE MOUNDS in "Vision Quest Sites."

Brewster Stone Rows (24) Rows of boulders broken periodically by standing stones, near two ponds.

Burnt Hill Standing Stones (25) A collection of 14 standing stones in Heath, their bases wedged into crev-

New England: Enclosures and Cairns

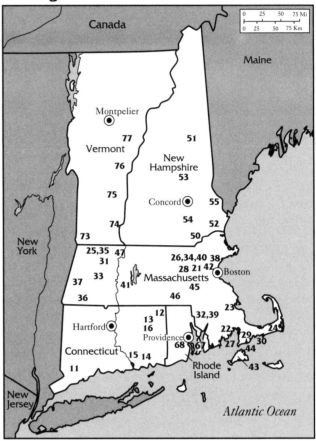

ices in quartzite bedrock, some of which have been shown to be aligned to solstice events as marked by natural features on the distant horizon.

Elizabeth Brook Stoneworks (26) Complex of stone and earth structures associated with Elizabeth Brook, a stream that connects two swamps, one 39 feet lower than the other.

Elizabeth Islands Perched Boulder (27) Boulder with serpentine marks oriented to natural features and cairns that mark solstices and equinoxes.

Esker Stoneworks (28) In Boxborough, a complex of stone and earth structures associated with a pond, swamp and esker. Solstice sunsets are marked by stone rows. See ESKER STONEWORKS under "Vision Quest Sites."

Falmouth Boulder Ridge (29) A variety of manmade stone features, perhaps the remains of a primitive observatory.

Falmouth Great Rock (30) Large boulder on hilltop overlooking several kettle holes, with standing stones or natural peaks on the horizon marking solstice and equinox sunrise and sunset. Great Rock is one of several similar sites on Cape Cod.

Franklin Indian Fort   (31) A complex of stone rows and cairns by a river that probably served as a sacred enclosure rather than a fort.

Freetown Stone Mounds   (32) A group of cairns, in and near cedar swamps, probably part of an ancient ritual site.

Goshen Counterfeiter's Den   (33) A stone chamber deep in the side of a hill just west of the Goshen Cemetery. The name Counterfeiter's Den derives from a legend that counterfeiters were caught a few miles away.

Harvard Indian Fort   (34) Complex of earth and stone structures, located near a spring.

Heath Indian Fort   (35) Complex of earth and stone structures, including a standing stone, that may have served as an observatory.

Indian Point Indian Wall   (36) A wall of boulders on a projection into Lake Onoto.

Monument Mountain Stoneworks   (37) A heap of stones, at the end of a 50-yard-long row of stones, located on a promontory in Great Barrington and visible for miles around, to which each passing Indian added a stone.

North Salem Balanced Rock   (38) Giant boulder supported by four smaller stones on the crest of a hill.

North Watuppa Pond Mound   (39) Oval stone mound, 65 feet long and seven feet high, on the site of a former American Indian reservation in Freetown.

Oak Hill Ridge Stone Chambers   (40) Stone chambers located on northern and southern ends of Oak Hill Ridge in Harvard, the northern aligned to the winter solstice and the southern to the summer solstice.

Pelham Beehive Cave   (41) One of New England's many beehive-shaped stone chambers.

Phaeton Rock   (42) Giant boulder supported by three smaller stones in Lynn.

Quitsa Cromlech (Quitsa Dolmen)   (43) Stone chamber set into a hillside on Martha's Vineyard, with an entrance facing due south.

Shanks Pond Rock Stacks   (44) Line of cairns in Falmouth aligned to the winter solstice sunrise and equinox sunset.

Southborough Stoneworks   (45) Group of stone rows and stone and earthen mounds, some as much as 20 feet in diameter, in and around a swamp.

Upton Chamber   (46) Famous beehive stone chamber aligned to observe the setting solstice sun and stars of the Pleiades, as marked by cairns on nearby Pratt Hill.

Wendell Beehive Cave   (47) One of New England's many stone chambers, near a well-known mineral spring.

Montana   ✢

Blackfeet Reservation Landslide Butte Three-Legged Figure   (48) A 45-foot circle of stones with a 12-foot circle on one side and three lines of stones on the other, lying inside a humanoid ground figure, located on Landslide Butte. See entry under "Ground Figures."

Nebraska   ✢

Blackbird Hills   (49) A stone fireplace and earth altar mark this place, sacred to the Omaha. See entry under "Sacred Mountains" in Power Points and Sacred Places.

New Hampshire   ✢

America's Stonehenge   (50) A complex in North Salem of stone chambers and walls of the sort found throughout New England, formerly called Mystery Hill. The entire complex covers about 20 acres of hills and woodland, through which runs an apparently haphazard collection of low stone walls. The site's central feature is an acre dominated by 22 stone chambers, several with astronomical alignments.

Bartlett Balanced Rock   (51) A giant boulder supported by smaller stones on the crest of a ridge.

Kingston Stone Structures   (52) Stone chamber and other structures resembling those in North Salem (see AMERICA'S STONEHENGE above).

Lochmere Indian Fort   (53) Wide stone rows form a pattern of enclosures and avenues on the bank of the Winnepisogee River. Compared to other New England Indian forts, this site is relatively large and systematically laid out, and may show Hopewellian influence.

Raymond Stone Structures   (54) Stone structures resembling America's Stonehenge (see entry above).

Sanbornton Indian Fort   (55) Complex of manmade stone features, near a river, probably a sacred enclosure rather than a fort.

New Jersey   ✢

Kennelon Perched Rock   (56) Giant boulder supported by two smaller stones, on the edge of a cliff.

Tripod Rock (57) A 160-ton perched boulder in solstice alignment with other perched stones in Pyramid Mountain Natural and Historical Area, Morris County.

New Mexico ✤

Chicoma Mountain Rain Roads (58) An elliptical circle of stones with stone-bordered paths leading outward from it, intended to guide water toward pueblos in the valley below. See entry under "Sacred Mountains" in Power Points and Sacred Places.

New York ✤

Atoharo's Duff (59) Huge mass of white marble in Pittsfield, formerly a balanced rock that, when rocking, would cause the earth to vibrate.

Montauk Indian Fort (60) A complex of stone and earth-stone structures by the sea, probably a sacred enclosure rather than a fort.

North Salem Balanced Rock (61) A magnificent, 2,240-cubic-foot pink granite boulder set on five smaller supporting stones.

Oneida Stone (62) A large boulder set on a low earthen mound, a place of worship for the Iroquois peoples.

Rocking Stone (63) A large half-spherical boulder balanced precariously on a flat-topped earthen mound near Peekskill.

Ohio ✤

Ross Stone Wall (64) A slightly oval-shaped stone wall, with an opening partially blocked by two cairns at one end, and at the opposite end, outside the enclosure, a group of five parallel stone rows 200 feet long and 65 feet wide.

Spruce Hill Works (65) A hilltop site near Bourneville with three stone mounds, completely enclosed by a stone wall.

Oregon ✤

Susan Creek Indian Mounds (66) A concentration of stone mounds near Glide, identified as vision quest cairns, used in historic times by the Upper Umpqua.

Rhode Island ✤

Newport Old Stone Mill (or Stone Tower) (67) Held by some to have been constructed by the Norse in the

Old Stone Mill tower, Newport, Rhode Island (photograph by Rebecca Matlock, courtesy James G. Matlock)

1300s; excavations turned up only early English colonial artifacts dating the structure to about 1640.

Queen's Fort (68) Two rows of piled-up boulders connecting larger boulders on the summit of a spectacular natural mountain of stones, 50 feet high, the product of glacial action. Known as Queen's Fort, after the Niantic queen Quaiapen.

South Dakota ✤

Codington County Humanoid Figures (69) A network of paths leads from male and female ground figures to four rock piles that circumscribe an area of several hundred square feet, within which are several artificial depressions resembling vision pits. See also entries under "Vision Quest Sites" in Power Points and Sacred Places and "Ground Figures" in this section.

Medicine Knoll Snake Effigy (70) A snake effigy made of 825 stones, on the north end of Medicine Knoll near Blunt. The Dakota, whose traditional land this is, say that the snake was made in commemoration of a great war speech after a successful hunting season.

Pavement Circle (71) A circle of stones, 17 feet in diameter, on a hill two miles from Turtle Peak in the Wessington Springs vicinity. (See TURTLE PEAK BOULDERS under "Ground Figures.")

Snake Butte Rock Row (72) A 500-yard line of rocks running northward along the side of the butte near Pierre, said by the Dakota to represent the blood that dripped from an Arikara chief as he fled, mortally wounded, from a fight with the Dakota.

Vermont ✣

Hobomock's Shrine (73) On Rattlesnake Ledge of The Domlet, in Pownal, a great heap of broken pieces of quartzite bedrock. Local Indians, associated seismic noises with the site and built stone piles at the places they heard the noises.

Putney Indian Fort (74) A complex of earth and stone structures, located near a spring, which may have served as an observatory.

South Woodstock Calendar One (75) One of the most studied ancient observatory sites in New England. It consists of a complex of stone chambers, stone walls, standing stones and cairns in a natural bowl surrounded by hills and ridges, on many of which stand other stone structures.

South Woodstock Calendar Two (75) A complex ancient observatory site, including one of the largest stone chambers in Vermont.

History of Old Stone Mill (photograph by Rebecca Matlock, courtesy James G. Matlock)

South Woodstock Indian Fort (75) A complex of stone and earth structures, including a standing stone, located near a spring, probably a sacred enclosure or observatory rather than a fort.

South Woodstock Standing Stone (75) A slender stone 10 feet, six inches tall standing alone in a field.

Tunbridge Indian Fort (76) A complex of stone walls and cairns, aligned with standing stones on the horizon, located on a promontory of a northwest-southeast ridge overlooking a branch of the White River and the hills surrounding the Calendar One bowl (see SOUTH WOODSTOCK CALENDAR ONE, also in Vermont).

Washington Stone Chamber (77) Built into a hillside at 2,000 feet, this stone chamber is at the highest elevation of any known in New England.

West Virginia ✣

Mount Carbon Stone Walls (78) The "walls" are really dominolike rows of loosely piled slabs and blocks. They form fragmentary broken circles, semicircles, and U-shaped features that run east-west for about three miles in Fayette County. In the center of the complex are several mounds, fashioned from both earth and rocks. One of the rock mounds has the shape of a turtle.

Omar Stone Wall (79) A stone "wall" complex similar to the Mount Carbon Stone Walls in Fayette County.

Raleigh County Stone Wall (80) Another stone "wall" complex similar to the Mount Carbon Stone Walls in Fayette County, located on the summit of a nameless peak.

Rush Creek Stone Wall (81) A stone "wall" complex similar to the Mount Carbon Stone Walls in Fayette County, situated on a natural terrace below Rush Creek in Kanawha County.

Wisconsin ✣

Rock Lake Pyramids (82) Stone pyramids were reported to be in Rock Lake near Madison by a diver in 1976, but an underwater archeological expedition the following year failed to find evidence of any. Nevertheless, pictures taken from the air show dark shapes in the water that may represent stone piles on the bottom.

CANADA

Alberta ✣

Viking Ribstones (83) Two quartzite rocks carved to resemble a pair of buffalo, located in a field southeast of Edmonton. They are thought to be about 1,000 years old. The Plains peoples believed the stones were sacred and had a relationship to the Lord of the Buffalo Spirits. All other sacred rocks were descendants of these stones. The Blackfoot used "buffalo stones" in rituals to "call" the buffalo before a hunt.

Newfoundland ✤

L'Anse Amour Burial Mound (84) A stone burial mound, over 4,000 years old, on the Labrador coast.

L'Anse aux Meadows (85) Cairns and remains of stone structures in the only well-established Norse site on the North American mainland, dated to about A.D. 1000.

Nulliak Island Stoneworks (86) A stone chamber, similar to those common in New England, and a stone burial mound, on the Labrador coast.

Nova Scotia ✤

Yarmouth Stone (87) A 400-pound boulder with strange markings found in a cove in 1812. The markings, which remain unidentified, have been thought to be Mycenian, Japanese, Micmac, Norse and Basque. The stone is on display at the Yarmouth County Museum and Historical Research Library.

Ontario ✤

Henry Invocation Site (88) Semi-permanent invocation site at White River, with various stonework structures, including vision pits.

Otter Island Invocation Site (89) A massive rock enclosure as well as other structures, including several vision pits, on an island in Lake Superior.

Otto Cove Invocation Site (90) An assemblage of stone structures, some rectangular, others circular or crescent-shaped, with stone-lined floors, associated with cairns, on a desolate stretch of beach.

Rock Lake Puckasaw Pits (91) Groups of stone-lined pits and cairns, in Algonquin Provincial Park resembling those at the Lake Superior sites described above.

Tecumseh Cairn (92) The remains of the great Shawnee chief, Tecumseh, are buried here on Walpole Island. Tecumseh, who sought to unite all American Indian tribes against the white people, was killed by the British in the battle of Thames, Ontario, on October 5, 1813. His remains initially were buried in a secret location, then moved to Oklahoma, and in 1941 were moved again to their present cairn. According to legend,

Tecumseh, like many other real and legendary heroes, will return someday to lead his people, the Shawnee, to victory.

Wright Ceremonial Site (93) Major ceremonial site on Oiseau Bay near Lake Superior with stone structures and stone-lined vision pits between two long stone rows.

Québec ✤

Hammer of Thor and Imaha (94) This stone monument of unknown origin—possibly Norse or Inuit—consists of a vertical shaft eight feet high, topped by a cross-member 4.5 feet long, and a capstone. It was discovered in 1964. The site is about 15 miles from Payne Bay village near the west coast of Ungava Bay. Imaha is Inuit for "maybe."

GROUND FIGURES

Ground figures are depictions of humans or animals, or else geometric designs, often of considerable size. There are two basic types of ground figures. Some are piles of stones or boulders. Others are created by digging into the ground, then piling stones or desert gravel around the edges so that it outlines the figure. The latter are often called intaglios, indicating they were produced by incisions in the earth.

The world's most famous ground figures, the Nazca lines of Peru's coastal desert, are intaglios. For centuries, researchers have been baffled by these enormous drawings. They are more than 1,000 years old, centuries older than the Inca empire. Thousands of shallow lines run across the desert into the hills, straight as arrows, or zigzag and spiral into mazes. Giant trapezoids, rectangles and triangles are formed by the crossing lines, decorated with dozens of drawings of monkeys and birds—and a whale, a hummingbird, a heron and a cat with a fish's tail.

Since most of the drawings can be appreciated only from the air, Danish writer Erich von Däniken has argued that they were landing strips for extraterrestrial spacecraft. But according to the German mathematician Maria Reiche, who has studied the lines since 1946, the area is a giant calendar keyed to the movements of the sun, moon and constellations. Reiche maintains the calendar helped the ancients know when to plant and irrigate crops. She believes that the drawings were made to be viewed from the air by the gods thought to be responsible for the community's well-being.

Similar considerations may explain the meaning of the North American intaglios and other ground figures, such as those at the Bannock Point Petroform Site in Manitoba's Whiteshell Provincial Park. Who made the

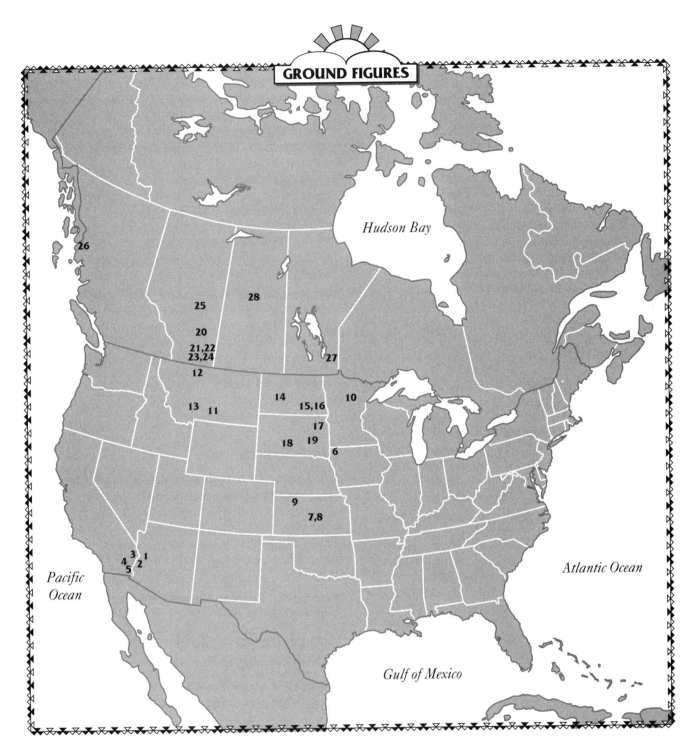

designs and why they made them are still a matter of dispute. They were once called the Ojibwa Boulder Mosaics, after the group of American Indians who occupied the region in historical times, but they are probably much older, perhaps as much as 3,000 years old. Recent studies have shown that some of the stones are aligned to the summer solstice and to a point one lunar month past the summer solstice.

Other ground figures may represent shamanic visions. A group of intaglios of men and panthers near Blythe, California, may be a form of hunting magic, because panthers seen in dreams before a hunt were considered a good omen. At least one ground figure appears to be an accidental creation—the Snake Dance Pattern in Imperial County, California, was produced by the regular footwork of dancers over a period of centuries. The following is a list of major ground figure sites.

UNITED STATES

Arizona ✣

Parker Rattlesnake (1) A 165-foot serpent intaglio, rendered realistically with a forked tongue, several sets of stone rattles and two quartz eyes.

Ripley Intaglios (2) Sixteen immense anthropomorphic, zoomorphic and geometric intaglios, some 35 by 80 feet, probably Yuman in origin, near Ehrenberg.

California ✣

Blythe Desert Intaglios (3) Three groups of enormous figures of men and animals with long tails, probably meant to suggest panthers. The designs may have been inspired by a Yuman belief that if one dreamed of a certain supernatural who had two forms—man and panther—one would have luck in hunting.

Imperial County Snake Dance Pattern (4) A serpentine intaglio, six feet wide and nearly three-quarters of a mile long, created by dancers who stood side by side and moved in a regular sequence over the earth. It may have been in use for thousands of years.

Winterhaven Stickman (5) An 80-foot-long anthropomorphic intaglio figure said by the Mohave to represent a mythological monster.

Iowa ✣

Gitchie Manitou (6) Scattered among the remains of abstract mounds and boulder ground figures near Larchwood are a complex array of circles, ellipses and connecting lines.

Kansas ✣

Lyons Great Horned Serpent (7) A snake intaglio, 160 feet long and cut three to 10 inches deep, on a bluff overlooking the headwaters of the Little Arkansas River.

Lyons Minor Serpent (8) A smaller snake intaglio, forming a teardrop shape, on the same bluff as the Great Horned Serpent.

Penokee Stone Man (9) A giant figure of a man, with pronounced ears and phallus, outlined in small stones, many of them now partially buried in the earth.

Minnesota ✣

Turtle Oracle Mound (10) This so-called mound near Inger in Chippewa National Monument is actually an intaglio in the shape of a turtle. Dating from the late 18th century, it is said to have been used by the Ojibwa, or Chippewa, as a council area and later by the Dakota (Sioux) as an oracle in their war against the Ojibwa.

Montana ✣

Billings Humanoid Figures (11) Along the road between Pryor and East Pryor are three humanoid ground figures, outlined by rocks. A cairn of boulders stands near each. See also entry under "Vision Quest Sites" in Power Points and Sacred Places.

Blackfeet Indian Reservation Three-Legged Figure (12) A three-legged humanoid figure (the third "leg" perhaps a phallus) on Landslide Butte that is said to have been constructed by a man who wanted to immortalize himself.

Three-Legged Figure (13) A three-legged humanoid ground figure near Bozeman, the third "leg" of which may represent a phallus.

North Dakota ✣

Fort Berthold Indian Reservation Hoofprint Intaglios (14) A series of impressions, each about two feet in diameter and several inches deep, resembling the tracks of a giant horse, near the Mandan Dakota village of Fishhook on the reservation. The tracks are said to commemorate a major war with other Dakota groups in 1853.

Montpelier Circular Figures (15) Several groups of large circles of boulders. One group comprises circles 16 feet and 13 feet in diameter, with adjacent openings. Each has a pair of "horns" or "ears"—smaller circles— with their openings facing outward.

Montpelier Stone Parallelograms (16) Two closed parallelogram structures on the east side of the James River, four miles south of the group of circular figures described in the previous entry.

South Dakota ✣

Codington County Humanoid Figures (17) Boulder outlines of two giant figures, one evidently male and the other female. South of these two figures there is a network of trails linking four cairns. According to Dakota legend, this complex marks a romantic tragedy. A young bride and her lover had run away, only to be killed at the spots of the respective male and female figures by the woman's husband. See also entries under "Enclosures, Walls and Cairns" above, and "Vision Quest Sites" in Power Points and Sacred Places.

Snake Butte Figures (18) On the north side of Snake Butte near Pierre is the boulder outline of a giant turtle. At the edge of the bluff, there is a large complex of stone squares, circles and parallelograms. See also SNAKE BUTTE ROCK ROW under "Enclosures, Walls and Cairns."

Turtle Peak Boulders (19) On the southwest side of the high knob known locally in the Wessington Springs area as Turtle Peak are abstract boulder outlines of a woman and some type of four-legged animal, 15 and 20 feet long, respectively.

CANADA

Alberta ✚

Cluny Ground Figure (20) Three-legged humanoid ground figure.

Grassy Lake Cairn (21) A prominent burial cairn, over 20 feet in diameter, near the Grassy Lake Medicine Wheel and possibly associated with it.

Grassy Lake Medicine Wheel (22) A turtle effigy is located outside the ring of the medicine wheel. See also entry under "Medicine Wheels."

Miner Turtle (23) Possible turtle effigy on the prairie between Miner 1 and Miner 2 medicine wheels.

Ross Medicine Wheel (24) An anthropomorphic stone figure is located inside the ring of the medicine wheel.

Rumsey Medicine Wheel (25) An anthropomorphic stone figure is located inside the ring of the medicine wheel.

British Columbia ✚

Metlakatla Man (26) Full-sized outline in intaglio in rockface on the southwestern tip of Robertson Point in Prince Rupert. According to Tsimpean legend, the imprint was made by a chief who went to visit the sky. He found no food there, and in returning to earth, fell and indented the rock.

Manitoba ✚

Bannock Point Petroform Site (Ojibwa Boulder Mosaics) (27) In Whiteshell Provincial Park on granite bedrock that may be the oldest exposed rock in the world, having been scoured clean of soil during the last Ice Age, are a group of designs composed of small rocks and boulders, themselves vestiges of the Ice Age. Some of the designs are geometric in form, whereas others are human and animal effigies, including turtles and snakes.

Saskatchewan ✚

Turtle Petroform (28) Rock and boulder outline of a turtle on the edge of high plains near Big River.

MEDICINE WHEELS

Medicine wheels form a special class of ground figure. They are not a type of megalithic monument of the sort found in Europe, but rather arrangements of stones on the surface of the earth. The term has been used to cover various configurations, but properly speaking it includes at least two of the following three features: a prominent central cairn; one or more stone rings surrounding the cairn; and two or more spokes leading outward from the cairn or ring. Medicine wheels with all three features are fairly rare. Most also have other stone structures in them or near them—rings of stones used for anchoring tipis (tipi rings), anthropomorphic ground figures or secondary cairns.

Medicine wheels vary greatly in size. Some are small and compact, but others are some 300 feet in diameter and have massive central cairns—as much as 30 feet or so across and several feet high. The central cairn at the famous medicine wheel in the Bighorn Mountains of Wyoming is estimated to contain 1,000 tons of rock.

Some medicine wheels may be as much as 3,500 years old. Many were not constructed all at once, but over a period of time. The most extensively excavated medicine wheel cairn, at Majorville, Ontario, indicates that this site was in more-or-less continuous use from about 2500 B.C. to historic times. Thus, it is contemporary with the Egyptian pyramids and Stonehenge. Other medicine wheels were probably built much more recently, but dates are not certain.

The word "medicine" implies a magical or supernatural function and is probably an adjective applied for want of a better one; medicine wheels are old enough that their original use has been forgotten. They are found predominantly on the northern Plains, from Alberta and Saskatchewan down through the Dakotas to Montana, Colorado and Wyoming. The culture that built them was drastically changed with the introduction of the horse and the arrival of Europeans, and there have been great population movements into and out of the region. Present-day Algonquians know only that the medicine wheels were there when they came and often consider them sacred places.

The Blackfoot associate medicine wheels with mortuary practices, and indeed several medicine wheels, such as the Ellis medicine wheel in Alberta, were used as burial places. Many—but by no means all—medicine wheels seem to have served as observatories, their spokes oriented to astronomical events such as sunrise and sunset on equinoxes and solstices. In a few cases—notably the Bighorn Medicine Wheel in Wyoming and the Majorville Cairn in Alberta—there are small clusters of stones that have been named starburst mosaics at the ends of certain spokes. These mosaics mark the spokes used to site key events, such as summer solstice sunrise, the start of the Algonquin new year.

The term "medicine wheel" was first coined in reference to the Bighorn Medicine Wheel, which is especially well formed, with 28 spokes radiating from its massive central cairn to meet in a large outer circle. Many sites are not so elaborate, and few resemble wheels. The only other one with 28 spokes is that at Majorville. In general, Canadian medicine wheels—which are the vast majority—are less developed than American ones. Many Canadian sites are simply large cairns, not all of which have spokes, rings or other associated features. Their spokes point in various directions, not primarily the cardinal directions (although there appears to be a slight preference for southwest), but have other features that could be summer solstice registers. All the sites lie on hilltops or high mesas and have clear horizons. Canadian medicine wheels are never found in mountains, but on the prairie.

Canadian researcher John Brumley classifies medicine wheels in eight subgroups, based on their basic features. Subgroup 1 sites are characterized by a prominent central cairn surrounded by a ring of stones. Subgroup 2 sites are similar to those of Subgroup 1, except that two stone lines extend outward from the ring, forming a passageway directed toward the cairn. Subgroup 3 sites have a prominent central cairn from which lines of stones radiate in various directions, but there is no outer circle. Subgroup 4 sites consist of a circle of stones from which two or more lines extend outward. Subgroup 5 sites consist of stone rings dissected into segments by four or more interior lines of stone; again, there is no central cairn. Subgroup 6 sites have a prominent central cairn and a stone ring with interior lines connecting to the cairn. Subgroup 7 sites have a prominent central cairn surrounded by a stone ring, with two or more stone lines extending outward from the margins of the stone ring. Subgroup 8 sites have a prominent central cairn surrounded by a stone ring and two or more lines extending outward from the cairn and passing through the ring before terminating.

The individual entries and table that follow include Brumley's 67 sites as well as some others that fit his definition of medicine wheel but are not mentioned by him.

UNITED STATES

Colorado ✤

Gold Hill Medicine Wheel　(1) A 10-foot-diameter circle of stones on a ridge, apparently constructed as a solstice register.

Trail Ridge Road Medicine Wheel　(2) A rudimentary medicine wheel that marks the summer solstice sunrise, unusual for being at an altitude of 11,400 feet, located in Rocky Mountain National Park.

Michigan ✤

Beaver Island Stone Circles　(3) Stone circles resembling medicine wheels, discovered in 1988 at Lake Michigan, dated to about 3000 B.C. The largest circle is 397 feet in diameter, composed of boulders two to 10 feet tall, with a hollowed-out central cairn.

Colorado, Montana, Wyoming: Medicine Wheels

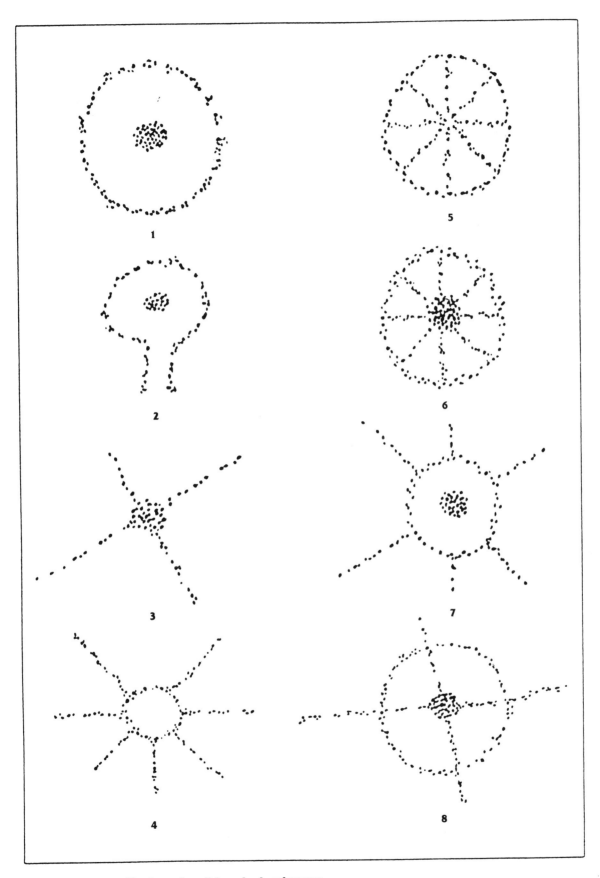

John Brumley's classifications of medicine wheels subgroups

Montana ✤

Belle Creek Medicine Wheel (4) This medicine wheel sits atop a prominence rise in the prairie grassland. It lacks a prominent central cairn.

Fort Smith Medicine Wheel (5) A rudimentary medicine wheel, three feet in diameter, that marks the summer solstice sunrise, with a lichen-covered cluster of stones or sunburst mosaic opposite its pointer.

Sun River Medicine Wheel (6) The eroding river bank near Lowry has destroyed three of the 10 spokes of this wheel.

Wyoming ✤

Bighorn Medicine Wheel (7) A 70-foot diameter circle with 28 36-foot spokes of stones half sunk in the ground, radiating from a hollowed-out central cairn. Six cairns outside the circle establish alignments that mark the summer solstice sunrise and perhaps the rising of certain stars. Constructed at an altitude of 9,640 feet near the summit of Medicine Mountain near Sheridan, it was used from about A.D. 1200 to 1700.

CANADA

Alberta ✤

Anderson Medicine Wheel No. 1 (8) A large central cairn surrounded by a ring of stones, with a smaller second ring on the southwest. An opening to the southeast is flanked by rows of stones.

Michigan, Ontario: Medicine Wheels

Bighorn Medicine Wheel, Wyoming. Illustration by David Anstey (courtesy Cynthia Parzych Publishing, Inc.)

Anderson Medicine Wheel No. 2 (8) A large central cairn surrounded by a circle of stones. There are no prominent radiating spokes, although short stone lines up to about seven and a half feet in length extend outward from the ring wall.

Antelope Hill Medicine Wheel (9) A hollowed-out central cairn surrounded by a ring of stones with an opening from which leads rows of stones, producing a keyhole shape.

Barry Medicine Wheel (10) Near Calgary, a 36-foot circle of boulders with a stone-bordered walkway leading outward from a gap in the circle, producing a keyhole shape.

Buffalo Bird Medicine Wheel (11) A hollowed-out central cairn with a hemispherical line of stones to the south, and a vertical row running from the cairn south through and past the line.

Jamieson's Place Medicine Wheel (12) Located along the Bow River, the wheel lacks a prominent central cairn and is a subgroup 5 medicine wheel.

Majorville Cairn (13) A 100-foot-diameter wheel whose central cairn appears to have been built up through 4,000 years of continuous use beginning about 2500 B.C.

Manyberries Medicine Wheel (14) A cairn with a long, meandering line of stones leading away from it.

Other, smaller cairns and stone alignments are in the vicinity.

Many Islands Lake Medicine Wheel (15) On the prairie bordering a prominent escarpment with a commanding view over a glacial lake basin, the 36-foot circle has six spokes, varying from 54 to 435 feet in length. The low central cairn is seven and a half feet in diameter. Several stone circles, perhaps tipi rings, and several cairns are located outside the circle.

Miner Medicine Wheel No. 1 (16) On the prairie along the edge of Red Deer River Valley, this large central cairn is surrounded by a stone ring 45 feet in diameter with 22 radiating spokes. It has small cairns at the ends of three of them, and one especially long one passing through another, smaller circle that appears to be a tipi ring. Two gaps in the circle are often referred to as doorway openings.

Miner Medicine Wheel No. 2 (16) A hollowed-out central cairn surrounded by a ring of stones with two cairns, resembling ears, along it. Two other smaller cairns lie to the northeast.

Miner Medicine Wheel No. 3 (16) A large hollowed-out central cairn surrounded by a ring of stones, but without radiating spokes.

Ross Medicine Wheel (17) A cairn with a semicircular line of stones above it and an anthropomorphic stone effigy just below it.

Alberta, Saskatchewan: Medicine Wheels

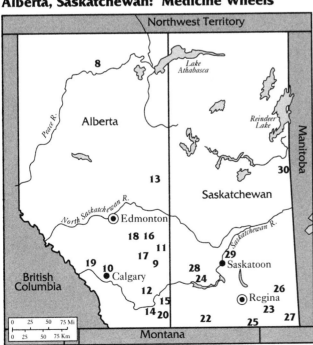

Rumsey Medicine Wheel (18) A large central cairn topping a burial place surrounded by a stone ring, but without radiating spokes.

Sundial Hill Medicine Wheel (19) A central cairn surrounded by two concentric rings of stones, broken by an "entrance way" lined by rows of stones. A small cairn lies between the entrance way and the central cairn.

Twin Peaks Medicine Wheel (20) The central cairn of this wheel encloses a burial evidently made at a later date than the cairn itself.

Ontario ✤

Ellis Medicine Wheel (21) A burial was found beneath the central cairn. The small central ring is simply a tipi ring that was used to secure the cover of a burial lodge. Other tipi rings surround the site, some at the end of the radiating lines.

Saskatchewan ✤

Canuck Medicine Wheel (22) A central cairn from which six spokes radiated, this wheel is located near a river that was destroyed by cultivation.

Halbrite Medicine Wheel (23) A central burial cairn with four radiating lines of stones.

Hughton Medicine Wheel (24) Circle of boulders 25 feet in diameter with a stone-bordered walkway leading outward from a gap in the circle, producing a keyhole shape.

Minton Turtle (25) A conventional medicine wheel to which have been added a head, feet and tail. Its principal axis, from tail to head, is aligned to Sirius rising at the summer solstice. Two cairns and a starburst stone mosaic point to the summer solstice sunrise. Sunset is marked by the joining of the tail and body as viewed from the mosaic.

Moose Mountain Medicine Wheel (26) Two thousand years old, on a ridge that from a distance looks like the humped back of a moose. The summer solstice sun rises over a massive central cairn as seen from a starburst stone mosaic at the end of one of the wheel's "spokes."

Oxbow West Medicine Wheel (27) This wheel has a three-foot-diameter central cairn surrounded by a 30-foot-diameter circle. A prominent "doorway" gap is present. Seven stone lines, varying from 45 to 225 feet in length, radiate outward from the cairn, through and past the circle.

Plenty Medicine Wheel (28) A cairn stands at the intersection of two long stone rows.

Tipperary Creek (29) A prominent central cairn in the Saskatoon area, surrounded by a stone ring and a scattering of other stones, but without radiating spokes.

Wilson Russell Medicine Wheel (30) This structure is unusual in that the ring is composed of a thick band of stones, between one and two yards in diameter, enclosing a central area no more than 11 feet across.

ADDITIONAL MEDICINE WHEELS

State/Province	Site	Subgroup
Montana	Eagle Butte Medicine Wheel	2
	Grassy Knoll Medicine Wheel	4
	Montana Medicine Wheel	3
	Montana Medicine Wheel	1
Alberta	Alberta Medicine Wheel	1
	Alberta Medicine Wheel	1
	Alberta Medicine Wheel	3
	Alberta Medicine Wheel	1
	Buffalo Hill Medicine Wheel	1
	Darkhorse Medicine Wheel	4
	Eagle Child Medicine Wheel	4
	Jim Allen Medicine Wheel	1
	Loose Wheel Medicine Wheel	1
	Many Spotted Horses Medicine Wheel	4
	Murphy Medicine Wheel	4
	Steel Medicine Wheel	4
	Suffield Medicine Wheel	4

State/Province	Site	Subgroup
Alberta	Suitor Medicine Wheels Nos. 1 and 2	4
	Suitor Medicine Wheel No. 3	4
Saskatchewan	Birdfoot Medicine Wheel	3
	Oxbow East Medicine Wheel	3

PETROGLYPHS AND PICTOGRAPHS

Ancient depictions of the hunt, agriculture and daily life, religious ceremonies, or maybe messages from deities or even extraterrestrials? No one knows for certain, but rock art left by ancient American Indian peoples testifies to their desire to leave a written record about themselves.

Rock art commonly appears in two forms: pictographs or petroglyphs. Pictographs are drawings on rocks or cave walls using early forms of paint and applied with sticks, plants, fingers or brushes made of hair. No matter what group of people drew the pictographs, most of the artists used red, black or white, occasionally all three. Red tones came from iron oxide hematite; black from manganese ore or charcoal; and white from any chalky material. These minerals were then ground in mortars into powder and mixed with oil to bind them into paint. Pictograph artists usually chose protected locations to display their works, as the delicate drawings suffered from exposure.

Petroglyphs, also called rock writings, are made by incision; the dark, patinated rock surfaces were removed to reveal the lighter color beneath. Petroglyph artists used stone hammers and chisels to create their work, and could display the pictures in larger, more open locations.

Europeans first discovered North American rock art in the Massachusetts Bay Colony. The pious Puritans believed the carved human figures covering what is now called Dighton Rock represented works of vanished races, symbols of ancient astrology or diabolism or signs from God. The more romantic believed Norse, Phoenician, Scythian or Portuguese explorers had left the writings as keys to buried treasure. In truth, we now know, the carvings were made by Algonquian peoples.

However, Puritan theories, while perhaps colored by their faith, were not far off. Today, anthropologists believe the drawings and carvings variously represent clan symbols, identification of prayer locations, depic-

PETROGLYPHS

143 145,144 146
142 140 141 139 127
2 6 7
4   9   5 3   70,71
8   11 10
1

196

Hudson Bay

201
200
202
198 199
197
189 195
184 185 73 92
182 183 91
186 188 187 72 96
137 95 94
138 93
135 94
136
74 193
63, 65
67 64 66
68 77
148 151 153
147 150 154
155
149,152

215 203 204 206 205
216 210 211 85
129 207
84 209 208
83 191 192 82 132 131 130 190 133
89 88 86 76
90 75 87
134
181

214
213
212 78
81 80 79

Atlantic Ocean

see inset above right

69

Pacific Ocean

Gulf of Mexico

■ Detailed map of state appears within chapter

tions of the hunt and manifestations of hunting magic, astronomy, visions by the artist or a shaman, puberty and fertility rites and desires, records of important events in the life of the tribe, communications with deities or the spirits, ancient calendars or solstice markers, and even simple doodling. Many of the designs seem no more than geometric shapes or decorations. But then no one knows for sure.

Centuries of wind, sun and rain have not destroyed the ancient messages, but modern man is quickly accomplishing what the elements cannot. Graffiti drawn near and even over the rock art not only defaces the works but insults those who recognize the sacred nature of the writings.

Although the pictographs and petroglyphs of each region of North America exhibit a particular style, there

Petroglyphs at Bandelier, New Mexico (courtesy National Park Service)

are commonalities to each. Most are concerned with the success of the hunt and crops, the necessity of sex and birth and communication with the spirits.

The Pacific Northwest

Coastal Indians of Washington State, Oregon and British Columbia left art depicting sharks, whales, bears, eagles, other birds, dragonlike sea monsters, people, salmon, beavers, sheep, stylized masks and other geometric patterns. Rock artists created both petroglyphs and pictographs, employing combinations of red, white and black paints. Gods and deities appeared also. A favorite theme, besides the success of the hunt or fishing, was sex and fertility. The artists portrayed men with enormous phalluses, and women were shown with spread legs and vulvae.

According to stories from the Salish Indian tribes of Washington State, rock art commemorated significant dreams and visions of young people entering adulthood, especially boys. At puberty, boys were sent into the wilderness to pray and fast. They desired to see visions of the supernatural being who would be their guardian spirit throughout life. If the devotee was successful in his vision quest, he would record the dream or depiction of the guardian spirit on the rocks. These drawings could also show what qualities the boy desired, such as strength or wisdom, upon reaching adulthood. Girls also underwent puberty ceremonies, but were kept secluded and schooled in the mysteries of childbirth. Rock art for females usually showed married life, sex and fertility and common household tasks.

The Great Basin

The Indians of northern California, eastern Washington and Oregon, Nevada, Utah and Wyoming used mainly pictographs to depict humans, deer, snakes, abstract patterns and most especially bighorn sheep common to the Rocky Mountains. Deities often appeared as twins. In California, pictographs also show vulva forms and fertility symbols. Much of the rock art in caves in this region seems to have served as solstice markers.

The Desert Southwest

The tribes of the desert and pueblo regions of southern California, Arizona and New Mexico, as well as northern Mexico, used rock art extensively to decorate their homes and record events and religious rites. Common themes include anthropomorphic male figures (females appear rarely), birds, snakes, flute players, lizards, bighorn sheep, abstract forms, turkeys, kachina masks and historical events in the life of the tribe. Horned or feathered serpents, like Quetzalcoatl, appear frequently, as well as other horned serpent gods. In Hopi rock art, the flute players are humpbacked, representing the god Kokopelli. Star patterns and pictures of constellations also figure prominently, lending credence to the pictographs' use as calendars or astronomical tools.

One puzzling petroglyph appears near Hopi villages near the Casa Grande Ruins National Monument northwest of Tucson, Arizona. Casa Grande, a four-story structure believed to be an observatory and part of a larger village, was built by the ancient Indians of the Southwest, known only as the Hohokam. A similar petroglyph has been found in Nayarit, Mexico, and the pattern appears in basketry designs of the Pima Indians and in Hopi silverwork. The glyph is a circular, compli-

Cree rock painting of the Great Manitou

cated maze pattern believed to be a cult symbol of the Bronze Age and first discovered in Ireland, Cornwall and Italy. The pattern has also appeared on a silver coin found in Knossos, Crete. No one has yet ventured an explanation of how a European Bronze Age design crossed the ocean to the New World.

Mississippi Valley rock art (Squier & Davis, 1847)

Cliff dwelling ruins at Casa Grande, Arizona (photograph by Fred E. Mang Jr., courtesy National Park Service)

Another strange pattern can be found near Blythe, California, in the desert. The design is an enormous gravel drawing of men and animals and can be viewed far better from the air than on the ground. How it was made, by whom, or how it was to be seen remain a mystery.

Northern Great Plains

The Indian rock artists of Montana, North and South Dakota and Minnesota drew anthropomorphic figures, deer, bears, horses, animal tracks, their tipis and scenes of war: great battles, rifles, shields and shield bearers. Strangely, the buffalo associated with these tribes through stories and movies are rarely depicted.

Southern Great Plains

Tribes in Kansas, Oklahoma and Texas depicted themselves as anthropomorphs, also drawing horned figures, deer, bears, rattlesnakes, thunderbirds, buffalo and atlatls, or spear-throwers. Artists used the pictographs to keep records of the great influx of European expansion, showing guns, wagons, priests and church symbols. In fact, the themes of hunting and warfare dominate the southern Great Plains drawings. Stars and abstract patterns appear as well.

Texas and New Mexico

A great many of the best-preserved pictographs in the southern Great Plains can be found throughout the lower Pecos River area of Texas and New Mexico. One of the best spots is at Hueco Tanks State Historical Park, about 32 miles east of El Paso. Huecos are natural rock basins that furnish trapped rainwater, and travelers dating from the early Anasazi hunters to more recent Mescalero Apache have left 2,000 pictographs and symbols there in 44 separate sites. Scholars attribute most of the existing drawings to the Apache, dating back some 200 years, although some are 4,000 years old.

The park's high, challenging rocks appeal to climbers as well, and unfortunately to vandals. Many of the priceless pictographs have been defaced, some with gang graffiti, and park authorities and the local Tigua

Indians are currently working on the best plan to save the sacred spot. Graffiti began at the tanks during the days of the Forty-niners, when thirsty miners left messages (misspelled) noting "Watter Hear."

Anthropologists speculate that many of the more enigmatic symbols found in the lower Pecos pictographs represent shamans and other participants in a mescal bean cult. Mescal beans are powerful narcotics and hallucinogens. The ceremonies involve body painting, dancing with weapons, gourd rattles and feather adornments, and most likely inspired great hunting and fearless courage against the white man's invasion.

The Eastern Woodlands

Pictographs from this area, encompassing far eastern Canada and New England, show round-headed humans, birds and bird tracks, turkeys, cranes, rattlesnakes and other serpents, footprints, animal tracks, abstract patterns, mythical thunderbirds, ovals, vulvae, fish, bison, arrows, maces and batons. Like their brothers further west in the Northern Woodlands, these rock artists also employed turtles as fertility symbols and drew pictures of Mishipizhiw, the Great Water Lynx or mythical water panther. Many of the drawings from this region show "power lines" connecting human forms with symbols, believed to represent the connections between Indian shamans and the spirit world.

The Northern Woodlands

The Algonquin Indians of the Great Lakes regions were prolific artists. They drew animals such as deer, bison, moose, turtles and lizards and anthropomorphic figures with raised arms and bird wings. Very often these anthropomorphs were horned or connected by lines to the bison or other animals. Pictographs also tell of the coming of white men, probably the French, into the region, showing men and canoes and horsemen with rifles: a new invention. Algonquin artists also drew Mishipizhiw, the water panther, and Maymaygwayshi, a mischievous spirit who lived in rocky areas around the Great Lakes and robbed fish traps.

Some of the best-preserved petroglyphs and pictographs are in Peterborough, Ontario, Canada. These rock artists often depicted sex and copulation, with the men having enormous phalluses and the females with widespread vulvae. Genitalia separate from complete human forms also appears. Turtles, with their wide shells, represent vulvae and fertility, as did turtles with eggs. Such abundant fertility symbols, especially in connection with drawings of the shamans, may represent the shaman's ability to tap into the secret, sexual power of nature. One of the petroglyphs at Peterborough shows a canoe with its mast topped by a sun disk. Rays extend

outward. This glyph resembles the rock art of the far northern polar regions, Siberia and Scandinavia. The canoes are probably magical boats that can fly throughout the cosmos, carrying the souls of shamans and other supernatural beings. Here is a list of major petroglyph and pictograph sites in North America.

UNITED STATES

Alabama ✦

Blount County Petroglyphs (1) Incised, pecked and rubbed glyphs on an exposed sandstone ridge over a spring.

Colbert County Petroglyphs (2) Glyphs representing human hands and feet, snakes and other features are located on a boulder in a shelter floor.

DeKalb County Pictographs (3) Five pictographs in yellow and red on the ceiling of a small sandstone shelter with a southeast view.

Franklin County Petroglyphs (4) Incised, pecked and rubbed motifs including concentric circles, circles with cup holes, spirals, crosses and wavy lines.

Jackson County Pictographs (5) Red pictographs, including spirals, horned snakes and rectangles, on the vertical wall of a high bluff with a view to the east.

Lawrence County Petroglyphs (6) Incised petroglyphs resembling stick figures on the flat surfaces of a sandstone boulder.

Madison County Petroglyph (7) A three-dimensional life-sized face is carved on the projecting point of a limestone rock at ground level.

Marion County Petroglyphs (8) Petroglyphs produced by pecking or rubbing represent such things as the mace, monolithic axe, bi-lobed arrows, crescents, birds, animals and human legs.

Marshall County Pictographs (9) Pictographs on the vertical face of a limestone bluff overlooking the Tennessee River include geometric forms, animal forms and sun circles.

Tallapoosa County Petroglyphs (10) Pecked and incised in a boulder in an open area are pit-and-groove circles in association with stumps remaining from steatite bowl quarrying operations.

Walker County Petroglyphs (11) Incised petroglyphs of bows and arrows and various drilled and pecked holes on the flat roof of a sandstone shelter.

Alaska ✣

Baranof Island Petroglyph   (12) Complex petroglyph that recalls the Tlingit Indian creation myth, of an older regional style.

Kalinin Bay Petroglyphs   (13) Site with bold, older and newer style petroglyphs. The older are more complex and more deeply cut than the newer. One of 10 sites known in southeastern Alaska.

Arizona ✣

Canyon de Chelly National Monument   (14) Among many Navajo pictograph sites in the Chinle vicinity, Standing Cow Ruin has a blue and white pictograph of a cow. Another painting depicts a shamanic curing ceremony. Some of the petroglyphs may have astronomical significance.

Canyon del Muerto   (15) This site includes drawings of Spanish horsemen as well as Anasazi paintings of large human figures with head-top ornaments and left-ear appendages that may represent shamans and shamanic power.

Arizona: Petroglyphs

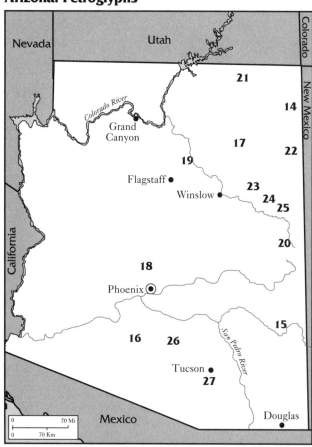

Casa Grande National Monument   (16) Ruins of a Hohokam village and a possible observatory lie northwest of Tucson.

Hagoe Canyon Petroglyphs   (17) At Ruin 5 there is a pictograph panel including Kokopelli and a stylized deer with tracks following along behind it, in Navajo County.

Hieroglyphic Canyon   (18) Drawings here in Phoenix resemble cave drawings found in France.

Inscription Point   (19) Located in Wupatki National Monument near Flagstaff, these petroglyphs include pairs of anthropomorphic figures copulating, probably some form of fertility magic.

Lyman Lake   (20) Area of abundant rock art apparently of Anasazi provenance.

Monument Valley Navajo Park   (21) Dozens of petroglyphs appear on sites throughout the park.

Newspaper Rock Petroglyphs   (22) A large sandstone boulder near Adamana covered with petroglyphs in many designs—geometric units, quadrupeds, foot- and handprints, creatures and numerous fine lines. Surrounding boulders display similar designs.

Painted Desert Petroglyphs   (23) A habitation site with several Anasazi ruins and boulder terraces and slopes covered with petroglyphs depicting geometric units, animals, hand prints and human design motifs.

Painted Rocks State Park   (24) Indian rock art drawings of snakes, lizards, men and geometric figures, in Holbrook.

Petrified Forest National Park   (25) Many petroglyph sites here interact with sunlight at solstices. The most frequent images are pecked and include elaborate geometric designs, rounded masks, animals and birds with long beaks.

Picacho Mountain   (26) Various anthropomorphic petroglyphs, some horizontal, others upside down, perhaps representing death or illness. One panel depicts a shamanic curing ceremony. A pecked petroglyph on Picacho Point appears to be a map of the surrounding area.

Picture Rocks Retreat   (27) A variety of petroglyphs in Tucson on a rock in a retreat run by Redemptionist Fathers.

Puerco Ruin Petroglyphs   (22) A prehistoric Pueblo village site near Adamana with boulders decorated with petroglyphs leading to the structures.

Ruins at Wupatki National Monument, Arizona (photograph by Fred E. Mang Jr., courtesy National Park Service)

California ✣

Andreas Canyon (Rincon Village) (28) Village site with pictographs and pit-and-grooved petroglyphs in Riverside County.

Spring Shelter (28) The sun interacts with petroglyphs at this site in Riverside County around winter solstice.

Anza Borrego State Park Pictograph Site (29) At the end of a well-maintained mile-long trail near Borrego Springs, a small group of symbols, painted in red, cover the vertical face of a large boulder.

Burro Flats Painted Cave (30) Pictograph panels at this Chumash site near Santa Susana depict a comet as it approaches and departs from the sun. Petroglyphs of concentric circles may represent the upper and lower worlds that are traversed by shamans on out-of-body journeys.

Buttercup Farms Pictographs (31) Two polychrome pictograph panels featuring anthropomorphs, chain designs and handprints appear in rock shelters at this site near Perris.

Chalfant Canyon (32) Unusual, pecked petroglyphs of figures with long pointed snouts or beaks and appendages that appear to be either ears or head feathers, possibly representations of Coyote, the "father" of the Owens Valley Paiute, and more generally the Trickster.

Chumash Painted Cave (33) At San Marcos Pass near Santa Barbara, a grotto about 15 feet deep in a rock outcropping 20 feet above the road contains paintings of many brilliant, colorful figures and designs. One is of a centipede, a sign of death for the Chumash. Adjacent paintings depict burial practices.

Coso Range (34) Mountains and canyons, including Little Petroglyph Canyon (see separate entry), on the China Lake Naval Weapons Range. Among the petroglyphs are realistic-looking medicine bags.

Cow Creek Petroglyphs (35) Various designs on a rock face behind a midden deposit in Shasta County.

California: Petrophyphs

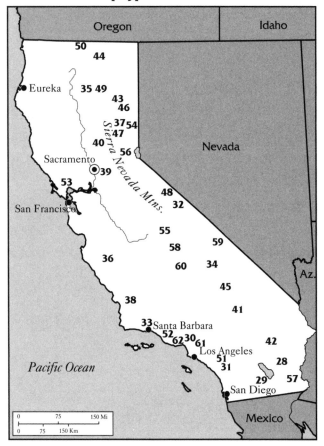

Cueva Pintada (Painted Cave) (36) Located near King City in the Hunter Liggett Military Reservation, this cave is covered with polychromatic pictographs on walls and ceiling.

Hawley Lake Petroglyphs (37) One of the largest petroglyph sites in the northern Sierra Nevada in Sierra County.

Honda Ridge (38) Located in Santa Barbara County, on Vandenberg Airforce Base, a pictograph site that once may have been a solar observatory.

Indian Grinding Rock (39) A limestone outcropping in Amador County with mortar pits and petroglyph designs.

Indian Stone Corral (40) Numerous petroglyphs are associated with this site in Orangevale, perhaps once a ceremonial center.

Inscription Canyon (Black Canyon) (41) Beautiful and unusual petroglyphs carved on basalt cliffs may be seen in the canyon near Barstow.

Joshua Tree Petroglyphs (42) Located in Joshua Tree National Monument near Twentynine Palms, this

site has numerous petroglyphs hidden from general view. (See also JOSHUA TREE NATIONAL MONUMENT entry under "Sacred Places.")

Lakes Basin Petroglyphs (43) At least 83 designs on six large panels appear at this Plumas County site.

Lava Beds National Monument (44) At Fern Cave there are a large number of rock paintings, some of which may represent the explosion of the A.D. 1094 supernova, and at Symbol Bridge there is a pictograph with three crescents that may portray the same event.

Little Petroglyph Canyon (45) One set of pictographs at this China Lake site depicts a pair of archers aiming their arrows at each other. The set either represents supernaturals doing battle, or records a specific conflict of some sort.

Maidu Indian Boulder (46) Rock art appears on this 50-yard-long boulder, in Graegle near a place once used as a summer hunting camp by the Maidu.

Meadow Lake Petroglyphs (47) Three hundred ninety pecked design units surround the lake in Nevada County.

Mono Crater Petroglyphs (48) At the summit of this volcanic cone are vulva forms carved in high relief, possibly made in association with girls' puberty initiations. In Diego rites, such forms protect initiates from evil and ensure safe and easy childbirth.

Olsen Petroglyphs (49) Various designs associated with a precontact Wintu Indian village in Shasta County.

Petroglyph Point (50) Petroglyphs in geometric and zoomorphic forms extend for about 25 miles along the cliffs of an isolated volcanic zone near Tulelake.

Puberty Rock (51) This rock in Perris is decorated by monochromatic paintings made by girls following puberty rituals that included ingestion of hallucinogens, one of two major rock-painting traditions in prehistoric southern California.

Rancheria Saca Rock Art (52) This art at Alamo Pintada Creek includes a rock slab with crosses and centipede motifs, dating to the historical period. Also at this site is a large serpentine boulder with pit-and-groove markings, a type of petroglyph rare in Chumash country.

Ring Mountain (53) This site in Tiburon, used as a fertility ritual site, has an unusual display of Miwok rock art.

Sardine Valley Archeological District (54) This area in Sierra County contains several granite boulders decorated with petroglyphs.

Sequoia National Park (55) Interesting pictographs can be seen near Fresno at Hospital Rock and at Potwisha Camp. At Hospital Rock, in addition to paintings, there are small pits carved in the rock that may have been used by shamans.

Strap Ravine Nisenan Maidu Indian Site (56) Grooved petroglyph and probable burial mounds in Placer County.

Sun Cave (57) Sunlight interacts with petroglyphs at this Imperial County site at winter solstice.

Terminus Beach Petroglyphs (Tulare-2) (58) This site is said to be guarded by a shamanic spirit helper whose likeness appears in paintings perhaps made by shamans in altered states of consciousness.

Titus Canyon (59) The petroglyphs here seem to have been made long before contemporary American Indians, who regard them with superstitious awe.

Tule River Pictographs (60) The Tule River Indian Reservation includes one of the most spectacular Yokuts pictograph sites, with cave paintings that may have been made by shamans in altered states of consciousness. Painted Rock has a picture of an evil spirit.

Vasquez Rocks (61) The rocks of this area of Los Angeles County are covered with pictographs.

Ventura 195 (62) This Santa Monica Mountain site has many paintings of frogs and other animals that may have been produced by shamans in altered states of consciousness.

Colorado ✛

Cañon Pintado (63) Pictographs and petroglyphs appear in this region of seven rock shelters near Rangeley.

Carnero Creek Pictographs (64) At this site near La Garita is a pictograph panel with 54 anthropomorphic, zoomorphic and geometric figures drawn on rock flow from the San Juan Volcanic Field.

Carrot Men Pictographs (65) This site near Rangeley is a campsite with two panels of pictographs and petroglyphs, depicting stylized zoomorphic and anthropomorphic figures.

Indian Rock Art (66) Vertical rock panel containing both pictographs and petroglyphs near Penrose.

Mancos Canyon (67) A great procession of men, birds and other figures carved into a rock here may document the migration of a people.

Pictograph Point (68) One stylized line drawing here shows a chief who has passed away. A jagged line above

him denotes water, and out of his mouth grows a spruce tree, into which he has transformed himself at death. This site is near Cortez, in Mesa Verde National Park.

Florida ✛

Leverock's Altar Stone (69) Two human faces were carved almost 2,000 years ago on the face of this rock that now sits in front of Leverock's Restaurant in New Port Richey.

Georgia ✛

Track Rock Archaeological Area (70) Located in Chattahoochee National Forest, near Blairsville, in a 50-acre area, there are preserved petroglyphs of ancient origin, resembling animal and bird tracks, crosses, circles and human footprints.

Track Rock Gap (71) At this site in Union County are several large bedrock boulders with deeply incised figures, principally bisected ovals, but also a rayed sun, a cross within a circle and other features.

Idaho ✛

Buffalo Eddy (72) Sites on both sides of the Snake River near Lewiston contain more than 500 separate petroglyphs and a few pictographs. Humans are shown on horseback in this area more often than elsewhere on the Columbian Plateau.

Lake Pend Oreille (73) This is one among 130 rock art sites so far discovered in northeastern Washington and northwestern Idaho. Small pictographs and small clusters of petroglyphs are common. At seven locations, petroglyph panels depict bear paws.

McCammon Petroglyphs (74) This site on Interstate 15 has several large boulders on which prehistoric peoples pecked designs and pictures. It is one of the few rock art sites in Idaho.

Illinois ✛

Gorham Petroglyphs (75) Petroglyphs of animals and human hands decorate an imposing bluff at this site in the Shawnee National Forest.

Piasa Rock (76) On this rock in the Mississippi River near Alton is a painting of a demonic figure, perhaps representing a river spirit.

Kansas ✛

Indian Hill (77) There are a series of petroglyphs at this village site in Ellsworth County.

Maine ✥

Monhegan Island Petroglyphs (78) Cryptic rock carvings over a spring.

Massachusetts ✥

Assawompsett Pond (79) Rock carvings appear on submerged rocks here in Middleboro.

Dighton Rock (80) A variety of strange symbols are incised on the 7-by-11-foot face of this waist-high reddish-brown rock near Berkley.

Rock Ledge (81) This freakish-looking chunk of rock in Westford bears an unusual combination of holes, lines and discolorations.

Michigan ✥

Sanilac Petroglyphs (82) One of several curious images carved in rock in Sanilac Petroglyphs State Park seems to link a spiderlike creature to a human being through an umbilical cord. According to contemporary Indians living in the area, other figures represent the Water Panther.

Minnesota ✥

Jeffers Petroglyphs (83) This site in Cottonwood County is the largest known concentration of rock art in

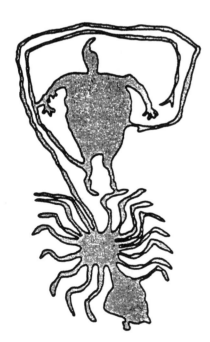

Sanilac "Spider Man" drawn in violet. "Spider" is believed to symbolize a campfire

Minnesota, consisting of more than 2,000 figures, many of which may have been made before 3000 B.C.

Kensington Rune Stone (84) Found in Alexandria in 1898 by a farmer who proclaimed it to be a Norse relic.

Nett Lake Petroglyph Site (85) About 150 pecked glyphs decorate the rocks here in Koochiching County.

Missouri ✥

Holliday Petroglyphs (86) Four groups of wall carvings are associated with a woodlands campsite.

Jacob's Cavern (87) Stylized drawings on deer bone fragments are to be seen in this cave near Pineville.

Mitchell Petroglyph Archeological Site (88) This small rock shelter in Cairo contains petroglyphs.

Thousand Hills State Park Petroglyphs Archeological Site (89) This Kirksville site is one of the largest and best preserved petroglyph sites in the northeastern section of Missouri.

Washington State Park (90) Hundreds of petroglyphs appear on outcrops of dolomite here. The designs include human figures, spirals, birds, footprints, mace, bi-lobed arrows, meanders, snakes, zoomorphs and phallic figures.

Montana ✥

Flathead Lake Rock Art (91) Western Montana's only petroglyph, a large geometric abstract slightly abraded over red pictographs, is at this site. The abrasion may have been intended to cancel the effects of the painting.

Kila Pictographs (92) This site consists of two pictograph sites one-half mile apart, on high cliffs that border the Ashley Creek Valley. Of special interest are depictions of bison and other animals, along with men in canoes.

Petroglyph Canyon (93) Anthropomorphic and zoomorphic petroglyphs decorate the limestone cliffs for a distance of about 800 feet near a habitation site near Warren dated to the 18th and 19th centuries.

Pictograph Cave State Monument (94) This cave near Billings, the home of prehistoric hunters, has designs of men and animals painted in red, white and black.

Smith River Rock Paintings (95) Pictographs show stylized stick figures, but also handprints and geometric designs, painted in red and black.

Sun River Rock Paintings (96) On the upper Sun River, near the Continental Divide. A large number of handprints and anthropomorphs, zoomorphs and tally marks, all painted in red.

Nevada ✥

Black Canyon Petroglyphs (97) Petroglyphs on rock ledges near Alamo surround rock rings or hunting blinds, dating before 1865.

Carson River Petroglyphs (98) The petroglyphs at this site are predominantly circles and wavy lines typical of the Great Basin curvilinear style.

Grimes Point (99) Markings on rocks here in Churchill County are believed to have been used in hunting rites.

Hickson Summit Petroglyphs (100) Some time between 1000 B.C. and A.D. 1500, five different groups of Native Americans pecked designs and pictures of animals on the cliff at the south edge of the present picnic ground near Austin.

Humboldt National Forest Petroglyph Trail (101) Interpretive signs take the visitor on a self-guided tour of rock carvings.

Kachina Cave (102) Painted anthropomorphs in red ochre—groups of distinctive, abstract, horned humanoid figures with tapered or triangular bodies, some holding small shields—located in White Pine County.

Lagomarsino Site (103) Hatchmarks and zigzags here in Story County are typical of the Great Basin rectilinear style.

Lake Mead National Recreation Area (104) Among other subjects, these petroglyphs in the Glendale vicinity show the elusive bighorn sheep, highly prized by hunters, and may represent hunting magic.

Pahranagat Lake Petroglyph Panels (105) The rock art here depicts highly stylized anthropomorphic figures, holding atlatls, and mountain sheep, as well as ticked lines with animal and other figures, perhaps representing a game drive. The art is a good example of the Great Basin representational style.

Sheep Mountain Range Archeological District (106) This is a large area in the Las Vegas vicinity containing numerous petroglyphs and pictographs as well as campsites and roasting pits for mescal, both prehistoric and historic.

Tim Springs Petroglyphs (107) This canyon area near Indian Springs contains numerous petroglyphs and pictographs of bighorn sheep, deer and abstract symbols.

Valley of Fire State Park (108) In the park are a large number of petroglyphs left by Anasazi peoples on

Nevada: Petroglyphs

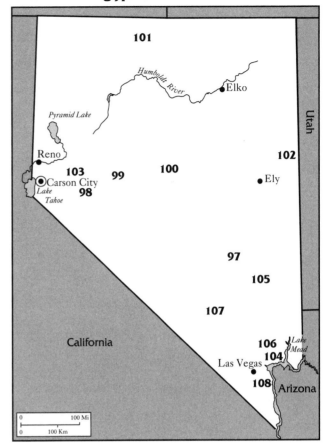

periodic visits, particularly in Petroglyph Canyon, in the Las Vegas vicinity. Some designs are geometric; others portray hands, feet, mountain sheep, other animals and special devices for throwing spears called atlatls.

New Mexico ✥

Bandelier National Monument (109) Pictographs and petroglyphs are to be seen among the Anasazi cliff dwellings here in Los Alamos.

Carlsbad Caverns National Park (110) Prehistoric American Indians made black and red paintings on the rock wall of the entrance to the caverns, although they appear not to have ventured far into them. In the Slaughter Canyon area of the park is Painted Grotto, a pictograph site.

Chaco Canyon National Park (111) Among the petroglyph sites is Atlatl Cave, where there are many painted handprints, animals, fertility themes and humpbacked flute players. Other sites in the vicinity of Bloomfield have apparent astronomical representations.

Petroglyphs on bank of Rio Grande at Bandelier, New Mexico   (photograph by Fred E. Mang Jr., courtesy National Park Service)

Crow Canyon Archeological Site   (112) Sixty panels of Navajo and Pueblo petroglyphs are to be seen at this site near Farmington.

El Morro National Monument   (113) This site includes a stone "bulletin board," used by both American Indians and white settlers. A sandstone butte is covered with 500 Spanish inscriptions.

Feather Cave   (114) This is a ceremonial cave near Lincoln decorated with petroglyphs of hands and masked dancers.

Heshoda Tsina (Place of Writing)   (115) Pictographs, mostly handprints painted in a variety of colors, and petroglyphs, many of them in highly unusual geometric designs, are to be found on the Zuñi Indian Reservation.

Indian Petroglyphs State Park   (116) Perhaps 900 years ago, hunters camping in the Albuquerque area carved a variety of realistic and symbolic drawings in the face of the basalt escarpment created by a lava flow from a nearby volcano.

Inscription Rock   (117) A black-top basaltic mesa in Los Lunas on the top of which are huge boulders, on one of which are inscribed the Ten Commandments in Phoenician and other unlikely languages. Although the inscriptions are now known to be a hoax, the area still retains its mysterious aura.

Kyakima   (118) This rock art on the Zuñi Reservation dates from the late 17th century; it is mostly petroglyphs of large masks or shields, anthropomorphic figures and elaborate geometric designs.

Largo Canyon   (119) At this site are various petroglyphs of supernaturals. Among the most frequently depicted is the Humpbacked God, usually shown holding a staff. He is horned, horns being an insignia of supernatural power.

Petroglyph Canyon   (120) Besides being a good source of potting clay, this canyon on the Zuñi Reservation contains many panels of petroglyphs. Included are a large number of anthropomorphs that show the influence of the Rio Grande style, with rounded heads and horns.

Petroglyph National Monument (121) This Montano site includes Petroglyph [State] Park, West Mesa and Boca Negro Canyon Unit, all with rock art sites.

Pine River Canyon (Los Pinos) Pictographs (122) Born for Water, one of the Slayer Twins, is depicted in an 18th-century pictograph in the Navajo Reservoir District.

San Cristobal Petroglyphs (123) The art at this site includes depictions of supernatural figures called mudheads, two-horned and one-horned masks, other masks with jagged teeth and stars.

Scholle Petroglyph (124) This rock art panel includes a crescent and a star that may represent the A.D. 1094 supernova explosion.

Three Rivers Petroglyph State Park (125) Some 20,000 carvings here in Carrizozo depict wildlife, including a fish, ceremonial figures and geometric designs.

Village of the Great Kivas (126) Petroglyphs that seem to represent the exploding of the A.D. 1094 super-

nova are to be seen here on the Zuñi Reservation. There are also vivid paintings of masked kachina dancers as well as pecked petroglyphs that evoke stories and interpretations from modern Zuñis.

North Carolina ✚

Judaculla Rock (127) A soapstone boulder in Cullowhee covered with pictographs that, according to Cherokee mythology, were made by a giant named Tsul'kula.

North Dakota ✚

Medicine Rock State Historic Site (128) Petroglyphs carved on a large rock and what is called a dance ring, 200 feet in diameter in the Elgin area.

Writing Rock State Historic Site (129) Two large glacial boulders in Fortuna, on which are carved petroglyphs probably representing the mythical thunderbird.

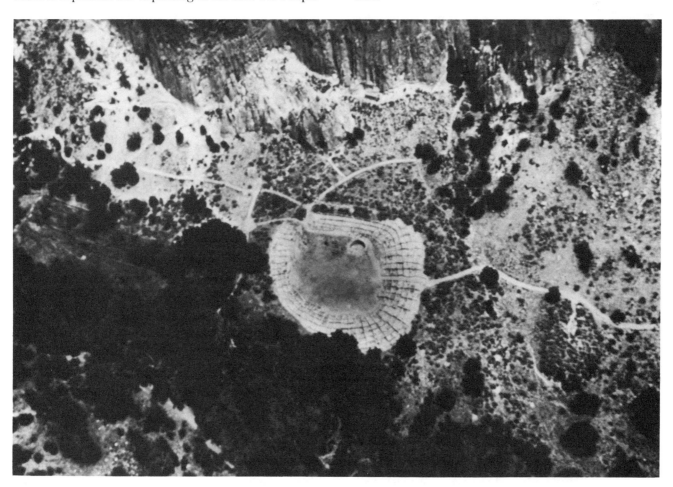

Tivony Ruin at Bandelier, New Mexico (photograph by Fred E. Mang Jr., courtesy National Park Service)

New Mexico: Petroglyphs

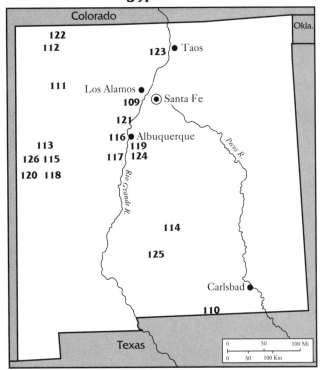

Ohio ✛

Barnesville Petroglyph (130) Outcropping of large sandstone rocks covered with carvings of footprints, animal tracks, snake figures, star or sun signs, stylized human faces, hands and feet, in association with Adena artifacts.

Hammondsville Hieroglyphics (131) A large slate wall filled with untranslatable hieroglyphic-like rock paintings.

Kelley's Island Inscription Rock (132) A large limestone boulder with stylized humans, pipes and amorphous designs, attributed to the Erie, and interpreted as a depiction of several tribes smoking pipes in a ceremony.

Leo Petroglyph (133) Symbols and figures carved on a stone slab, similar to Kelley's Island Inscription Rock.

Oklahoma ✛

Heavener Runestone (134) This so-called runestone contains eight "runic" symbols carved between A.D. 600 and A.D. 900.

Oregon ✛

Albert Lake Petroglyphs (135) Several boulders with a series of pecked petroglyphs of geometric forms.

Greaser Petroglyph Site (136) A cluster of boulders with pecked petroglyphs of human and animal figures, possibly the site of rabbit or antelope drives in prehistoric times.

Hell's Canyon (137) Pictographs of guardian spirits or other supernaturals finger-painted by vision quest supplicants as well as a variety of lightly scratched petroglyphs.

Horsethief Lake State Park (138) Here in The Dalles area is one of the Columbia Plateau's largest concentrations of rock art still existing in its natural setting. A pictograph site near here is unusual in having eight pairs of twins, who were thought to be born with shamanic powers.

Tennessee ✛

Bradley County Sandstone Petroglyphs (139) A wall of red sandstone inscribed with unknown characters and drawings for about 16 feet of its length.

Franklin County Sandstone Shelter (140) A small sandstone shelter with grooved marks on walls and ceiling, opening to the west; apparently a shrine.

Hamilton County Cave Pictographs (141) Classic southeastern ceremonial complex motifs—including encircled cross, mace, monolithic axe, woodpecker, crescent and bird-man warrior—on the ceiling of a cave at the head of the Sequatchie Valley.

Lawrence County (142) Two figures, a life-sized hand and a figure resembling a rattlesnake rattle or a medicine pipe, are incised in bedrock.

Mound Bottom Petroglyphs (143) Petroglyphs on a bluff in Cheatham County overlooking Mound Bottom and evidently associated with this Mississippian site (see MOUND BOTTOM under "Platform and Temple Mounds" in Earthworks and Mounds).

Van Buren County Sandstone Shelter (144) The walls of the shelter contain about 50 predominantly linear incised lines and two vulva-shaped carvings.

Warren County Sandstone Shelter (145) Petroglyphs appear on two sandstone boulders in this small rock shelter, dating to the Mississippian period.

White County Cave Petroglyphs (146) This cave has many distinctive petroglyphs on its limestone walls, evidently of Mississippian provenance.

Texas ✛

Big Bend National Park (147) Along the Hot Springs Nature Trail in the Marathon area, pictographs may be seen.

Hueco Tanks State Park   (148) In the El Paso vicinity, on the walls of caves and in rock shelters around natural hollows used to collect water in prehistoric times, are painted pictures, some lively and graphic, others merely designs.

Lower Pecos Canyon Archeological District (149) Numerous rock shelters and caves here in the Comstock area contain pictographs.

Meyers Springs Pictographs   (150) This site in the Dryden area includes a pictograph panel with prehistoric designs of handprints and human and animal figures. Later elements, such as crosses and churches, indicate European contact.

Painted Rock Indian Pictograph Site   (151) Important central Texas pictograph site, covering some 1,000 feet of a limestone bluff overlooking the Concho River. Contains geometric shapes, animal and human figures and negative and positive handprints painted in red, orange, yellow, black and white.

Panther Cave   (152) Remarkably detailed pictures, predominantly of deer and panthers, cover the whole wall and part of a ceiling of a water-filled cave in the Amistad Recreation Area. The cave takes its name from a gigantic panther visible from the shore of the lake in the Comstock area.

Pictograph Cave   (153) A rock shelter near Lake Whitney whose back wall is painted with three groups of red stick figures, dated from the 12th to the 16th centuries A.D.

Satan Canyon   (154) Symbolic depictions of fishing are to be seen in this canyon in Val Verde County.

Seminole Canyon State Park   (155) This rock art site at Diablo Dam in Alamo Canyon near Del Rio has spear and animal motifs that appear to reflect shamanic hunting magic. At Seminole Canyon, there are red paintings of greater than human-sized shamans associated with hunting motifs. The drawings date to between 8000 B.C. and A.D. 500.

Utah ✤

Arches National Park   (156) This park near Moab contains several pictograph and petroglyph sites, including some unusual paintings five or more feet tall, similar to those at Horseshoe Canyon.

Buckhorn Wash Rock Art   (157) Paintings and carvings on stone left by people of the Freemont culture between A.D. 900 and 1300.

Canyonlands National Monument   (158) The rock art here near Moab includes both pictographs and petro-

glyphs, some of which may have been used to mark game trails.

Capitol Reef National Park   (159) Among the rock art here in Torrey are two crescents and a bright object or sun symbol that may represent the explosion of an A.D. 1094 supernova.

Clear Creek Canyon Rock Art   (160) Many panels of petroglyphs decorate the canyon in the Fort Cove vicinity.

Courthouse Wash Pictographs   (161) This pictograph panel in the Moab area contains designs representing several distinct cultures. Among the figures are anthropomorphs up to five feet tall.

Davis Gulch Pictographs   (162) At this site near Glen Canyon is a 60-foot sheltered pictograph panel with 35 figures, including some anthropomorphs, assigned to the Anasazi period.

Dinosaur National Monument   (163) Freemont pictographs and petroglyphs may be seen at several sites in the Vernal vicinity.

Dry Fork Creek Petroglyphs   (164) This major petroglyph site boasts nearly life-size anthropomorphs pecked in rows across the cliff face, probably shamanic in origin.

Utah: Petroglyphs

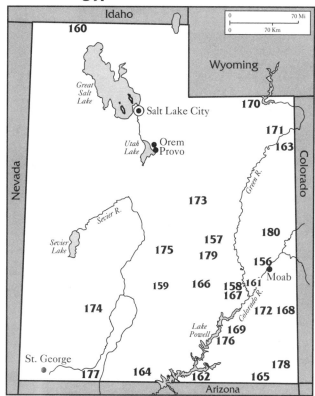

Peculiar stones called the Marching Men at Arches National Park, Utah (courtesy National Park Service)

Grand Gulch Rock Paintings (165) Abstract designs in red and black, including lines, zigzags, and circles, attributed to Archaic peoples, and uncommon in this region.

Horseshoe Canyon (166) In Canyonlands (West) National Park, throughout Horseshoe Canyon and Barrier Canyon, which are part of the Green River area, are large paintings of human figures on sandstone cliff walls. These are believed to have been done by shamans and to have had religious significance.

Hot Springs Picnic Site (167) Near the picnic site is a rock shelter containing Indian pictographs, one of which is called the Moki Queen by the local residents in the Hanksville area.

Indian Creek Petroglyphs (168) At this site near Monticello in Indian Creek State Park is a large petroglyph panel that includes trapezoidal-bodied anthropomorphs, birds, stick men and wavy lines.

Kachina Bridge (169) In Natural Bridges National Monument at Rock Ruin, there are a series of panels in which Twin War Gods go through various adventures, losing their power-giving feathers in the process.

Manila Petroglyphs (170) These are 200-foot-long discontinuous petroglyph panels depicting anthropomorphic, zoomorphic and geometric figures.

McKee Springs (171) In Dinosaur National Monument in the Vernal area is rock art by Freemont people.

Newspaper Rock State Historical Monument (172) This cliff face near Monticello with some 350 carvings appears to mark the passage of people and tribes and to record events, serving as a stone tabloid of the history of the place over 1500 years, most dating from A.D. 900 to 1200.

Nine Mile Canyon Rock Art (173) Sites near Price and along the road to Myton, near Wellington, include many rock-art panels attributed to Freemont people.

Parowan Gap Indian Drawings (174) Drawings and designs on rock, evidently by Freemont people. Anthropomorphic and geometric figures are executed with rare precision over the sandstone cliff face.

Rochester–Muddy Creek Petroglyph Site (175) Petroglyph panels on sandstone outcroppings depict anthropomorphic, zoomorphic and geometric figures.

Rock Ruin (176) Petroglyphs in Natural Bridges National Monument depict the emergence of the people from the womb of the earth.

Salt Creek Archeological District Rock Art (177) Pictograph and petroglyph sites in association with camping sites and habitation structures.

Sand Island Petroglyphs (178) Large panel of petroglyphs overlooking the San Juan River near Bluff. Among the figures is Kokopelli, the humpbacked flute player.

Temple Mountain Wash Pictographs (179) A pictograph panel, 60 feet by eight feet, lies above a narrow ledge at the bottom of a sandstone cliff near Hanksville.

Thompson Wash Petroglyphs (Sago Canyon Petroglyphs) (180) Extensive panels of both carving and painting appear on rocks in this area.

Virginia ✤

Indian Paintings (181) A prehistoric site near Maiden Springs consisting of pictographs of birds, animals, women and warriors, halfway up Paint Lick Mountain.

Washington ✤

Cowiche Creek Pictographs (182) Has some of the better Yakima-style polychrome pictographs in south-central Washington. Also in the Yakima vicinity is a display of Indian-painted rock art beside a modern highway that follows an ancient Indian trail.

Indian Painted Rocks Pictographs (183) Located near the Little Spokane River, and similar to those near Yakima.

Lake Chelan (184) This site is notable for depictions of hunting and game drives. One scene shows a communal game drive, another a lone hunter pursuing a herd.

Long Lake Pictographs (185) Red-pigment pictograph panels with a variety of anthropomorphic, zoomorphic and symbolic designs in the Ford vicinity.

Roosevelt Petroglyphs (186) In a special park, residents of Roosevelt have installed and protected a group of petroglyphs collected from nearby sites.

Snake River Archeological District Rock Art (187) Pictograph and petroglyph sites appear in association with seasonal campsites near Asotin.

Telegraph Island Petroglyphs (188) Site near Paterson with petroglyphs inscribed on basalt rocks now lining the John Day Pool.

Wedding Rock Petroglyphs (189) Twenty-five carvings, including fertility symbols, hunting figures, boats and whales, associated with a nearby Ozette village in the Forks vicinity known for its whale hunting.

West Virginia ✤

Indian Cave Rock Art (190) Numerous anthropomorphic, zoomorphic and geometric petroglyphs and pictographs, in an oval rock shelter near Goodhope.

Wisconsin ✤

Gullickson's Glen Petroglyph Site (191) In a narrow gouge on high sandstone cliffs at Black River Falls is a large collection of petroglyphs. Among the figures are bison, elk, cranes, a wild turkey, a human figure with bow and arrow, an eagle dancer and a thunderbird.

Roche-a-Cri State Park (192) Petroglyphs are carved into the side of a mound in the park near Friendship.

Wyoming ✤

Dinwoody Canyon Pictographs (193) This site includes hundreds of pictographs, accumulated over a long period of time; later panels include feared Water Ghost beings and Rock Ghost beings. In historic times, this was a shamanic healing site.

CANADA

Alberta ✤

Ribstone Petroglyphs (194) Boulders with incised ridges, like ribs, in the Viking vicinity.

Writing-on-Stone (195) Among other subjects, petroglyphs in the Lethbridge vicinity depict men on horseback, probably dating after A.D. 1730. Representations of men with bows and shields may have been made earlier. Animal figures may have been drawn as part of a vision quest.

British Columbia ✤

Atlin Lake Petroglyph (196) Two outlined circle-faces, supposedly of a frog and a human, along with one animal figure reported to be a caribou. The carving relates to a place constructed to catch caribou.

Cranbrook Petroglyphs (197) Rock carvings near a lake and a well-traveled trail include anthropomorphic, zoomorphic and geometric figures. There are numerous pecked and abraded animal tracks, stylistically different from other rock art in the region.

Gibbs Creek Petroglyphs (198) Over 90 boulders have petroglyphs at this, the largest petroglyph site known in British Columbia. Many of the boulders are submerged for part of the year, but are revealed during salmon fishing season. They include fishing motifs.

Kootenay Lake Pictographs (199) One of the larger pictograph sites in British Columbia. One panel has a realistic representation of traveling deer and fawns.

Jump Across Creek Petroglyphs (200) This site includes several human figures, one about seven feet long, incised in bedrock.

Port John Pictographs (201) The largest rock art site recorded on the central coast of British Columbia.

Protection Island Whale Petroglyph (202) A single zoomorphic design crudely pecked into a large slab of sandstone, evidently representing a killer whale, radiocarbon dated to about A.D. 1675.

Manitoba ✤

Deer Strand Pictographs (203) Well-known pictograph site at Minago River.

Kapitopaskahk Site (204) Red ochre swaths and crosses on a cliff facing Cross Lake.

Molson Lake Pictographs (205) Largest rock painting site in Manitoba.

Moswacask (Moose's Ass) Pictographs (206) A rock formation at Little Playgreen Lake resembling the hind portion of a moose, at whose anus native peoples would shoot for good luck on their way out to hunt. Faint paintings were observed on the inside surface of each of the legs.

Ontario ✤

Agawa Indian Rock (207) In Lake Superior Provincial Park, Native American pictographs at one of Canada's most sacred sites.

Peterborough Petroglyphs (208) A squatting figure with a hole in the abdomen here may be symbolic of death and rebirth. Other petroglyphs represent supplication to the Great Spirit. There are also some unusual inscriptions interpreted by Barry Fell as having a Scandinavian origin.

Petroglyphs Provincial Park (209) Carvings on marble bedrock along Highway 28.

Sunset Channel Pictographs (210) A bird of omen painting at this Lake of the Woods site is characteristic of the Ojibwa.

Tranquil Channel Petroglyphs (211) Paintings here at Lake of the Woods depict female figures with prominent genital regions, taken to be fertility symbols, as well as male stick figures with prominent phalluses. There is a recurring motif of three male figures grouped around one female. The site was visited by the Ojibwa as late as 1977.

Québec ✤

Lake Memphramagog Petroglyphs (212) Boulder with petroglyphs and linear markings that may have recorded celestial observations.

Lake Wapizagonke Pictographs (213) Schematic human figures, a turtle and a triangular morph, near Shawnigan. A moose and a figure with a bird's head are among the figures now destroyed.

Rochers aux Oiseaux (Bird Rock) (214) Paintings of schematic human figures, fishes, canoes with people, a bird figure, an arched figure and other pictures, now faded; in the 17th century, native peoples threw tobacco offerings while passing the rock.

Saskatchewan ✤

Larocque Lake Pictographs (215) Among the pictograph panels on Canadian Shield bedrock here is one with stick figures and a caribou standing above a horned serpent.

HAUNTED PLACES

What is a "haunting"? Generally, a place or structure is considered to be haunted when it acquires a reputation over a period of years for being plagued by repeated bizarre and unexplained phenomena. Such phenomena are the reported presence of ghosts, poltergeists or spirits, or the repeated sightings of mysterious and monstrous creatures. Haunting phenomena also include strange lights, noises and smells, as well as "bad" or "evil" atmospheres. There is no question that some areas of North America are haunted zones, where mysterious phenomena occur again and again.

According to lore, the ghosts, spirits or other entities that cause hauntings are attached to specific places, or their "homes." In some cases, haunted sites literally are homes—countless houses and dwellings have been reputed to be haunted places where things go bump in the night, year after year, generation after generation.

What Places Are Haunted?

Haunted sites can be virtually anywhere: lakes, wells, swamps, forests, mountains, canyons, roads, cemeteries and buildings. Haunted sites can be in remote locations, or near or in cities—sometimes a particular neighborhood of a city acquires a reputation of being haunted. Some haunted places are discovered to be the sites of ancient American Indian burial grounds or hunting grounds, or have been associated by American Indians with evil spirits or powers. As in the movie *Poltergeist*, a haunted place might be on top of an old and perhaps forgotten cemetery, or on the former site of a church or other place of worship. Many of the areas considered to be power points or sacred places, covered in the first section of this book, are haunted.

Houses that are haunted do not necessarily have to be old or spooky in appearance, despite what novelists and Hollywood filmmakers would have us believe. Modern, even newly constructed houses can be haunted, especially if they have been built over a burial ground or sacred spot.

Objects as well as sites may be haunted. These include skulls and skeletons, or possessions cursed or associated with tragic events.

Haunted places sometimes can be identified by their names. Researcher Loren Coleman noticed that the same names cropped up in connection with various unexplained phenomena, and called this syndrome the Name Game. For example, if the word "Devil," or its Spanish equivalent, "Diablo," appears in a place-name, as in Devil's Canyon or Diablo Road, it may indicate that the area has a reputation for strange events or sightings of spirits. Other names that often appear in this context are "Mason," which is associated with Freemasonry; "Hob," which refers to "hobgoblin," a type of mischievous spirit; and "Lafayette" or "Fayette," which derives from the French term *fée* (fay), for fairy. Some haunted areas come to be known as triangles, probably after the famous Bermuda Triangle located between Bermuda, Florida and Puerto Rico, where many unexplained disappearances of ships and planes have occurred. While the Name Game may seem odd, just remember these names the next time you read about some mysterious event. One of them may appear in the story.

What Haunts a Place?

Hauntings are attributed to ghosts, spirits, poltergeists or mysterious creatures. Ghosts generally are believed to be spirits of the dead who are trapped on the earth plane. According to lore, souls of the dead become trapped when they do not accept death, or they are being punished for a terrible crime. They are tied to a spot, oftentimes the place where they died, or a place that they loved during life, and either drift about without apparent purpose, or reenact their deaths or other traumatic events. Another belief about ghosts is that they have no intrinsic personality, but are impressions created by intense emotion, thus explaining the mechanical and repetitive motion of some ghosts.

Some haunting ghosts have motifs, such as the phantom traveler or phantom hitchhiker. These ghosts may be male or female in appearance, and travel along lonely roads or rail lines. Supposedly, they interact with living persons, seeking rides or asking directions. Their destination is likely to be the cemetery where their bodies are buried, or their former home.

Spirits are believed to be nonhuman entities that often are part of nature. They may be essences or embody the spirit of a place, such as a mountain or lake. They may be invisible but have a palpable presence, or they may appear in various guises, some of them humanlike and some of them monstrous. Fairies, elves and working spirits—those who toil away in households, mines, etc.—resemble humans. They may act kindly toward human beings, or may be mischievous or downright malicious, such as spirits that attempt to lead travelers astray. Spirits are part of the mythical landscape—literally the spiritual energy of a place. Their guises and activities are empowered by local mythologies, that is, the beliefs of humans in them. Thus, it is not unusual for spirits to be more active in areas that are remote rather than urbanized, and where folklore beliefs that have been accumulated over generations are still held.

Poltergeists, or noisy spirits, are said to be invisible entities that plague a place, usually a house or building, with violent acts and noises. Their assaults upon a site—and often the persons there—usually have a finite period of time. Poltergeists are most active at night. Some long-term ghost hauntings have poltergeist characteristics. Psychical researchers believe that at least some poltergeist disturbances are created by human beings who unwittingly project repressed emotional and sexual tension, anger and frustration.

Mysterious creatures belong to a shadowy realm that seems to bridge our physical world and another dimension. Such creatures may resemble known animals, or be grotesque shapes that incorporate both animal and human features. It is possible that mysterious creatures are in part shaped by generations of human belief and folklore.

Characteristics of Hauntings

Hauntings follow no pattern; rather, each haunting is unique. Some hauntings seem purposeful, such as a spirit that guards a place, or the ghost of a person that lingers in a location favored in life. Other hauntings seem to be tied to violent events: murder, accidents, suicides and severe emotional shocks. Still others are aimless, having no apparent purpose or cause.

Hauntings can involve entities who seem benign or even friendly, such as ghosts of beloved family members or even pets. These ghosts may seem to be watching over the residents and protecting them from harm. At the other extreme, a place may seem to be infested with malignant entities that do everything possible to terrify and drive out the human inhabitants.

Haunting phenomena can include mysterious blobs of light, filmy forms, dark shapes or exotic spirits or creatures. The majority of hauntings, however, consist mostly of strange noises such as thumps, moaning and crying and animal sounds, as well as strong odors, such as flowers, perfume, charred wood, decaying organic matter or meat or sulphur. In addition, there may be changes in the atmosphere of a haunted place that cause witnesses to feel intense cold spots, to have their hair stand on end or to experience discomfort or unseen presences.

Ghosts seem to vary in their behavior. Some mechanically repeat the same actions over and over, almost like images on a moving picture film. Other ghosts seem to respond intelligently to events around them. Ghosts appear in period costumes and in modern dress, and come in both sexes and all shapes and sizes. Some ghosts appear as phantoms in black hoods and robes. Some ghosts appear solid and completely normal, while others seem vague, misty and semitransparent.

Such phenomena often seem to be related to persons who once lived at a site, or to events that took place there. For example, a house reputedly haunted by the ghost of a woman who loved roses might seem filled with a strong scent of roses from time to time, even though no roses are present.

Hauntings sometimes seem to affect the physical environment. Doors and cupboards may be found open, apparently having opened by themselves, and furniture may be relocated around a room by unseen forces. Objects at a haunted site may disappear and later reappear in a distant location. Objects affected in such a manner are called apports, from the French word *apporter*, which means "to bring." Supposedly, spirits and ghosts do the transporting by unknown means.

Poltergeist hauntings are characterized by the violent movement of objects, usually small; breakages of objects; electromagnetic malfunctions; physical assaults; and noises and smells. Sometimes people witness the movement of objects by unknown means. In most ghost hauntings, however, the movement of objects is not witnessed.

The phenomena of hauntings may occur over a limited period of time, such as a few months or years, or may go on for centuries. Sometimes haunted sites become dormant for unexplained reasons, and then reactivate. Some hauntings occur only on certain anniversary dates, such as a person's death, or the date of an accident or battle.

How Can We Explain Hauntings?

Many hypotheses attempt to explain hauntings, but none are conclusive—we don't know what causes hauntings and why. The failure of science to explain hauntings prompts skeptics to say that hauntings are not paranormal, but can be attributed to tricks of light and mind, natural phenomena or hoaxes. But, as researcher and author Ivan T. Sanderson said of poltergeists, "It is no use saying these things don't actually happen, because they do." Footsteps on the stairs when nobody is there, lights burning in the windows of empty houses, fuzzy shapes floating about the darkness, mysterious cries and moans in the night, even the melodramatic rattling of chains—all these phenomena occur in

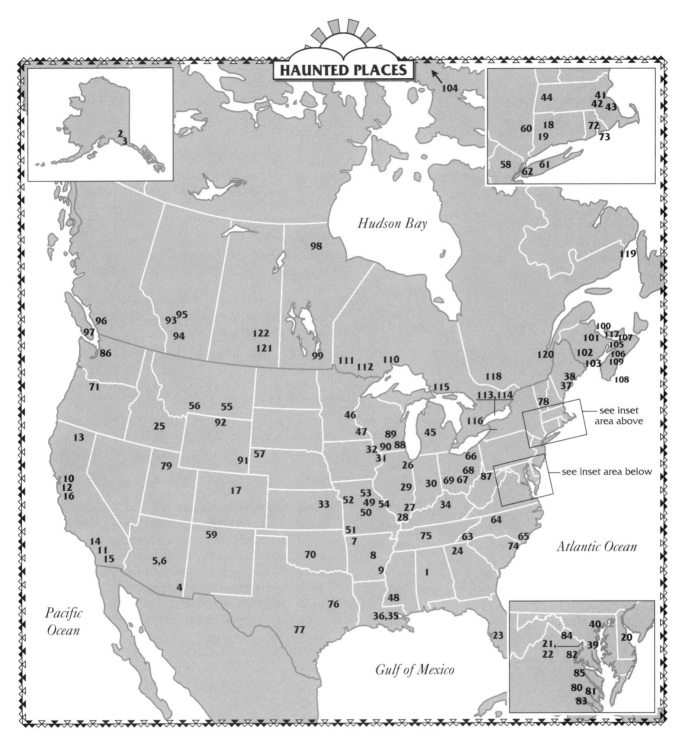

haunted places, despite the lack of convincing explanations for them.

Complicating the matter is the fact that no two persons experience the same haunting in quite the same way. In fact, two persons can be at a haunted site together, and one person will experience unexplained phenomena while the second party experiences nothing. Such disparate experiences make it difficult to prove

hauntings. It is likely that psychical and emotional sensitivities influence our receptivity to haunting phenomena.

Thousands of hauntings have been systematically investigated by psychical researchers and parapsychologists since the late 19th century. Many explanations have been proposed, but there is no conclusive evidence to support one more strongly than another. Frederic W.

H. Myers, one of the founders of the Society for Psychical Research (SPR) in London, believed that most hauntings are fragmentary and meaningless, the residues of postmortem energies. One of Myers's colleagues, Eleanor Sidgwick, former secretary of the SPR, suggested that hauntings are comprised of recordings in space of human thoughts, actions and feelings. These can be accessed by psychically sensitive individuals, who perceive them replayed as a haunting.

The hypotheses popular with the public view hauntings as spirits tied to a place; spirits of the dead trapped on the earth plane for various reasons, such as failure to accept their deaths; and psychic recordings of events, thoughts and emotions, similar to the idea proposed by Sidgwick.

Researchers further have been unable to agree on definitions of ghosts or apparitions, and poltergeists.

In modern times, we tend to regard hauntings as something to be feared: They are manifestations of the Unknown, and the Unknown, we have convinced ourselves, is full of dread. In the mythic landscape, however, hauntings have a much different tenor. They are not fearful, but are merely phenomena that occur in an alternate reality separated from our material world by the thinnest of veils. The things that go on in hauntings coexist with us in the universe, but just beyond the pale of our waking consciousness. Haunted places provide window-areas, or openings into another world or dimension that allows strange beings to pass back and forth between our world and theirs.

We *can* experience these openings into other dimensions under certain conditions—when we are in the right place at the right time and in the right frame of mind, which usually is a state of relaxation or even distraction. For a moment, our consciousness is expanded and we glimpse another landscape. We may even help create what we experience by projecting our own thoughts, which may explain why two or more persons do not experience a haunting in exactly the same way.

The following are some of the notable haunted places in North America. Attention is devoted here to ghosts, poltergeists and spirits. For creatures, see Mysterious Creatures.

UNITED STATES

Alabama ✛

Moundville (1) A 40-mile section of Interstate 65 is said to be haunted because of the hundreds of accidents that have occurred there, with at least 208 persons injured and 23 killed. Legend has it that the highway

is built over a Creek burial ground, and the spirits of the dead dislike the disturbance of the roadway.

Alaska ✛

Gakona (2) A ghost that opens and closes doors, makes the sounds of footsteps and plays with electromagnetic equipment haunts the Gakona Lodge and Trading Post. The smell of smoke sometimes permeates the premises, though no fire can be found.

Tonsina (3) The Mangy Moose Saloon boasts the ghost of a mustachioed man who is tall, dark and thin. He appears in both day and evening, and opens doors for people.

Arizona ✛

Douglas (4) The basement of the Gadsden Hotel is haunted by a man in a khaki uniform, seen moving around the corridors at night.

Lost Dutchman Gold Mine (5) Located somewhere in the Superstitions, this fabulously rich vein of gold was discovered by an eccentric prospector named Jacob Walz in the years after the American Civil War. Walz, known as The Dutchman, died before he could claim his treasure. Ever since, would-be treasure hunters have been swarming into the Superstitions to search for the lost mine. Some of them turn up dead—without their heads. Apache Indians shun the Superstitions as evil.

Superstition Mountains (6) The Superstition Mountains are only 40 miles east of Phoenix, yet they seem to lie in a different world. Cowboys searching for stray cattle sometimes come across human skeletons. No one knows how they got there, and few can be identified. In 1949, a prospector named James Kidd disappeared here. His estate of about $174,000 was willed to organizations for research to prove survival after death. One beneficiary, the American Society for Psychical Research, used the funds to research near-death experiences.

Arkansas ✛

Fayetteville (7) This small community is the site of numerous strange phenomenon, including skyquakes (vibrations felt in the air), phantom panthers, UFOs, lake monsters and unexplained interference with car engines and railroad trains, which frequently derail.

Little Rock (8) The Old State House, 300 West Markham Street, was the scene of a murder in 1837 when Speaker John Wilson fatally stabbed Representative Anthony. A ghost in a long black coat drifts about the

House Chamber on the second floor, where the murder took place.

Monticello (9) The Allen House, 705 North Main Street, is haunted by a ghost believed to be that of LaDell Allen, who committed suicide by poisoning herself in the 1940s. Predominant phenomena are noises. The house, built in 1900, has been divided into apartments.

California ✣

Alcatraz (10) A former federal prison, located on an island in San Francisco Bay, is haunted by the sounds of its previous inmates, America's toughest criminals. The prison has been a tourist attraction since it closed in 1963. Visitors report hearing screams, moans, clanging doors, whistling, footsteps running down corridors and even ghostly banjo music, perhaps once played by Al Capone. Cold spots are felt where prisoners were kept in isolation.

Escondido (11) The Elfin Forest here is haunted by the apparition of a woman in white, often seen floating above the ground. She has also been observed to pass through the walls of houses. A retired minister, Corinne Pleasant, saw the woman floating about 15 inches off the ground.

Moss Beach (12) Located in a small town near San Francisco, the Moss Beach Distillery is a restaurant and bar. It is haunted by the ghost of a woman in blue, who was killed there in a fight in the 1930s. Apparitions of the Blue Lady in a blood-stained dress are seen frequently, especially in the ladies' room and on the highway outside. Employees of the restaurant report being tapped on the shoulder while working alone in the kitchen.

Mt. Shasta (13) Mt. Shasta, a dormant volcano 14,162 feet high, is the focus of many strange legends and beliefs. The Hopi believe that a race of lizard men have a city underneath the volcano, as well as beneath the city of Los Angeles. The mountain also is said to be the home of legendary Lemurians, who survived the catastrophic sinking of the lost continent of Lemuria in the Pacific Ocean thousands of years ago. Many sightings of ape men and of hooded phantoms have occurred.

Alcatraz   (photograph by Richard Frear, courtesy National Park Service)

Orange County   (14) The Peters Ranch, located in the Loma Foothills, near Peters Canyon Reservoir, is haunted by the apparition of a giant owl.

San Diego   (15) The Whaley House, now a museum in Old Town, near the intersection of U.S. 101 and Interstate 8, is plagued with strange noises and nasty odors, as well as ghostly footsteps. The principal ghost is "Yankee Jim" Robinson, who was hanged in 1852 for stealing San Diego's only pilot boat. Robinson died an agonizing death due to an improperly built scaffold. He dropped only five feet instead of 15, and he kicked and strangled for about 15 minutes while hanging in the noose.

San Jose   (16) At 525 South Winchester Boulevard is the Winchester House, one of the strangest-looking houses in the United States, with an even stranger history. It was built by Sarah Pardee Winchester, widow of Oliver Winchester, founder of the Winchester Repeating Arms Company. Convinced that the spirits of Native Americans killed with Winchester rifles were pursuing her, Sarah Winchester built her house with 2,000 doors, 160 rooms, 47 fireplaces, 40 staircases and dozens of secret passages. Her intent was to confuse the spirits so they wouldn't be able to find her. Theodore Roosevelt visited Sarah Winchester at her home, although what he thought of it is not recorded. Today, most of the rooms are sealed, but it is possible to take a guided tour of a small portion of the house.

Colorado ✛

Denver   (17) The tranquil Cheesman Park in the center of town stands atop an old and ruined cemetery, and reportedly is haunted by the ghosts of the restless dead. The 320-acre site was mapped out as Mount Prospect Cemetery in 1858, and was renamed City Cemetery in 1873. While it was under private ownership, it was divided into three sections, Catholic, Jewish and city. The latter portion deteriorated over time, and Denver

Winchester Mystery House, San Jose, California   (courtesy Winchester Mystery House)

officials decided to have the dead buried there dug up and relocated. Five thousand bodies remained unclaimed, and in 1893, the city began to exhume them. Workers mixed various remains in small coffins. Graves were looted of personal mementoes. Health concerns and a media scandal ensued, and work was halted. Some of the abandoned graves still remain beneath the park. Stories circulate that the moans and cries of the unhappy dead can be heard at night, and an air of sadness lingers about the land.

Connecticut ✛

Dudleytown (18) Reached from Torrington on the Dudleytown and Dark Entry Roads, Dudleytown is an abandoned community of stone cellars in ruined houses. The town, founded by the titled Dudley family of England in the 18th century, has been empty since 1924. According to legend, numerous residents committed murder and suicide. One suicide was Mary Cheney Greeley, wife of newspaper publisher and 1872 presidential candidate Horace Greeley, to whom the famous saying, "Go West, young man!" is attributed. Another strange case concerns a doctor from New York City, William Clark, who bought 1,000 acres of land in Dudleytown in 1924, but regretted it when his wife went insane. Since then, nobody has lived here, or wanted to. Phantom shapes have been reported, as well as spook lights. Real estate in this part of Connecticut is valuable, yet the Dudleytown area remains unclaimed. It may be that Dudleytown's troubles are due to its location on former Mohawk Indian burial or hunting ground.

Stratford (19) The Phelps House, at 1738 Elm Street, near the American Shakespeare Theatre, is one of the most remarkable haunted houses in North America. Its haunting made international headlines in the 1850s. The house was purchased by Rev. Phelps in 1849, who moved there with his large family from Belchertown, Massachusetts. Soon after the Phelps family moved in, bizarre poltergeist manifestations began, including the appearance of eerie little puppets or dolls made from bits of clothing. They were often found arranged in tableaux of people praying, as if to mock the Rev. Phelps. Nothing quite like these manifestations has ever been recorded since in poltergeist cases. The children were attacked in their beds by unseen entities, and objects flew around the house, including a heavy set of tongs and shovel from the fireplace. Between 1947 and 1967, the Phelps House was used as a convalescent nursing home. Nurses complained of hearing strange whispers in the darkness, and a heavy cellar door would swing open by itself. In 1968, the house was abandoned,

and was invaded by hordes of hippies seeking psychic thrills. The badly vandalized house was to have been torn down, but was saved in order to be turned into part of a hospital complex.

Delaware ✛

Dover (20) The Governor's House, called Woodburn, at 151 Kings Highway, has at least four ghosts, one of whom rattles chains and another of whom loves to sip the owners' wine. The chain rattler may have been a slave kidnapper who raided the house, which was part of the Underground Railroad. Other ghosts are a Revolutionary War colonel, who died there while the house was in use as a war hospital, and a little girl who tugs at visitors' clothing.

District of Columbia ✛

Capitol Building (21) The basement here is haunted by a phantom black cat that suddenly expands in size if encountered. Some guards are said to be reluctant to patrol the basement of the Capitol alone at night.

Decatur House (21) Located in Lafayette Square, the house is haunted by the ghosts of its original occupants, Stephen and Susan Decatur. Stephen Decatur had reached fame as one of America's greatest naval heroes by the turn of the 19th century. He was fatally shot in a duel in 1820, and died at home. His widow, Susan, could not bear to remain in the house. Stephen's ghost is seen looking gloomily out a window, and departing through the back door with his gun in a box as he had the morning of his duel. Susan's ghost is heard weeping.

Georgetown (22) 3400 Prospect Street is known as Halcyon House, built in 1783 by Benjamin Stoddert, first Secretary of the Navy. It is now a women's dormitory and is part of Georgetown University. Haunting phenomena include ghostly footsteps in the attic; lights that switch themselves on and off; doors that open and shut when no one is near them; and ashtrays that unaccountably are found filled with water.

White House (21) The ghost of little Willie Lincoln, who died in the White House at age 12, is sometimes seen in the corridors at night. When Queen Wilhelmina of the Netherlands was a guest of Franklin D. Roosevelt in the White House during the Second World War, she answered a knocking on her bedroom door late at night to find the ghost of Abraham Lincoln standing in front of her. Strange cackling laughter is heard in the Rose Room, which used to be Andrew Jackson's bedroom.

The White House, Washington, D.C. (Rosemary Ellen Guiley)

Florida ✤

Mound Key (23) Mound Key is an American Indian shell-mound where tribesmen abandoned the shells of edible sea creatures in vast numbers. Located in Charlotte Harbor, some 15 miles southeast of Punta Gorda, Mound Key is shunned by the local population. Rumors of buried pirate treasure attract all sorts of hunters and curiosity seekers. Ghost lights and Skunk Ape sightings (see Mysterious Creatures) are common here.

Georgia ✤

Calhoun (24) A wide range of bizarre haunting phenomena plague the Worcester House, an historic site at New Echota, once the capital of the Cherokee Nation. The house was built in 1828 by Samuel Worcester, a Vermont missionary. It served as home, post office, church and school. Worcester was a champion of Cherokee rights, and when they were removed from Georgia by the government, he was imprisoned for a short while. Upon his release, he moved west to be with the Cherokee. The house was reputed to be haunted as early as 1889. Two murders were alleged to have occurred there, and bloodstains allegedly covered a floor upstairs. The ghost of a short, thin man has appeared, and strange sounds, footsteps and rattling chains are heard. Doors open and close by themselves. Visitors say they feel watched by unseen presences. While rattling chains seem to occur in some hauntings for no particular reason of historical fact, it is interesting to note that when the Cherokee were removed, many were taken away in chains.

Idaho ✤

Blaine County (25) In September 1975, unidentified figures in long black robes were observed here by a Forest Service employee. This incident took place near the town of Cove Creek. Mutilated cattle have been found in the area. On October 9, 1975, a local motorist reported that a group of men in masks had attempted to block his car on U.S. Highway 95, but he managed to escape.

Illinois ✛

Chicago (26) Bachelor's Grove Cemetery, a tiny one-acre plot near the Rubio Woods Forest Preserve, is one of Chicago's most haunted spots, with more than 100 reports of unusual phenomena. The cemetery has been inactive since 1965. Among the ghosts—and there are many—is the figure of a woman called the White Lady or Madonna of Bachelor's Grove. She is seen only on nights of the full moon, sometimes carrying a baby in her arms. Other ghosts emerge periodically from a nearby lagoon, and a phantom farmhouse appears and disappears. Ghost lights also are reported.

Resurrection Cemetery (26), at 7200 South Archer Avenue, boasts as its most famous ghost Resurrection Mary, a phantom hitchhiker. Men driving alone at night near the cemetery are flagged down by a beautiful young woman in a white dress, and asked to take her to her home. "Home" turns out to be the cemetery gates, where the specter disappears. In December 1977, a motorist reported to police that he had seen a young woman, dressed in white, apparently trapped behind the cemetery gates and trying to get out. When police responded, they found nobody there.

Hull House (26), now a museum located at 800 South Halstead Avenue, is haunted by hooded phantoms that have been seen on the staircase. Built as a settlement house in 1856 for poor immigrants, it was turned into a welfare house by Jane Addams and Ellen Starr in the 1880s. At the turn of the century a Devil Baby with horns and a tail was supposedly born here, causing a panic in the immigrant neighborhoods. Modern ghost hunters report capturing ectoplasm and unusual lights in photographs, although the staff deny any hauntings.

Equality (27) The Old Slave House, also known as Hickory Hill, is haunted by the ghosts of slaves who died here. A pair of U.S. Marines who volunteered to spend the night here in 1966 fled in terror. Moaning and ghostly voices crying out the name "Julia" are heard.

Little Egypt (28) This region of southern Illinois near the town of Cairo is known as Little Egypt. Phantom wagons pulled by black horses are seen at night on Dug Hill Road. The Devil's Bake Oven near Grand Tower is haunted by a screaming female ghost. The area is full of supernatural beliefs and folk tales, and has also been the site of many "unknown animal" encounters.

Decatur House, Lafayette Square, Washington, D.C. (Rosemary Ellen Guiley)

Resurrection Cemetery, Chicago environs, behind the bars
(Rosemary Ellen Guiley)

Mattoon (29) In 1944, the small Illinois city of Mattoon was haunted by a sinister phantom entity known as the Mad Gasser. Women sleeping alone in their houses were attacked with a sickly sweet-smelling gas that induced nausea and fainting. The attacks continued over a period of several months, generating great fear. Police, unable to stop or even find the gasser, accused the women of hysteria. Nonetheless, police called in a State Department of Public Safety crime specialist, Richard T. Piper, who publicly admitted that the case was the strangest he had ever worked on, and that there was a definite pattern to the attacks. After some of the incidents, victims reported seeing a tall male figure running into the night. Oddly, these descriptions matched those of Spring Heel Jack, a real gasser whose activities terrorized women in London, England, in the 1840s. Had the ghost of Spring Heel Jack moved to the Midwest 100 years later? The attacks eventually stopped of their own accord. A witness claimed that on the last occasion the gasser had been a woman.

Indiana ✚

Indianapolis (30) The Hannah House on Madison Avenue in Indianapolis was built in 1858. The owner, a wealthy state legislator named Alexander M. Hannah, used the house to hide runaway slaves in the years

Hull House, Chicago, Illinois (Rosemary Ellen Guiley)

before the Civil War, and it is rumored that slaves who died there were buried in the basement. The house stood vacant from 1962 to 1967, when new owners moved in and found the house was haunted. Sounds of breaking glass are heard in the basement, and there is a lingering smell of rotting flesh in one of the upstairs rooms.

Iowa ✤

Clinton (31) Located on the west bank of the Mississippi River, Clinton is haunted by the ghost of a World War II bomber that flies silently over Eagle Point Park. A seven-foot-tall ape man has been reported. A house across from the Longfellow Elementary School was plagued by poltergeist activity, when stones from a nearby field began pelting the house, apparently by themselves.

Dubuque (32) The Ham House, 2241 Lincoln Street, is a 23-room Victorian mansion built before the Civil War by Matthias Ham, a wealthy miner, lumberman and farmer. Legend has it that a pirate intruder was shot to death on the premises by Sarah Ham after she was widowed in 1889. Since 1964, the Ham House has been a museum. Workers from the County Historical Society report lights going on and off without explanation, doors opening by themselves and the sound of organ music. Also reported are icy breezes and cold spots, and shuffling noises.

Louisiana ✤

Hahnville (33) The Vie Fortune Plantation is haunted by the ghost of Josephine Darrell, a wronged woman who hanged herself from a white oak tree now known as the Moaning Oak because of the odd sounds that are heard near it. Local people will not use the bayou road near Vie Fortune at night.

New Orleans (34) Not surprisingly, New Orleans has many haunted houses. The home of voodoo priestess Marie Laveau at 1020 St. Ann Street is haunted by its former mistress, while the home of General Pierre G. T. Beauregard has ghostly manifestations every night at 2 A.M. The home of notorious sadist Delphine La-Laurie, who whipped slaves to death in her attic, is at 1140 Royal Street. Passersby late at night say they hear terrible screams coming from the house.

Kansas ✤

Manhattan (35) The theater at Kansas State University is haunted by a ghost known as Nick. Tape recorders turn themselves on and off, scenery shifts itself and footsteps are heard backstage when no one is there.

Kentucky ✤

Frankfort (36) Liberty Hall, 202 Wilkinson Street, has a gray lady, believed to be the ghost of Margaret Varick, the aunt of the first Mrs. Brown who lived in the house. In 1817, Varick arrived to comfort the Browns after the death of their eight-year-old daughter, and she died of a heart attack within three days. Her ghost, a small trim figure, is seen doing chores and gazing out a window. Other phenomena include phantom music and doors that open and close by themselves.

Maine ✤

Cape Elizabeth (37) Beckett's Castle, at 1 Singles Road, hosts a multitude of haunting entities. The house—not really a castle—was built in 1871 by Sylvester Beckett, a Portland lawyer, publisher, arts supporter and Spiritualist. Legend has it that Beckett himself has haunted the place since his death in 1882, to prove survival after death. A painting is repeatedly found reversed and wedged behind the kitchen stove, and a bedroom door refuses to stay shut, even when nailed. Bedclothes are ruffled. Other ghosts include a child, who may have been one of Beckett's children who died young, as well as various artists who had worked at the house.

Portland (38) A gentleman ghost wanders about the Portland Art Museum, 7 Congress Square, formerly the McLellan-Sweat House. At the former Clapp House at 97 Spring Street, now the Portland School of Art, an invisible presence makes the sounds of heavy footsteps and boxes being pushed about. Some believe the ghost is that of Captain Asa Clapp, a wealthy man, who bought the house in 1817 but never lived in it—at least during his life.

Maryland ✤

Annapolis (39) The James Brice House was built in 1767 by James Brice, a wealthy merchant, on East Street, near the intersection of Prince George Street. The house is haunted by the ghost of Brice's son, who was murdered by a servant, and by the spirit of a young woman that glides around the 14-room house. In 1940, the skeleton of a woman was found sealed up in a wall. A workman named Thomas Murdock also claimed to have been terror-stricken when he ran into a gigantic spider in one of the cellars.

Baltimore (40) The Edgar Allen Poe House, at 203 North Amity Street, was occupied by the horror writer from 1832 to 1835. Visitors see lights on when the house is empty, feel tapped on the shoulder by invisible

Edgar Allen Poe House, Baltimore, Maryland   (photograph by Jonathan Scott Arms, courtesy National Park Service)

presences, hear mysterious voices and noises and observe windows and doors that seem to have opened or shut by themselves.

Massachusetts   ✛

Boston   (41) Charlesgate Hall, a dormitory of Emerson College in Boston's Back Bay district, has an old elevator that is haunted by a specter of a man in black with an injured arm. Students avoid the area. Blankets have been pulled off sleeping students at night by an unseen hand, and it is rumored that when Charlesgate Hall still belonged to Boston University, a suicide occurred there, and many residents belonged to a sinister cult of some kind.

Dover   (42) In April 1977, this prosperous suburban community only 15 miles from Boston was haunted by a demon that became known as the Dover Demon. Between April 21 and April 22, local teenagers had encounters with a weird humanoid being with a huge

head, glowing round eyes, and long, thin arms and legs. The being was seen walking atop a stone wall by a road, and later in a forest near a stream. It was about the size of a monkey, was hairless and peach-colored. The youths, who had never seen anything like it before, were considered by police to be reliable witnesses. The Dover Demon was never explained.

Hockomock Swamp   (43) The Hockomock Swamp, located between Rehoboth and Abington, Massachusetts, figures in many Native American legends. Spook lights are seen near the Reynham Dog Track, and giant birds have been reported by police. Farmers in nearby Bridgewater have had sheep and pigs inexplicably mutilated. In 1970, state police staged a hunt for a giant bear, even though there are no bears native to the area. In 1939, workers in the Civilian Conservation Corps reported encountering a giant snake. Bigfoot sightings have taken place in Hockomock Swamp. A stone with indecipherable hieroglyphics, known as the Dighton Stone, was found here, as well as an 8,000-year-old burial ground.

Lenox (44) Edith Wharton's mansion, at the intersection of Route 20 and Plunkett Street, is haunted by Wharton; her husband, Edward; and author Henry James, who was a frequent visitor. Their filmy apparitions are accompanied by noises. Also present is a sinister hooded figure who attacks people in bed and presses down upon them. After Wharton's death, the house was used as a girls' school, and girlish phantom laughter is heard.

Michigan ✛

Grand Rapids (45) The ghosts of a murder and suicide haunt the site where now stands the Michigan Bell Telephone Company, at Fountain and Vision streets. The ghosts have lingered despite the fact that the original building, the Judd-White rooming house, where the violence took place, was demolished in the 1920s to make way for the Bell building. The unhappy ghosts are said to be Warren and Virginia Randall, who had a stormy marriage. Their lives ended when Warren took off his wooden leg—he'd lost a leg in a railyard accident—and knocked her senseless. He then turned on the gas and sliced his own throat. Their ghosts harass Michigan Bell customers by making strange phone calls in the middle of the night.

Minnesota ✛

St. Paul (46) Minnesota's most haunted house is located at 476 Summit Avenue. The apparition of a child's head floating in the air has been seen, and sleepers have awakened to find sinister men in black standing by their beds. Some psychics who have investigated the house have refused to spend the night there.

Winona (47) Heffron Hall, a dormitory on the campus of St. Mary's College, is plagued by the ghost of a priest who went mad and attempted to murder a bishop here in 1915. Students living here hear strange tapping noises in the hall at night and have seen a phantom in a dark cloak and hood. Papers on bulletin boards flutter when there is no wind.

Mississippi ✛

Natchez (48) Magnolia Hall, 215 South Pearl Street, is an historical site haunted by strange smells and a ghost who likes to sleep on one of the beds. The house was built in 1858 by Thomas Henderson, a planter and merchant. Henderson's ghost may be the haunting entity, since the bedclothes that are found mussed are in Henderson's old room. A sweet odor that may be laudanum wafts about.

Missouri ✛

Columbia (49) Room 310 of the Sigma Phi Epsilon fraternity house is haunted by the ghost of a girl who committed suicide. Students sleeping alone in the room have had covers pulled off their beds and have heard ghostly giggling in the darkness.

Fayette (50) Lilac Hill is haunted by the ghosts of the family that built it 160 years ago, the Morrisons. The present owners avoid the upstairs floors, where strange noises are heard at night and cold spots are found.

Hornet (51) Near Hornet is a gravel road known locally as the Devil's Promenade. Mysterious balls of light of varying sizes are seen here at night. A bus carrying children home from a carnival in Quapaw, Oklahoma, was pursued by one of the lights.

Kansas City (52) In May 1981, Kansas City was struck by a plague of phantom clowns, sinister figures dressed in clown costumes, often with a picture of the Devil on the front, who chased children and tried to lure them into unmarked vans. Despite intensive police efforts, none of the mysterious clowns was captured.

Paris (53) The streets of this small town were haunted for 70 years by the specter of a woman in black, wearing a bonnet and carrying a cane. The ghost appeared all over town and was seen by numerous residents. The hauntings came to an end in 1934, and the ghost has not been seen since.

St. Louis (54) The Lemp House, on De Mencil Street, is haunted by the ghosts of several members of the wealthy Lemp brewery family who committed suicide there. There is a rumor in St. Louis that the Lemps kept a deformed child, known locally as the Monkey Boy, imprisoned in the house. Images of a monkey-like face turn up on photos taken inside the Lemp House.

Montana ✛

Custer Battlefield National Park (55) Ghosts of those who died in the Battle of Little Bighorn in 1876 still linger here. At a section called Reno's Crossing, one specter has been tentatively identified as that of Second Lieutenant Benjamin Hodgson, Major Marcus Reno's adjutant, who died a particularly sad death. A bullet killed his horse and shattered his leg. While he was crawling away, he was shot again and killed, and his body rolled down a bank.

Pray (56) A noisy and pesky ghost who likes to scatter kitchen dishes and cutlery haunts the Chico Hot Springs Resort, built at the turn of the 20th century. An apparition of the face and upper body of a man has been seen hovering over the floor. The ghost may be that of the original owner, William E. Knowles, who emigrated from Pennsylvania in 1880 in search of gold.

Nebraska ✦

Hat Creek (formerly Warbonnet Creek) (57) Phantom Cheyenne and soldiers of the U.S. Calvary still fight here, carrying on a bloody battle that took place in July 1876, one month after the massacre at Little Bighorn.

New Jersey ✦

Butler (58) The cemetery here is plagued by ghostly voices, some crying out for help, some moaning as if in pain. Demonic laughter is also heard. An investigating committee was formed in July 1924 to check out the stories, and a police officer testified to hearing the voices. A ludicrous attempt was made to explain away the phenomena on the grounds that the noises were being made by a scientist with a mechanical amplifier.

New Mexico ✦

Chaco Canyon (59) The ruins of this Anasazi settlement are haunted by the ghosts of ancient residents, and by spirits from the lower world that were conjured in rituals.

New York ✦

Kinderhook (60) This quiet old Hudson Valley town was the setting for Washington Irving's ghost story about a headless horseman, "The Legend of Sleepy Hollow." Residents say they still see phantom riders along Route 9H and on the grounds of the Van Alen House, built in 1737. The Lindenwald mansion is haunted by the ghost of President Martin Van Buren, and residents have complained of ghostly violin music in the night. The entire Hudson River Valley, with its long history of Dutch settlement going back to the 17th century, is home to numerous haunted houses and eerie legends.

Mt. Misery, Long Island (61) Located near the affluent suburban town of Huntington, Mt. Misery has long had a haunted reputation, as its name suggests. Apparitions of hooded phantoms, gorillas and silent black limousines gliding along the roads late at night have been seen here. Henry L. Stimson, a prominent Wall Street banker and Secretary of War 1940–45, kept a home here.

New York City (62) The Morris-Jumel Mansion at 160th Street and Edgecombe Avenue is haunted by the ghosts of Eliza Jumel and her second husband, Aaron Burr. Students on tours of the house frequently ask the tour guide who is the lady in white they see standing on the balcony. The Old Merchant's House on East 4th Street is so haunted that caretakers cannot get any sleep there, while on Gay Street in Greenwich Village there is a house that is home to a top-hatted ghost who is seen strolling up and down the alley at night.

Also in New York City is the Dakota Apartments (62) on West 72nd Street and Central Park West. This remarkable Gothic-style building, complete with hideous gargoyles, was used as the setting for the horror film *Rosemary's Baby*. The upstairs servants' quarters are said to be haunted, and occupants reportedly have refused to use the basement laundry room. John Lennon was murdered outside the main entrance in 1980, and the building has now become a shrine to his memory, with crowds of the faithful gathering every year on the anniversary of his death.

The Michael C. Rockefeller Wing of primitive art at the Metropolitan Museum of Art on Fifth Avenue and East 81st Street (62) is haunted by black shapes that some guards have seen floating through the air at night. The collection is named for the son of Nelson Rockefeller, former governor of New York, who disappeared mysteriously while on an expedition to collect tribal art in New Guinea.

North Carolina ✦

Asheville (63) In 1908, prisoners here petitioned the warden for protection from the ghosts that were leering at them, and from the strange noises in the building at night.

Thomasville (64) A furniture factory here is haunted by the figure of a six-foot man in a checkered shirt, seen many times. The workers refer to the specter as Lucas. Owners say that the ghost is better than a watchdog for keeping unwanted intruders away from the factory.

Wilmington (65) The New Hanover County Library is haunted by the ghost of a genealogist who frequently used the library when she was alive. The librarian has complained of hearing books being moved around when the library is closed.

Ohio ✦

Cleveland (66) At 4308 Franklin Boulevard N.W. is the Franklin Castle, or Tiedemann House. A family living there was advised by a Catholic priest to leave when they began receiving weird phone calls and hearing music in the middle of the night. Mirrors fog over by themselves, doors fall off hinges and a female specter has been seen in an upstairs window.

Fayette County (67) Cherry Hill, also known as Haunted Hill, is the site of a haunting by a headless horseman, the ghost of a rider who, according to legend, was murdered for the gold in his saddlebags. In June 1953, a headless skeleton was dug up, but the mystery surrounding it was never solved.

Granville (68) The old Buxton Inn is haunted by an entity that throws pitchers off tables and opens locked doors.

Loveland (69) On the banks of the Little Miami River, this oddly named town seems to be a psychic window for the supernatural. In March 1955, a motorist reported to the FBI that he had seen a group of small, hunchbacked trolls engaged in some mysterious activity under a bridge in Loveland. In March 1972, police officers reported seeing a four-foot-tall manlike frog in Loveland. And in September 1978, two volunteer firemen captured a live penguin that was wandering around town. Police issued a statement that the penguin had escaped from a zoo, although there were no penguins in any zoo in Loveland. In fact, few zoos have the special refrigerated facilities needed for keeping penguins.

Oklahoma ✛

Lawton (70) Lawton, a small town near the U.S. Army's Fort Sill, is haunted by a werewolf. In February 1971, a housewife went out on her back porch and found the werewolf standing there. Another witness had a heart attack and was taken to Comanche County Hospital for treatment. Two soldiers walking along Lawton's commercial strip said they were attacked by the werewolf as they passed the cemetery. Lawton police consider the case still open.

Oregon ✛

Oregon City (71) The McLoughlin House, 713 Center Street, is haunted by the ghost of its famous resident, Dr. John D. McLoughlin, founder of Oregon City and one of the West's preeminent pioneers. McLoughlin's hulking shadow has been seen, and he reportedly has

John D. McLoughlin House, Oregon City, Oregon (courtesy National Park Service)

tapped people on the shoulder. Objects have been apported, and noises and voices are heard. The Barclay House, next door at 719 Center Street, is haunted by Uncle Sandy, a 19th-century seaman who was brother to Dr. Forbes Barclay, a physician who worked for the Hudson Bay Company. A phantom dog leaves paw prints on the carpet.

Rhode Island ✤

Exeter   (72) A vampire reputedly haunts Chestnut Hill Cemetery, behind the Chestnut Hill Baptist Church on Route 22. The vampire is said to be Mercy L. Brown, who died of consumption at age 19 on January 18, 1892. At the time, wasting-away illnesses such as tuberculosis were sometimes blamed on vampires. Mercy's mother and an older sister died first, followed by Mercy. When a brother fell ill, the three bodies were exhumed and examined for signs of vampirism. Mercy's heart and liver were removed and burned, and the ashes were mixed in medicine for the brother, Edwin. He died

Newspaper article about the Rhode Island vampire

despite the measures. Moaning is heard at Mercy's grave.

Newport   (73) Twenty-five Greenough Place is haunted by the ghost of President Harding's ambassador to Italy, Richard Washburn Child. Child was a prominent New York lawyer and writer. He was said to have died of pneumonia in a hospital, but legend has it that he actually died in a mysterious fall in the house, and that his ghost remains there.

South Carolina ✤

Murrells Inlet   (74) The ghost of a young girl who died of malaria in the mid-1800s searches for her lost engagement ring at The Hermitage, located on Route 1. The girl was Alice Belin Flagg, younger sister of the original owner of the house, Dr. Allen Belin Flagg. Alice fell in love with a man of whom her brother disapproved, and she wore her engagement ring around her neck concealed beneath her clothes. After she fell fatally ill with malaria, Flagg discovered the ring and threw it in the creek in a rage. On her deathbed, Alice begged friends to find her ring. She died without it, and now her ghost looks constantly for it.

Tennessee ✤

Stones River Battlefield National Park   (75) Phantom Civil War soldiers still fight here. The battle at Chickamauga took place on September 18, 1863, when General Braxton Bragg's Army of Tennessee met General William Rosencrans's Army of the Cumberland. Approximately 130,000 men clashed, and casualties were heavy on both sides. The Confederates won a major victory. One phantom is Old Green Eyes, said to be a soldier who was decapitated and his torso blown up by a cannon ball. His head was buried, and now its ghost roams the battlefield on misty nights. A lady in white drifts about, looking for her lover. Phantom sounds of moans and gunshots are heard.

Texas ✤

Houston   (76) The Houston Public Library is haunted by the music of a phantom violinist. Violin music is heard when no one but the library staff is around.

San Antonio   (77) Two museums in San Antonio, the Witte and the McNay, are haunted. Guards report being tapped on the shoulder by a person who isn't there, and papers left on desks are found distributed in locked rooms.

Vermont ✛

Mt. Glastenbury (78) Located near the college town of Bennington, Mt. Glastenbury has become known as a place where hikers go but don't come back. Between 1945 and 1950, seven hikers disappeared here without a trace. The entire Green Mountain State Forest area is regarded as cursed by residents of the small local town of Shaftsbury, who avoid it. The area contains two ghost towns, abandoned for unknown reasons.

Utah ✛

Salt Lake City (79) A raven-haired woman haunts the Utah State Historical Society at the Denver & Rio Grande Railroad Depot. She wears a period purple dress. Legend has it that she met her fiancé at the depot, and he broke off their engagement and threw the ring across the rails. She ran to retrieve it, and was killed by a train. Her ghost is sometimes heard singing in the ladies' room.

Virginia ✛

Amelia (80) Haw Branch Plantation near the small town of Amelia consists of some 15,000 acres. The manor house is haunted by the sound of women's voices in the library when no one is there, and by horrible screams coming from an attic room. The scent of oranges or roses is sometimes reported.

Charles City (81) The Shirley Plantation, built in 1723, is one of Virginia's numerous haunted houses. Strange noises in the house have been plaguing the Carter-Hill family for generations.

Fredericksburg (82) The Mary Washington House, bought by George Washington as a home for his mother, is haunted by that lady's ghost. The Rising Sun Tavern is haunted by the ghost of a Civil War–era prostitute who is seen climbing the stairs from the tap room. Also seen is the ghost of a man in a cowboy hat and string tie. The nearby Chatham-Lacy Manor is haunted by a woman in white whom guards have seen running across the lawn.

Gloucester County (83) Rosewell House is haunted by the ghosts of people who died mysteriously here in colonial times. Lettitia Baldridge, the wife of Fairfax Dalton, seems to have been involved in all of these deaths in some way. Dalton himself died in a mysterious fall. The events took place in a nearby house called Paynton Hall, which was burned down in the battle of York Plains Ford in the Civil War. In the 1830s, before Paynton Hall was destroyed, lamps were kept burning in the halls at night because so many people died there from unexplained falls on the stairs. Today, violin and piano music are heard at night in Rosewell House. The nearby slave cabins are also haunted.

Loudoun County (84) Noland House, built in 1750, is haunted by the ghost of "Mad Anthony" Wayne, the Revolutionary War general who surrendered to Burgoyne at Fort Ticonderoga. It is also haunted by the ghosts of two Hessian soldiers who escaped from a prison camp and took refuge here, but were tracked down and killed. Strangely, events prevented the house from ever being finished, and it remains uncompleted today.

Richmond (85) Westover, on the banks of the James River, is the family seat of the Byrd family, which included Richard E. Byrd, the famous explorer of the Antarctic. It is haunted by the spirit of Evelyn Byrd, who died in 1737. Her ghost, dressed in green velvet and lace, is often seen in the gardens and in the poplar grove. According to lore, she pines for a suitor rejected by her father. Richard E. Byrd's middle-aged son was found dead of starvation in a warehouse in Baltimore in the 1980s. His death was unexplained.

Washington ✛

Seattle (86) The Harvard Exit Theater, 807 Roy Street, is haunted by the ghost of an unknown turn-of-the-century woman. Poltergeist activities have disturbed boxes, furniture and equipment.

West Virginia ✛

Moundsville (87) Many strange phenomena have been recorded in West Virginia, a place where belief in the supernatural is unusually strong. In 1966, Moundsville was haunted by Mothman, a huge winged man with glowing red eyes (see Mysterious Creatures). The town also had reports of UFOs, men in black, phantom cars on the roads late at night and inexplicable interference with televisions and telephones. A period of bizarre encounters and events climaxed in 1966 with the collapse of a bridge over the Ohio River. Many of the people who had been witnesses to the Mothman encounters were killed.

Wisconsin ✛

Delavan (88) The dairy farm country around Delavan seems peaceful enough, but the region is haunted by a werewolf, or so residents claim. The werewolf is said to have a broad chest, human hands and a wolf's head. It travels on four legs at times, and at other times walks erect on two legs. It is most often seen crouching along

Bray Road at night. While there are a few timber wolves in northern Wisconsin, there are none in the area around Delavan. At about the same time that the werewolf sightings began in 1988, a burial ground filled with the mutilated bodies of domestic animals was found here, suggesting cult activity. However, local police insisted that the burial ground was just a pet cemetery. A hooded phantom on horseback, accompanied by a black dog, has also been seen.

Devil's Lake   (89) Devil's Lake State Park contains three effigy mounds of unknown origin. Nearby Baraboo is said to be haunted by the ghosts of elephants (dating from the time when Baraboo was headquarters for the old Ringling Brothers Circus). Campers at Devil's Lake have complained of shadowy forms, lake monsters and a phantom canoe on the lake. August Derleth, editor of H. P. Lovecraft's chilling horror tales, chose to live in nearby Sauk City because of its eerie atmosphere.

Mineral Point   (90) Graceland Cemetery is haunted by a tall vampire with a white face and a black cloak. In March 1981, a police officer saw the vampire and gave chase, but it escaped.

Wyoming ✤

Cheyenne   (91) A ghost lives in a room directly below the carillon bells of the bell tower of St. Mark's Episcopal Church, at 19th and Central. The original St. Mark's was built in 1868, and was expanded beginning in 1886. Workmen repeatedly quit the site because of unexplained disturbances. The rector, who lived on the ground floor, heard noises like tiny hammerings, and voices in the space above, though no one was ever in the attic. In the late 1920s, with work still going on, a decision was made to build a special chamber for the ghost in the hopes that he would leave the workmen alone. The chamber, difficult to access, apparently did the trick. Since then, however, visitors to the church report seeing apparitions and hearing voices that speak of bodies entombed within the church's walls.

Sheridan   (92) Sheridan Inn, now closed, is home to a phantom woman wearing an old blue dress, who stares out a guest room window on the third floor. She is Miss Kate, a scullery maid who lived and worked at the hotel for 65 years. She arrived in 1901, when Buffalo Bill Cody owned the place, and she loved it fiercely. When a new owner took over to renovate it after bad times, Miss Kate was promised her own room on the third floor. She died before she could occupy it, and the owner never rented it out, but buried Kate's ashes behind the wall and kept silk flowers there as a shrine. In more modern times, Miss Kate acted up with poltergeist disturbances if she didn't like changes made at the hotel. She was found disrupting the rock music played in the lounge. She also disturbed the silk flowers whenever she was unhappy.

CANADA

Alberta ✤

Banff   (93) The famous Banff Springs Hotel is the residence of several ghosts, and a lost room. According to legend, when the hotel was being expanded in the early 1900s, architects left space for a room without doors or windows. They altered the blueprints to disguise the error, and workers were told not to talk about it. A fire in the new wings in 1926 led to the discovery of the lost room. The corridor it occupies is said to be serviced by an elderly phantom bellhop, who drifts about at night. In the Rob Roy Lounge, ghostly residents include a headless bagpiper, a bride who fell down stairs and broke her neck, disembodied carollers in the men's room and a conscientious barman who tells guests they've had enough to drink.

Calgary   (94) The Deane House, the only surviving part of Fort Calgary, is haunted by the ghosts of a husband and wife who died in a murder-suicide. The house has caught fire mysteriously. Now a museum, Dean House is said to be located on top of an old Indian burial ground.

Phantom horses haunt two of Calgary's old firehalls, No. 3 in East Calgary and No. 6 in Hillhurst. Sounds of horses' hooves issue from areas where the horses were kept during the days of horse-drawn firewagons.

The Capitol Hill House, a small dwelling in the Capitol Hill district, is haunted and brings bad luck to anyone who lives there. The curse may be related to the disappearance of Thomas C. Hall in 1929. Nineteen years later, his body was found below the floorboards—he had been shot in the head. Occupants report a clammy phantom hand that pokes at people, strange sounds and feelings of discomfort.

The Canmore Opera House hosts a ghostly young man with long blond hair, dressed in turn-of-the-century clothing. He may be Sam Livingston, a homesteader on the park where the Opera House is located, who died in 1897. The ghost walks about and sits on the stairs.

Morley   (95) The ghost of White Eagle, a Stony leader, appears at certain times of the year in Ghost Hills, according to Stony legend. The story goes that after the Stony were defeated by the Cree and Blackfoot, White Eagle led them to safety in the mountains in the Morley area. During another attack by enemies, White Eagle was mortally wounded. He told his braves to bury him on the peak of Devil's Head Mountain, and loosen the boulders there. They did so, and the rocks rained down on the enemies and killed them. White Eagle's victorious ghost still appears out of the mist in Ghost Hills, drifts along Ghost Lake and Ghost River and disappears into Devil's Head Mountain. He is clad in flowing white robes, rides a white stallion and is followed by a white dog.

British Columbia ✛

Pitt Lake (96) Legend has it that at least 23 persons have died trying to find Slumach's Lost Mine, supposedly a huge gold deposit located northwest of Pitt Lake. The site was prospected by a Salish named Slumach. He reputedly took a squaw with him each time he went there, then killed her in order to insure the secrecy of the place. He either stabbed the women or shot them with gold bullets. Slumach shot and killed a half-breed prospector, and was hanged in 1891. Before his death, he is said to have revealed the mine's location to his son, with instructions that it be visited "only when times are bad." Supposedly, anyone who has attempted to find the mine since meets with tragedy or death. The Salish believe the mine is cursed and will never be found by a white man.

Victoria (97) Each spring, an assembly of ghosts visits a rocky point at Oak Bay, which overlooks the Strait of Georgia and is near the Victoria Golf Course. If the sea is calm, phantom voices are heard. The ghost of a lone woman stands apart from the group. She is believed to be a woman killed by her husband near the eighth tee in 1936—she had planned to divorce him because of his drinking problem. He strangled her and committed suicide. His body was found floating in kelp.

Manitoba ✛

Oldman River (98) A ghostly Cree village exists near Fort Walsh. All the inhabitants were massacred in a Blackfoot raid that left the village sacked and burned. The phantom tipis and their ghostly occupants have been seen, and their drumming and chanting heard. In 1875, Sir Cecil Edward Denny, of the Northwest Mounted Police, was boating on the Oldman River near Fort Walsh when a storm arose and he was forced to go ashore. He heard the drumming and chanting, and discovered the phantom village, its occupants oblivious to the storm. Denny went toward the village, but as he drew near he became enveloped in a flickering, blue flame and was thrown violently to the ground. He lay there helpless until the storm subsided. He then tried again to reach the village, only to find it had vanished. The only signs of an encampment were faded rings in the soil where tipis had stood, and some bleached bones.

St. François Xavier (99) A ghostly white horse forever haunts its namesake, the White Horse Plain, according to Cree lore. The white horse, a Blanc Diablo from Mexico, was a gift offered by one Cree chief to another for the hand of his daughter. A rejected suitor, a Sioux, brought a war party that sent all the Cree reeling. The bride mounted the white horse, and her Cree fiancé a gray horse, and attempted to lead the Sioux astray. Out on the open plain near St. François Xavier, the white horse was easily spotted, and the Sioux bore down and killed the couple and the gray horse. The white horse escaped and roamed wild on the plain for years. The Cree believed the soul of the bride had entered into it, and the horse became a ghost. The legend is honored by a 12-foot statue of a white horse that stands at St. François Xavier on the TransCanada Highway.

New Brunswick ✛

Beaubears Island (100) A headless nun haunts an old bridge across the upper end of French Fort Cove. Legend has it that she was decapitated by a crazed trapper wielding a knife. He buried her head in the woods. Her body was found, but not the head; the body was shipped back to France. The murderer was never caught. Her ghost wanders about holding its head, offering people 1,000 guineas (an old English coin) to send her head back to France.

Dungarvon River (101) The screams of a camp cook murdered in the 1860s sound up and down the river, despite at least one attempt at exorcism in the early 1900s. The cook, wearing his moneybelt, took a hunting trip with a young Irish logger, who murdered him for the money and buried the body in the snow.

Fredericton (102) A ghost, a poltergeist and a presence called Black Peter haunt the 21-room Glasier Mansion 10 miles from town. Phenomena include strange creakings, crackings and footsteps. Black Peter—the name of a servant of the original owner, John Glasier— has appeared as a little old white man with a potbelly, a fringe of white hair and nautical clothing.

At the Boyce Mansion (102), now student housing for the University of Newfoundland, a maternal ghost likes to visit sleeping male students and run her phantom fingers through their hair. She soothes them if they awaken. The ghost is said to be that of a mother of a boy who died at the school. He had sent her a letter asking her to come to his sickbed, but she never received it. Her grieving ghost continually searches for the letter.

Grand Manan Island (103) Numerous ghosts haunt this spooky island, the largest to lie at the entrance to the Bay of Fundy. On moonlit nights, generally November 19 and 25, the Rowing Man appears in a phantom dory in Little Dark Harbour, making the sounds of rowing. At Indian Beach, the Flaming Indian Woman appears every seven years, standing at water's edge and consumed by fire. Her name is Lemushahindu, and she is Passmaquoddy. The Little Man haunts Ghost Hollow south of Dark Harbour. He appears wearing a flat-topped hat on foggy nights, lunging out of the woods to fling himself in front of cars. Drivers slam on the brakes, but there is never an impact; the Little Man vanishes. Some two miles north of Dark Harbour lies buried pirates' treasure, according to lore. The pirates menaced a shipwrecked couple, Edmond Chatfield and Desilda St. Clair, from Maine, who spied them burying the hoard. Edmond was hanged from a tree in front of Desilda. The pirates released her, and she turned into a wild woman, living in the woods and luring the pirates one by one to murder them. Edmond's headless ghost prowls the shore, while Desilda's hysterical ghost rushes past him crying "Edmond! Edmond! Edmond!"

Northwest Territories ✣

Croker Mountains (104) A range of phantom mountains was "discovered" in 1818 by Sir John Ross, a British naval officer, during his Arctic expedition. He described finding a chain of mountains stretching from Baffin Island to Devon Island, which made Lancaster Sound landlocked. Subsequent explorers could not find the mountains.

Isle of Buss This phantom island was seen and mapped for two centuries, from its initial discovery in 1578 during Sir Martin Frobisher's Arctic voyage. In 1609, explorer Henry Hudson searched for it but could not find it. Nonetheless, his Hudson's Bay Company applied for a permit to extend its monopoly to the island, and it was granted by Charles II. In 1971, the island was declared nonexistent.

Nova Scotia ✣

Amherst (105) The Cox family cottage, at 6 Prince Street, was the site of one of the world's most famous poltergeist hauntings in 1878 and 1879. A nasty spirit who identified itself as Bob, the ghost of a former resident of the house, plagued one of the occupants, Esther Cox, 19 years old, as well as other members of her extended family, and anyone who tried to help her. Esther suffered a mysterious illness that swelled her body. Bob made loud noises, set skirts afire, levitated a cat, hounded exorcists off the premises and set other fires on the premises. The landlord, fearful of property damage, requested Esther to leave. She was charged with arson, convicted and sentenced to four months in jail, but was released after one month. Finally, she was successfully exorcised by a Micmac medicine man. Today a tire store occupies the site where the cottage once stood.

Big Indian Lake (106) The ghost of a man wearing a sou'wester, believed to have drowned in the lake, is seen walking across the dam.

Cape Blomidon (107) On the shore of Minas Basin, the rocky region of Cape Blomidon, is the haunt of Glooscap, the culture hero of the Micmac. The human-like Glooscap may be based in part on Henry Sinclair, an explorer, prince of Orkney and ruler of the Shetland Islands, who spent a winter among the Micmacs in 1398. Legend has it that it is bad luck to remove amethysts, called the eye of Glooscap, from Blomidon Mountain. Whoever does so will be compelled by sorcery to return.

Sable Island (108) Lying 180 miles off the coast of Nova Scotia, Sable Island is a sand spit that is a menace to Atlantic Ocean shipping. Heavy fog, shallows and sandbars have contributed to the destruction of at least 400 ships, and some 10,000 mariners are said to have lost their lives. Perhaps the most famous ghost is Dr. Copeland's wife. She and the doctor were aboard the *Princess Amelia* when it ran aground in 1802. Mrs. Copeland made it to shore, but was murdered by salvagers, who chopped off the finger that bore her wedding ring. Every 50 years, her ghost walks the beach, perhaps in search of her missing finger and ring. Today Sable Island is uninhabited except for a few scavengers, who have special permission from the Canadian government to live there, and a herd of shaggy wild ponies of obscure origins. Ghost lights and apparitions are frequent.

South East Passage (109) The Ghost House, located on the south shore overlooking the approach to Halifax, was built in 1910 from the wreckage of ships. Haunting phenomena include footsteps sounding downstairs at night, a team of phantom horses that gallops over the road, levitating bedcovers and heavy objects that crash mysteriously to the floor.

Ontario ✣

Bankfield (110) Old gold mines here are haunted. Flashing lights are seen in the mines when nobody is there, and hydraulic valves turn themselves on and off.

Workers have refused to enter the mines because of the hauntings.

Kenora (111) The so-called Windigo Capital of the World is haunted home to the Windigo, the terrible spirit of cannibalism of Algonkin-speaking tribes. Some eight Indian Reserves are located in the wooded lake region near the town of Kenora. The early white explorers recorded sightings of this specter, which likes to feast upon the flesh of stray travelers. The area rests on a ley line (supposedly marking earth energy), which may account for its reputation as a gathering point not only for the Windigo, but all sorts of spirits in American Indian lore.

Mameisgwess Lake (112) A spooky atmosphere here seems the perfect setting for resident Windigo specters (see KENORA above) and the Maymaygwayshi. The latter is a spirit variously described as a gnome, ghost, merman, monkey, little hairy man or Sasquatch-like figure. The Maymaygwayshi live behind waterside rock faces. Ojibwa shamans are said to be able to enter the rocks and give the spirits tobacco in exchange for potent rock medicine. The Maymaygwayshi like to eat fish, and steal the catch from local fishermen.

Niagara Falls (113) The ghost of Lewlawala, the Maid of the Mist, is seen in the swirling clouds of mist that rise up from the pit of Horseshoe Falls on the Canadian side. According to legend, Lewlawala, who did not want to marry a man she hated, attempted to commit suicide by paddling her canoe over the falls. She was rescued by He-No the Thunderer, who lived in a cave at the base of the falls. She was taken into the cave to live with him. In another version, Lewlawala is sent over the falls by her father as a sacrifice to end a plague. He-No rescues her and ends the plague.

Niagara-on-the-Lake (114) One of the most haunted areas in all of Canada. The historic community was once called Newark.

Sobbing Sophia is the ghost of Sophia Shaw, who was betrothed to General Sir Isaac Brock, administrator of Upper Canada. Brock was killed in the Battle of Queenstown Heights on October 13, 1812. Sophia spent the remainder of her life as a spinster, sobbing uncontrollably whenever she thought of her lost love.

At the Oban Inn is the ghost of Captain Duncan Mallory, who built the inn around 1824. He is only heard at night, walking about the halls, never seen.

The ghost of a murderer once haunted The Buttery restaurant, formerly a private home. Lloyd Burns, who abused his wife, Kate, was killed by her and her brother. They threw him down the stairs from the second floor. Kate was so upset over the crime that her ghost remained

to create poltergeistlike disturbances. It supposedly was exorcised in 1981.

The Angel Inn is haunted by the ghost of a British officer, Captain Swayze, who was killed on the premises of a log cabin that occupied the site before the inn was built. The cabin was destroyed when American troops burned the town in 1813. Swayze is mischievous and likes to make noise.

Sault Ste. Marie (115) The Bayview Hotel is plagued by the sound of a baby crying at night. Objects mysteriously appear and disappear. Legend has it that a retarded or deformed child was kept imprisoned here in the attic in the 19th century, and this may be the source of the haunting.

Toronto (116) At 82 Bond Street is one of Canada's most famous haunted houses. It belonged to Canadian Prime Minister William Lyon Mackenzie King, who concealed his obsession with the supernatural throughout his political career. The house is haunted by the ghost of his grandfather, a newspaper publisher and onetime mayor of Toronto, who died in 1861. Caretakers complain of hearing a printing press running in the cellar at night. Unexplained piano music is also heard. Beautiful female ghosts with long dark hair have been seen there as well.

Prince Edward Island ✤

Wellington (117) The Phantom Train of Wellington, an engine pulling three cars, appears sporadically during nights, especially in December. The train was first seen in 1885 crossing a railway bridge outside of Wellington. It stops at a station and phantom passengers get on.

Québec ✤

Hudson (118) A ghost named Maud haunts the Willow Place Inn, built as a private residence in 1820. The house was the scene of plotting by the Patriotes in the Rebellion of 1837. A servant girl named Mary, who was sympathetic to the military, overheard their plans. She was murdered and her body buried in the mud-floored basement. Her ghost—inexplicably named Maud—creates poltergeist disturbances to the present day, starting at Halloween and lasting through November. Doors slam shut, chairs are knocked over, rocks are piled up outside the door of Room 8—perhaps where the plotting took place—and mushrooms stored in the basement are mysteriously decapitated.

Île des Demons (119) This desolate island off the coast of Québec is sited on 17th-century maps, but not on modern-day ones. Most likely, it is one of the Îles

Harrington, desolate places. The Île des Demons is haunted by demons and imps who are perhaps tied to a local tale of doomed love. In 1591–92, Frenchman Jean-François de La Rocque de Roberval set sail for New France, with a company that included his niece, Marguerite de La Rocque. She took a lover aboard the ship. Roberval, a Calvinist, was so shocked that he abandoned her on the Île des Demons, with only her servant girl, Damienne. Her lover jumped ship and swam ashore to join them. There, Marguerite bore an infant that died. The lover and servant girl soon died. Marguerite pined for three years before being rescued by fishermen, who returned her to France.

Île d'Orleans   (120) The second-largest island in the St. Lawrence River is haunted by the ghost of Jean-Pierre Lavallée, the child of Indian and French parents who was reputed to be a sorcerer. In particular, he was gifted in weather prediction and spell-casting. According to lore, Lavallée used magic to create a dense fog that prevented British ships from attacking Québec City and the Île d'Orleans on August 24, 1711. Ghost lights, said to be the souls of fishermen mending their nets, appear in the sky in present times.

Saskatchewan ✛

Qu'Appelle River   (121) The ghost of a Cree brave paddles the river in his birch-bark canoe crying, "Who calls? Who calls?" Legend has it that the brave paddled through the river valley one night to claim his bride. He heard a girl's voice call his name, and he responded, "Who calls? Who calls?" but received no answer. When he arrived at his bride's village, he discovered to his horror that she had died the night before, uttering his name.

Yorkton   (122) The Girl of the Crossroads is the ghost of a girl three or four years old, seen often at the crossroads near Telsky Farm, located on the edge of town. The ghost stands by herself for long periods of time, then vanishes.

GHOST LIGHTS

Merely saying the words "ghost lights" brings to mind images of luminous, spectral figures floating through the air, perhaps holding a lantern in a skeletal hand or disappearing in a ball of fire and smoke.

In fact, the eerie illuminations—perhaps better called earth lights—do resemble balls or points of light that float through the air, although without gossamer mists trailing behind. They have been seen in various forms all over the world, and have been attributed to everything from UFOs to uranium to heat lightning to the spirits of Indians and even of Hitler. Many people have witnessed the lights, and nearly everyone has a theory about their origin.

The Ghost Research Society (GRS), based in Oak Lawn, Illinois, collects data on ghost lights and investigates activity. Most ghost lights are yellow or white, while others are red, orange or blue. The lights may change color as they are observed. They appear randomly or regularly at particular sites, varying in size and configuration, and may be active for years. Some appear and become inactive after short periods of time.

Research shows that regardless of location, ghost lights share some common characteristics: 1) they appear in remote areas; 2) they are elusive and can only be seen from certain angles and distances; 3) they react to noise and light by receding or disappearing; 4) they are accompanied by hummings, buzzings or emanations of gaseous material; and 5) they are associated with local folklore surrounding a haunting at the site where a terrible accident or tragedy involved loss of life. For example, a person loses his head in an accident, and his headless ghost returns to the site to look for it. The ghost light is the ghost's lantern.

Possible Explanations

Roman historian Pliny the Elder first recorded strange light phenomena in the first century A.D. Ancient and medieval scholars also saw the lights, believing them to be dragon fire.

Legendary sources of the ghost lights include: lost or massacred Indian chiefs and tribes, starcrossed lovers, the spirits of gold miners or trappers, Pancho Villa and his band, criminals whose spirits walk the earth, lawmen looking for the scoundrels, pioneers, settlers, soldiers and ranchers, lighthouses and ships, even Adolf Hitler with a lantern, leading German POWs into sanctuary in Mexico. The stories wax romantic and nearly always end tragically.

Possible natural explanations include escaping gases that somehow ignite; static electricity or St. Elmo's fire; reflections from mica or phosphorus found in rocks; uranium radiation; irregular air pockets; and reflections from faraway headlights.

Some of the more colorful explanations credit little volcanoes, reflections from a comet or meteor, mercury vapor lamps, reflections from old silver mines, luminescent bat guano and glowing jackrabbits that run through irradiated brush or pick up glowworms in their fur as the origins of the lights. Another hypothesis says that the lights are holes in the invisible barrier to the fourth dimension. Stories by oldtimers hoot at the idea of gas lamps or headlights as the source of the lights, as neither were around during the mid-1800s when recorded sightings first occurred. Few believe jackrabbits are responsible, either.

Perhaps the most likely cause of many ghost lights is a natural one, the earth lights phenomenon. There are three main categories of earth lights. *Ball lightning* can range in size from as little as a pea to bigger than a beachball. The light can also appear as a sphere with protrusions, as a cylinder or as a dumbbell. Ball lightning can be transparent, translucent, cloudy or even opaque. The lights float languidly, hover, move purposefully, rise and fall or remain suspended, stationary in space. Most ball lightning appears blue-white to yellow-white to orange in color and generally generates no heat. Even though ball lightning is most often associated with thunderstorm activity, it does not behave in ways that current physics can explain. It has been known to pass through windows, go down chimneys, through doors or, perhaps most frightening, enter aircraft while in the air and explode in the terrified passengers' faces.

Will o' the wisps, or swamp and marsh lights, usually appear near boggy ground where methane gas may escape. They often move against prevailing wind patterns and generate no heat.

Earthquake lights (EQLs) can appear before, during or after quake activity as far as tens of miles from the

GHOST LIGHTS

Hudson Bay

Pacific Ocean

Atlantic Ocean

Gulf of Mexico

epicenter. The lights may look like streamers or balls, fill the sky like aurorae or merely cause the air to glow or sparkle.

Two other scientific hypotheses may bring the ghost lights into the realm of acceptable science, although the second is still out of mainstream research. The first centers on the release of piezoelectricity from underground seismic pressure. One of the first to connect

earth lights with geological movement was Charles Fort, an American journalist who collected information on strange phenomena. In 1968, French scientist Ferdinand Lagarde—looking for connections with UFO sightings and seismic activity—published results of studies conducted in 1954 that found an 80 percent correlation between sighting locales and fault lines. Further research puts UFO sighting locales, seismic activity and the appearance of earth lights together 40 percent of the time.

Many scientists now associate the reporting of strange events with slight seismic activity, not large movement as in an earthquake. This Tectonic Strain Theory (TST) finds electricity, magnetic changes, gas production, emission of radio waves, sound and other energy effects all affected by these tectonic pressures.

Piezoelectricity, or energy caused by rock pressure, causes the earth to release electrostatic charges. German biophysicist Helmut Tributsch calls these emissions an "electrochemical glow discharge": Currents of earth's electricity, flitting along the ground in paths of least resistance (fractures or fissures in rock), pass through thin films of water held in the rock fractures. Electrostatic charges and even smells are released. Tributsch says that such passages of electricity from solids across air into the water cause a glow discharge, much like ionizing radiation, or X rays. He notes that animals detect these charges before humans, which could explain animals' erratic behavior prior to an earthquake.

The second hypothesis concerning ghost lights goes back to the Big Bang and the radio waves that resulted. All over the world, scientists and amateurs are tuning into the very low frequency (VLF) radio waves called natural radio, which have been around since time began but most often result from lightning. All a listener needs is a VLF receiver and a quiet, empty space away from civilization.

About 8 million lightning bolts strike the earth each day at 250 million volts each. Emissions cover the entire radio frequency spectrum, sending out atmospheric static, clicks, pops and squeaks known as *sferics*. Occasionally the sferics sound like chirping and barking, called *chorus*, caused by a harmonious chain reaction of VLF emissions. More infrequently, listeners catch a *whistler*, a strange descending pitch that is clear, distinct and gone before the listener realizes it was there.

Long-distance telephone operators in the 1880s noticed the whistlers when the sounds interfered with telephone transmission. During World War I, the whistlers—whose keening sound resembled incoming shells—thwarted German efforts to tap Allied communications lines. Physicists in the 1950s finally determined that whistlers result from lightning clicks that are stretched and distorted after traveling thousands of miles along the earth's magnetic lines. Listeners never know when to expect a whistler, but the sound signals that *something* is going on.

Edson C. Hendricks, a physicist in San Diego, believes that earth lights and whistlers may be related. Setting up receivers in the West Texas desert near Marfa, where some of the best ghost lights in the United States appear, Hendricks heard whistlers every time the lights shone.

In his book *Earth Lights Revelation: UFOs and Mystery Lightform Phenomena—the Earth's Secret Energy Force*, author Paul Devereux says that even with more scientific explanations of the lights, there are phenomena that still do not fit currently understood physical conditions. The lights seem to respond to thought and mental imagery, and can cause visions, confusion and memory loss in those who have seen them. They may take on form and appear as ghosts. Sometimes viewers convince themselves they have been abducted by aliens. Not only do earth lights occurrences spawn UFO sightings, but other paranormal and poltergeist activity accompany the emissions. The lights interrupt radio and television signals and can alter the gravity of electromagnetic fields. Mighty earth forces affected by extraterrestrial movement may combine to form unfamiliar types of energy, and unraveling the natures of these energies may reveal entirely new conceptions of geophysics.

Numerous ghost lights sites are reported throughout North America alone. Few remain active for any significant period of time. The following is a list of major sites of recurring activity.

UNITED STATES

Alabama ✤

Vernon (1) A single light 10 miles west of town.

California ✤

Julian (2) Multiple, moving lights above the Oriflamme Mountains.

Pinnacles National Monument (3) Watchers have seen earthquake lights in the Pinnacles, a park between Hollister and King City, probably because the Pinnacles sit across the San Andreas Fault.

Colorado ✤

Silver Cliff (4) Lights appear in the cemetery at Silver Cliff, a community 60 miles southwest of Colorado Springs in the Wet Mountains.

Florida ✤

Oviedo (5) Multiple moving lights on State Road 13.

Illinois ✤

Crestwood (6) West of here near the Rubio Woods Forest is a small, one-acre graveyard, Bachelor's Grove

Cemetery. The grounds are haunted by numerous specters, as well as bluish-white ghost lights seen bobbing along the ground. Red skyrocketlike streaks also have been seen in the air.

Iowa ✛

St. Mary's (7) Single light on a farm near town.

Louisiana ✛

Gonzales (8) Single light.
    Also, numerous ghost lights are reported throughout swampy areas.

Maryland ✛

Hebron (9) Single moving light west of town.

Missouri ✛

El Dorado Springs (10) Single moving light 10 miles east of town.

Joplin (11) Multiple moving lights 12 miles southwest of town.

Webster County (12) Strange lights began glowing off Interstate 44 between Northview and Marshfield in this rural county in the Ozark Mountains in December 1991, drawing hundreds of watchers and creating traffic hazards. Mysterious, almost surgical mutilations of at least 11 cattle began the same time, and some speculate the lights and killings are connected.

Nevada ✛

McDermitt (13) Multiple moving lights on a ranch near town.

New Jersey ✛

Lake Wanaque (14) Multiple moving lights in hills to the west.

Washington Township (15) Multiple moving lights have appeared to watchers in this urban community near Newark.

New Mexico ✛

Llano (16) Multiple moving lights along a river near town.

New York ✛

Hudson Valley (17) This area north of New York City has been famous for years for its breathtaking scenery and its spooky stories and sightings. Early Dutch settlers heard the ghostly ninepins that seduced Rip Van Winkle, and the valley is where Ichabod Crane met the headless horseman. Ghost lights appear throughout the valley.

North Carolina ✛

Big Laurel (18) Two to three moving lights near here.

Blowing Rock (19) On August 24, 1988, Dr. Donald Anderson and his wife, Hermine, saw what seemed like a command performance of the Rocky Knob phenomenon described below. For hours, the Andersons saw lateral flashes of orange-pinkish light, again resembling fireworks. No sound accompanied the lights.

Brown Mountains and Catawba Valley (20) Ghost lights have appeared near Morganton and Lenoir in western North Carolina, in part of the Appalachian range.

Chimney Rock Pass (21) Lights have been reported along U.S. Highway 74 in the Blue Ridge Mountains 25 miles southeast of Asheville.

Maco Station (22) Lights were spotted along railroad lines in this small community 14 miles west of Wilmington on the Atlantic coast.

Rocky Knob (23) Near Lenoir at Linville Ridge on Grandfather Mountain, three couples reported what seemed like fireworks lasting until almost dawn on August 23, 1987.

North Dakota ✛

Cass County (24) Single moving light along a road between Fargo and Kindred.

Ohio ✛

Loudonville (25) Single stationary light in woods near here.

Oklahoma ✛

Kenton (26) Single moving light eight miles east of town, plus a single moving light about 15 miles southwest of town.

Peoria (27) A ghostly white glow has been hovering over this northeastern Oklahoma town for years. The light typically appears about five miles northeast of the town and can be seen from a distance along a three-mile stretch of road running westward from Missouri. One local believer says the light passed right over his head, bright enough to read by, and disappeared when he honked his car horn.

Most of the legends about the Peoria lights center around decapitation. One story says the light is that of a luckless Indian who fell victim to his ax-swinging wife. Another says the light is a miner who lost his head in an accident. A third says it is a Civil War soldier left headless when he was hit between the eyes with a cannonball. Bob Whitebird, a former chief of the nearby Quapaw tribe, reports that a Seneca Indian did lose his head via the ax in a domestic dispute many years before. Then there are those who say the lights are the spirits of young Indian lovers who leapt to their deaths when they could not marry.

The lights can be dangerous, but only to local residents and onlookers. One man claims the troublemakers out at the viewing spot make the area unsafe, although sheriff's deputies patrol the road. Farmer Chester McMinn would not go down into the pasture at night to milk the cows, fearing someone would see his swinging lantern and take a potshot at the lights. McMinn admitted that he did some scaring of his own, however. He would drive his 1948 Chevrolet right up to the parked cars of the onlookers and turn on a spotlight he had mounted on top. Everyone would run and scream.

Sand Springs (28) Single moving light two miles west of town.

Oregon ✤

Union and Umatilla Counties (29) Single moving light along the road from Weston to Elgin.

South Carolina ✤

Summerville (30) Single moving light on Sheep Island Road.

Texas ✤

Angleton (31) Bailey's Light appears along Highway 35 about five miles west of Angleton, a small coastal town south of Houston near the Gulf of Mexico. Locals claim the light is the ghost of 19th-century settler Brit Bailey, who still searches the marshes for his whiskey.

Bell County (32) Single moving light along Leon River bank.

Chinati Mountain (33) Single moving light.

Kountze (34) The Ghost Light of Bragg Road outside Kountze, a small community about 30 miles northwest of Beaumont (and only about 150 miles from Angleton) attracted the same Japanese researchers that videotaped the Marfa Lights in 1989. Unfortunately, heavy rain and cold spoiled Professor Yoshi-Hiko Ohtsuki's efforts, but all the team's research appeared on the Nippon Television Network in April of that year.

LaSalle and McMullen Counties (35) Single moving light along Esperanza Creek.

Lufkin (36) Single moving light along railroad track.

Marfa (37) Probably the most famous ghost lights in America spook the residents and neighbors of Marfa, a small West Texas ranching community southeast of El Paso and north of Big Bend National Park. Actor James Dean looked for the lights when he was in Marfa filming the 1955 movie *Giant*.

The lights are the town's true celebrities. They appear most often out at Mitchell Flats, about 12 miles east of town on Highway 67 between Marfa and Alpine. The area served as an Army Air Force base during World War II. Usually the lights seem to come from the Chinati Mountains, about 50 miles south of the flats, and have been seen so often that the state of Texas installed a road marker to designate the official viewing spot. People come from everywhere to see the lights; professors from Tokyo's Waseda University videotaped the lights for 10 seconds in 1989.

The first recorded instance of the ghost lights, usually called simply the Marfa Lights, occurred in 1883. A young settler named Robert Ellison saw the lights while

Marfa Mystery Lights

coming through Paisano Pass in the Chinatis. He thought the lights were Apache campfires, but long-time residents told him that although many had seen the lights, further investigation revealed no ashes.

Another legend, told by Marfa resident Mrs. W. T. Giddens, finds Mrs. Gidden's father lost in a blizzard. Supposedly the lights appeared and spoke to him, telling the freezing man that he was off the trail three miles south of Chinati Peak, headed in the wrong direction. They guided him to a cave, where, accompanied by the largest light ball, he stayed through the night out of the snow. In the morning, he found he was indeed three miles south of Chinati Peak, and he safely returned home.

Explanations for the Marfa Lights include phospho-rescent reflections, gas emissions, electrostatic charges, ball lightning, chemicals left by the army and even irradiated jackrabbits. During the World Wars, locals speculated that the lights signaled German warplanes for bombing raids on the United States and Mexico. During World War II, pilots at the old airfield used Jeeps and supposedly dropped bags of flour from the air to mark the lights' location, but evidence was never found. Stories about the lights' ability to line up like runway markers and lead inexperienced pilots to crash into the Chinatis abounded; some believe the spooky lights were the reason the old base closed.

One hypothesis that mirrors the post–World War II terror of technological annihilation says that between 1942 and 1945, a scientist from the Massachusetts Institute of Technology, who came to the United States from the Middle East, was working on a very dangerous nuclear laser fusion device in a remote laboratory in the Chinati Mountains. During a failed test, the laser-generated light became lost in space and time. A gigantic explosion followed, which naturally destroyed the lab and scorched the earth for a seven-mile radius. Our government kept the accident secret, but the time-warped laser lights are the Marfa Lights.

Most of the legends, however, tell of wandering Indians and lost lovers. Some say the lights are the lanterns of vengeful Indians hoping to lure horse soldiers into a trap, or a lost tribe looking for its slain chief. Or the lights may be those of captured Apache chief Alsate, who disappeared into the desert during a forced march from Santa Rosa to Chihuahua in which many of his people died. Other stories attribute the lights to the souls of Indian braves and princesses, who died for love or are still signaling for a rendezvous. One legend says the lights belong to an Indian woman who gave her children to the devil in return for food and shelter during a famine.

Others say the lights represent a sheriff seeking revenge for his wife's murder, or a rancher in the 1850s who killed the bandits who had raped and murdered his family and plundered his homestead. The lights may be those of pioneers, settlers, miners and soldiers, or they may be signals to bands of scoundrels who stole and hid caches of gold. From a more distant past, some say the lights come from lighthouses that signaled ships eons ago when Mitchell Flats was an ocean (quite a while back for this landlocked area). More recently, the lights are said to be the carlights of a young man and woman who went parking on the flats and disappeared. Perhaps the most fanciful tale is that the lights are Hitler's lanterns as he searches for German POWs held at a nearby air base during World War II.

In January 1963, Jeff Henderson, then a student at Sul Ross University in Alpine, went out with his dorm buddies to find the lights. Most of the group doubted the lights' existence, and some of his friends thought they were being duped. But Henderson says that about 10 minutes after parking at the end of old runway 32, a pinprick of light appeared on the southern horizon. Soon the first light was joined by a second, then a third and a fourth—11 lights in all, bobbing out toward the Chinatis. Just seeing the lights at a distance made Henderson's skin tingle, but soon one of the lights separated from the others and streaked across the southern sky, then traveled back to the other lights.

As if responding to the doubters among the young men, one of the lights seemed to zoom toward them, growing in size and brightness as it approached. The ball's color changed from white to fiery orange, and grew so bright that the mesquite trees and yucca plants cast shadows. Henderson and the other young men hastily returned to the dorm.

San Antonio (38) Ghost lights have been reported on the outskirts of town.

Saratoga (39) Multiple moving lights along Bragg Road north of town.

Virginia ✤

Blue Ridge Mountains (40) Ghost lights abound throughout the mountain areas.

Suffolk (41) Single moving light along Jackson Road, south of town.

Washington ✤

Pasco (42) Single moving light.

Yakima Indian Reservation (43) Indians living here in the Cascade Mountain range report seeing ghost lights for many years. They also claim sightings of Sasquatch, or Bigfoot.

Wyoming ✣

Newcastle (44) In the 1940s, ghost lights were reported near here that rolled over the ground like tumbleweeds. Startled motorists would veer off the road in order to avoid hitting them.

Salt Creek (45) Bright yellow ghost lights have been reported near the Salt Creek Oil Field, 30 miles north of Casper, since the turn of the 20th century. The lights appear singly, and seem to glide along the outskirts of the field. They change from yellow to golden. The early sheep ranchers, many of whom were from Ireland and Scotland, believed the lights were lanterns carried by the spirits of the dead. In the 1920s, a popular story was that the lights were the lantern carried by a local resident named O'Rourke, who had died suddenly of a heart attack one night while sitting at the dinner table.

CANADA

Manitoba ✣
Woodridge (46) Single light in a forest near town.

Ontario ✣
Brechin (47) Single moving light along the shore of Lake Simcoe near town.

Niagara-on-the-Lake (48) Bright, deep-orange lights were seen frequently in the sky from 1975 to 1980. They moved at high speed and along erratic paths, sometimes executing 90-degree turns.

Saskatchewan ✣
Beechy (49) Single light in Buffalo Basin area.

PHANTOM AND MYSTERY SHIPS

Ghostly ships prowl the seas, lakes and rivers of the world. The ships are gray or white, sometimes luminescent, often appearing solid, sometimes seeming filmy or semitransparent. Some are full of figures going about their chores; others are eerily empty. They cut through the water silently, looming up suddenly out of the dusk or the darkness, disappearing just as suddenly.

Many phantom ships are tied to legends of disasters and wrecks. Such ships are forever tied to the site of their doom, racing through the water, reenacting their tragedies, such as striking rocks and sinking. Numerous phantom ships are seen afire.

Some ghostly vessels have legends with morals. Perhaps the best-known of these is the *Flying Dutchman*, a ship doomed to sail around the Cape of Good Hope, South Africa, forever with its dead captain and crew. The curse is due to either a foolish oath on the part of the captain, or as punishment for the captain's sins, depending on which variation of the legend you hear.

Some phantom ships seem only to wander about, like the four-masted ghost ship of Captain Kidd, which reportedly sails up and down the eastern coast as Kidd searches for his lost buried treasure. Other pirates—Blackbeard and Jean Lafitte—who plagued American shores in the late 17th and 18th centuries also sail about looking for their treasures.

There are literally thousands and thousands of reports of phantom ships, the majority of which are one-time sightings. A study of the logs of European merchant ships between 1831 and 1885 revealed 300 reports alone—and that was after the elimination of reports from other than reliable mariners, or observations made in fog or questionable weather conditions, or made too close to land. Some of the one-time sightings have no explanation, while in other cases the phantom ships seem to have appeared to avert a real disaster, or to provide a strange comfort to a ship in distress.

Consider the following example of a one-time sighting:

In July 1934, the 46-foot cruiser *Mary Ann* was traveling in the Strait of Georgia, British Columbia, enroute from Seattle to Alaska. A fog arose, causing the ship to reduce speed and sound its foghorn. Hours later in the mid-morning, just past Porlier Pass, the fog abruptly rose. Suddenly, a weather-beaten sailing ship appeared at the starboard bow. The captain of the *Mary Ann*, James Hampson, turned his wheel sharply to port, but saw with horror that a collision was unavoidable. To his further shock, the bow of his ship plowed straight through the phantom ship, which turned itself. The apparition lasted long enough for Hampson to see its deck and torn and faded sails clearly. There was no sign of life aboard, no noises. The ship vanished. Hampson then could see on the horizon a boat towing a raft of logs. What was more, he saw that a loose section of the tow boat's raft lay in the water on the course he had plotted. Had the phantom ship not caused him to turn sharply, the *Mary Ann* would have collided with the debris.

The frequency of phantom ships seen ablaze raises some interesting questions, for in some cases the factual basis of the legend includes no fire (for example, see the *Palatine* story under Block Island, Rhode Island, later in this section). Perhaps the ship on fire at sea is a symbol of ultimate disaster that resides in the human collective unconscious.

Here are some of the famous ghost and mystery ships reported in North American waters.

UNITED STATES

Connecticut ✤

New Haven (1) An unusual phantom ship appeared here in 1648, wrecking itself before a crowd of astonished witnesses. It was interpreted as a sign from God revealing the fate of a real ship that had disappeared. The ship was built in 1647 in Rhode Island to carry goods to England. It set sail in January 1648, bearing some prominent New Englanders, and presumably was lost at sea. In June a violent thunderstorm arose at New Haven, then the sky grew calm. About one hour before sunset, a ship sailing against the wind appeared to witnesses for about half an hour. The masts were shattered and broken. The ship then keeled over and disappeared in a smoky cloud.

Delaware ✜

Cape Henlopen (2) The ghostly H.M.S. *deBraak*, a Dutch-built, British-rigged 125-foot sloop reenacts its sinking off the point of Cape Henlopen on nights lit by the full moon. The ship sank in a gale on May 25, 1798. According to legend, the real cause of the sinking was the Bad Weather Witch, a sea sorceress who raises

terrible storms. The phantom sails silently, but reports have been told of the screams of the dying crew being heard in the night. The wreckage was raised in the 20th century, but no fortunes were found.

Port Mahon (3) A ghastly phantom ship from the early 19th century appears just off the shore of Port Mahon. The ship bears the corpse of its owner, Joshua

The ghosts of famous pirates sail in their phantom ships up and down the North American coastlines looking for their lost treasure

McCowan (or McGowan by some accounts), swinging from a rope on the bowsprit. According to legend, McCowan was killed by a crewman jealous of his romance with Sally Stout, the pretty daughter of the governor of Delaware.

Roosevelt Inlet (4) One of the many East Coast haunts of Captain James Kidd sailing about looking for treasure he is said to have buried in Sussex County.

Maryland ✤

Baltimore (5) The frigate *Constellation*, the oldest ship in the U.S. Navy, rests in the Inner Harbor as a tourist attraction. It reputedly is haunted, perhaps by more than one phantom.

The 176-foot *Constellation* had a distinguished service record. It was launched on March 27, 1797, with 36 guns. Her crew never lost a battle. The ship was engaged against the French, Barbary corsairs, West Indian and East Indian pirates and African and Caribbean slave traders. It fought in the Quasi-War with France, the Barbary wars, the War of 1812, the Mexican War and the Civil War. During World War II, it served as a relief

Many ships lost at sea due to storms and accidents enter folklore as ghosts, forever reenacting their tragedies

flagship of the Atlantic Fleet. It was decommissioned in 1955 and retired to Baltimore.

With such a fighting history, it should be no surprise that the decks would be haunted by ghosts. The ship saw plenty of bloodshed, pain, agony and terror in the nearly two centuries it plied the waters. Life aboard it was rough and cramped, and disease took nearly as many lives as battles.

In 1955, shortly after the ship's retirement, the Baltimore *Sun* reported that strange lights, shapes and noises were observed by persons aboard the nearby submarine *Pike.* Lieutenant Commander Allen Ross Brougham mentioned the phenomena to a friend who was interested in psychical research. The friend advised that the best time to observe apparitions was at midnight on nights between Christmas and the New Year.

On one of those nights, Brougham and others set up a watch with a camera. At midnight, Brougham detected a faint whiff in the air, like the smell of gunsmoke, accompanied by a muffled scurrying sound. A photograph was taken. When developed, it showed, according to Brougham's description, "a bluish-white radiancy, partly translucent, wearing a definitely dated uniform, gold-striped trousers, cocked hat, heavy gold epaulets and a sword. It—or he—was—or seemed to be a captain." The figure appeared to be crossing the quarterdeck. The ghost was thought to be one of the eight captains the *Constellation* had during her career.

In 1993, the *Constellation* was visited by the noted English clairvoyant and medium, Rosemary Gardner Loveday, who knew nothing of the ship's history. She detected the presence of an unhappy ghost who still prowled the ship, especially on the gun deck. She had the impression that he had killed himself, perhaps by hanging, for she could feel a sensation of choking and suffocation. He seemed to be a sad figure who was overwhelmed by the bad conditions aboard the ship, as well as harsh discipline that was meted out. Loveday described him as young and slim with dark brown, curly hair. He may have been an officer, but she perceived no uniform at all. Interestingly, U.S. naval crew and officers had no uniforms prior to the 1840s.

North Carolina ✤

Ocracoke Island (6) The famous pirate Blackbeard lived here, and the ghostly lights of his ship, the *Adventure,* are seen drifting about the waters of Pamlico Sound. Sometimes the outline of his ship can be seen in the light of the waning moon.

Blackbeard, born Edward Drummond in Bristol, England (he changed his last name to Teach), was one of

the most feared of privateers. Fearsome to behold and fearless in manner, he terrorized Atlantic shipping. He once blockaded the entire city of Charleston, South Carolina. With his plunder, he built himself a fabulous, two-story house on the island that became known as Blackbeard's Castle. Robert Louis Stevenson used him as the model for his pirate in *Treasure Island.*

Blackbeard met his doom in November 1718 in a bloody battle with the British navy. He sustained 37 wounds and kept fighting, until a blow to his neck from a sword nearly severed his head. His headless ghost wanders about Teach's Hole, a spot not far from the Ocracoke harbor, searching for its head.

Rhode Island ✤

Block Island (7) The Palatine Light is a legendary phantom sailing ship seen ablaze off Block Island since the late 18th century. Different legends explain the ghost as that of the Dutch ship, the *Palatine.* One version says the ship left Holland in 1752 with a load of immigrants bound for Philadelphia. Off the coast of New England, the ship suffered damage by storms. Then the crew mutinied, killed the captain, robbed the passengers and abandoned them, taking off in the lifeboats. The ship ran aground on Block Island and was

The U.S.F. *Constellation* c. 1900, probably offshore of Annapolis, Maryland

plundered by land pirates. The pirates saved the people aboard except for one insane woman who refused to leave the ship, despite the pirates' intentions to set it afire. She remained aboard, and as the tide carried the flaming wreck out to sea, her screams could be heard by those ashore.

Another version says that the ship bore German immigrants and was deliberately run ashore by the captain and crew for the sake of plunder. Still another version holds that the ship was lured aground one stormy night by the decoy lights of the land pirates. In both of these versions, the pirates did not save the survivors, but plundered the ship and set it afire with the living still on board.

Records show that no ship named the *Palatine* ever sailed into Block Island. However, the legend does have a basis in fact. A Dutch ship, the *Princess Augusta*, carrying Protestant Palatines from Germany, wrecked off Block Island on December 27, 1738. The ship had departed Rotterdam in August of the same year, carrying 350 passengers and 14 crew, bound for Philadelphia. Enroute, contaminated drinking water killed 114 persons, including the captain and seven crew, all of whom were buried at sea. The ship was left in the command of the first mate, Andrew Brook.

Storms blew the ship off course. Fighting broke out as food and water dwindled. Brook and the remaining crew extorted money from the passengers for provisions. On December 27, the ship struck a hummock off Block Island and took on water in the hold. Brook rowed ashore and secured the aid of islanders. The passengers were rescued, although Brook refused them permission to take their possessions. He then broke his agreement with the islanders that the ship would be anchored, and he cut the anchor and let it drift away—perhaps to cover up his own thefts of the passengers' possessions. A group of islanders pursued the ship and were able to recover some 20 trunks belonging to the passengers.

One woman did refuse to go ashore—Mary Vanderline, who seemed to have lost her sanity. It is not known why she was not forcibly rescued.

On December 29, the drifting ship crashed into a rock and sank, and Vanderline presumably drowned. It did not catch fire.

The first sighting of the blazing phantom ship occurred one year after the wreck of the *Princess Augusta*. It was observed by the crew of another ship, the *Somerset*. According to its captain, "we followed the burning ship to its watery grave, but failed to find any survivors." The glow of the phantom ship is seen periodically, and differs in size. Skeptics contend it is light emitted by gas rising from petroleum deposits on the ocean floor.

Texas ✛

Galveston   (8) Pirate Jean Lafitte's ghostly ship prowls the waters off Galveston, believed to be the area where his ship went down in the 1820s.

Wisconsin ✛

Washington Island   (9) The *Griffon* was last seen here before it mysteriously disappeared in September 1679 in the waters of Lake Huron. Its ghost still drifts about on some foggy nights. During its construction at Niagara, New York, the *Griffon* was considered by Iroquois as an affront to the Great Spirit, and was cursed. On her maiden voyage, the ship loaded fur at Washington Island in August 1679, and set out to return to Niagara. It never arrived, but "sailed through a crack in the lake," as seamen say about ships that vanish in the dangerous waters. In 1900, a wreck believed to be that of the *Griffon* was discovered off Bruce Peninsula in Lake Huron. The identity of the wreck was announced in 1955 after historical evidence had been examined; however, others have disputed the claim, and the true identity of the wreck remains unconfirmed.

CANADA

British Columbia ✛

Vancouver Island   (10) On November 2, 1957, a blazing fishing boat was spotted about 30 miles west of Vancouver Island by the Japanese freighter *S.S. Meitetsu Maru*, which was headed for Seattle. The fishing boat appeared to be completely engaged by flames from bow to stern.

The freighter dispatched a boat and crew members to row around the fishing boat. No survivors were seen. The craft was about 70 feet in length, which meant it should have a crew of at least 10. Its registry number, K-13-AC, indicated that the boat was Canadian.

The incident was reported. Strangely, all Canadian ships with a "K" registry were accounted for. For five days, U.S. Coast Guard and Canadian boats searched a 13,000-square-mile area for survivors. Not only were none found, no charred debris was found, either. Searchers did find two objects that only intensified the mystery: a chopping block imbedded with fish scales, and a ruptured fuel tank smelling of naptha. The tank was the sort used on foreign boats, and not by American or Canadian vessels.

The Japanese freighter crew reported that a strange white light or object had been seen near the burning boat, but that it rapidly retreated and vanished when the freighter got near. Other fishing boats in the vicinity reported seeing a white glow in the night. The incident remains a mystery.

New Brunswick ✤

Richibucto (11) The ghost of a dead seaman haunted the barque *Amity* for months while the ship was aground. In the 1860s, the barque left Richibucto loaded with timber, headed for Liverpool, England. It ran aground on a sandbar. The ship remained there for the winter, with only a watchman aboard. The watchman complained of hearing mysterious footsteps in the hold. In the spring, workmen who came to refloat the ship also heard the footsteps. The vessel was taken to port, unloaded, repaired and reloaded. It safely reached Liverpool. When the cargo was unloaded, the decomposing body of a sailor was discovered in the hold. It was never identified. Experts wondered why the body was not discovered the first time the ship was unloaded for repair.

Newfoundland ✤

Catalina (12) Did some unknown force snatch the crew of the *Resolven* in 1883? The brigantine was found drifting under full sail about 50 miles off Catalina on August 29, 1883, by the H.M.S. *Mallard*, only 36 hours after it had departed Harbour Grace en route to Snug Harbour. A boarding party found the crew and lifeboats missing, and the boat slightly damaged but still seaworthy. Most puzzling were a fire that still burned in the galley and the captain's logbook that lay open in his cabin. Experts speculated that the captain ordered the ship to be abandoned due to icebergs, but no lifeboats or survivors were ever found. The ship was towed back to Harbour Grace.

Nova Scotia ✤

Cape John (13) A phantom sailing ship afire has appeared in the Northumberland Strait, visible to residents of Cape John. It has appeared both at dusk and at night. For periods of about 30 minutes, it sits motionless on the water, flames rising from its rigging and hull. One legend recounts that it is a Scottish immigrant ship that set sail for Nova Scotia in the 18th century and was lost at sea. Another legend says that it was a pleasure ship that caught fire during a drinking bout. Natural explanations include optical illusion and gases rising from coal fields beneath the water.

Mahone Bay (14) The Teazer Light is a phantom ship in flames that appears at Borgals Point on Mahone Bay. The specter once was the *Young Teazer*, a pirate's ship that was trapped by British warships in Mahone Bay on June 26, 1813. The pirates set their ship afire rather than be captured. The ghost usually is seen in fog either prior to a storm, or within three nights of a full moon. It appears to be one to two miles offshore, although sometimes observers aboard ships think the phantom ship will ram theirs; it never does.

Merigomish (15) A phantom three-masted, full-rigged sailing ship of unknown identity has made regular appearances off the coast of this small fishing village, located south of Prince Edward Island where the eastern end of Northumberland Strait meets the Gulf of St. Lawrence. Traditionally, the ship appeared before or after the autumn equinox at dusk. If there is fog, the ship has a phosphorescent glow. It sails northeast at about 120 knots, with strange lights blinking on deck and in the rigging. Suddenly it seems to strike dangerous shoals, and fire bursts out on deck. Figures are seen jumping overboard. Quickly the entire ship is consumed by flame, and it sinks.

Pleasant Bay (16) A phantom sailing ship thought to be associated with legends of buried treasure once appeared in the shoals at Pleasant Harbour, a fishing village near Tangier. On clear moonlit nights, the ship would be seen and heard coming into the harbor and dropping anchor. Some fishermen from the village once went out to meet the ship, and saw a ghostly crew on deck, drinking and speaking in a foreign language. The ship then sailed up onto the land and disappeared in the woods, where it is thought the treasure might have been buried.

Prince Edward Island ✤

Charlottetown (17) On the morning of October 7, 1859, the bell of St. James Church tolled eight times for no reason. No one was found inside the church, and the bellrope was found secured. That evening, a passenger steamer, the *Fairie Queene*, failed to make its regular appearance in the harbor. The boat plied a route between Nova Scotia and Prince Edward Island. It had departed Pictou earlier in the day in good weather. Several days later, the news came that the boat had sunk, and eight passengers were drowned.

Lot Seven Shore (18) A flaming full-rigged phantom ship of unknown origin travels up Northumberland Strait at an impossibly high speed. It has been seen all along the south shore of the island. The specter manifests itself before storms, and also appears at the height of storms at sea.

Ontario ✛

Lake Superior (19) The ghost of the ill-fated *Bannockburn* is seen on stormy nights as it searches in vain for the lighthouse on Caribou Island. The steamer disappeared on November 21, 1902, in hazy and gusty weather. It had been loaded with grain at Port Arthur, and was bound for Caribou Island. The lighthouse there was out, however, and the ship ran aground on a reef and sank. All hands were lost.

The *Edmund Fitzgerald* also plies the lake as a phantom ship. An enormous freighter 729 feet long, the ship was loaded with iron ore pellets enroute from Superior, Wisconsin, to Detroit, Michigan, on November 10, 1975, when it hit stormy weather. It sank in two minutes near Whitefish Bay, right on the U.S.-Canadian boundary. There were no survivors.

Toronto (20) A phantom clipper ship in distress was seen near the mouth of Etobicoke Creek in August 1910. Eleven persons in yachts heard the ship's whistle and observed it traveling at about half-speed. Four witnesses boarded a dinghy and set out for the vessel, but it vanished into the night.

Québec ✛

Île d'Anticosti (21) This island that lies off the Gulf of St. Lawrence has shores so dangerous that they are called the Graveyard of the Gulf, claiming some 400 ships in the 17th and 18th centuries. All that remains of some of them are their ghosts. Perhaps the most interesting mystery wreck is the *Granicus*, driven aground by storms in 1828. The cabins were found filled with the remains of some 20 persons who had been butchered, cut up, hung, cooked and salted. The intact body of a man was found in a hammock.

WATER MONSTERS

Rumors of sea monsters, all over the world, have been around for ages. The creatures have been seen by fishermen, boaters and shoreline picnickers. They have been seen by veterans of the sea, who have spent their lives on the water and thought they had seen everything. They have been seen by large numbers of people at once. And, they have been captured on film.

What are these creatures, sometimes seen idling at the surface of the water, sometimes half on the rocks, apparently basking in the sun, sometimes seen swimming at amazing speeds? Although there is mounting scientific interest in the beasts, they have yet to be caught, and so remain in the category of myth.

Through the Eyes of Myth

Sea monster stories have existed as long as there have been methods, written and verbal, to record them. An octopus of tremendous size was first mentioned by Homer in the *Odyssey*. (The giant octopus lost its mythological status in the 19th century, when the first specimen of a giant squid was caught.) The Old Testament describes a "tortuous" sea monster called the leviathan; scholars disagree over whether it was a whale or a crocodile.

In 1723, a Danish Royal Commission was formed to determine whether mermaids and mermen existed; they decided that they did indeed exist. Folklorist Michel Meurger, in his landmark book, *Lake Monster Traditions: A Cross-Cultural Analysis* (written with Claude Gignon), points out that descriptions of mermen closely matched drawings of the sea god Neptune, which could be found on marine maps at that time. In 1753, Bishop Erik Pontoppidan of Norway wrote of "uncommon sea animals" in his *Natural History of Norway*. His study included the kraken (giant octopus), mermaids/mermen and sirens.

The sea serpent legend goes back at least as far as the *Aeneid*, in which Virgil tells of two large serpents that came from the sea. The Scandinavians have long believed in a water horse, or snake with a horse-shaped head, a description common in modern sea monster sightings. Nordic representations of a maned serpent, or *lindorm*, can be found as early as the Bronze Age. Nordic legend also tells of a terribly large, maned serpent that arose from Lake Mjosa in Norway in the 16th century, coinciding with other paranormal events taking place in the area. Other cultures also have their water horse legends: The Scottish *fuath* and the Finnish *nokk* are aquatic creatures with manes.

When the people from these cultures came to settle North America, bringing their legends with them, they found that the native North Americans had their own legendary water monsters. Theirs included a beast that was able to kill people with its smell; another had a huge pocket for storing its food, including humans.

Some believe contemporary sea monsters in North America are merely the product of these cultural myths. Settlers, particularly those raised on Gaelic folklore, wedded the beasts of their own cultural mythology with those of the American Indians. These hybrid monsters were then used to explain natural phenomena; for example, a floating log is mistaken for a sea serpent, and rumor grows into local legend. As Meurger says in discussing a Canadian lake monster, "This character of the 'sea monster' seems to have originated with the colonists of Saint-Eleuthere, at Pohenegamook, who came from Saint-Alexandre, a village near the Saint Lawrence Gulf. Therefore, one can interpret the 'beast of the lake' primarily as an importation of sea folklore to an inland lake."

Meurger suggests the function of a mythical sea monster is to symbolize the unknown; the myth also acts as a bridge to the "good old days." People who are disenchanted with the modern world cling to the magical possibilities of a sea monster. Meurger also points out that myth is not immune to modernization. At least one Canadian "monster lake" is rumored to contain an active submarine, due to sightings of a metallic, horse head–shaped periscope. It has even been suggested that the mystery sub is an aquatic UFO, indicating that one myth can blend into another—if indeed these sightings are merely the products of myth.

Through the Eyes of Symbolism

Another theory regarding sea monsters takes a Jungian approach, suggesting that these serpentine figures arise from the dark depths, not of the sea, but of the collective unconscious. This theory claims that sightings of certain paranormal phenomena, such as UFOs and sea monsters, are actually encounters with archetypal images. (It is noteworthy that UFO sightings have occasionally been associated with images of dragons in the sky.)

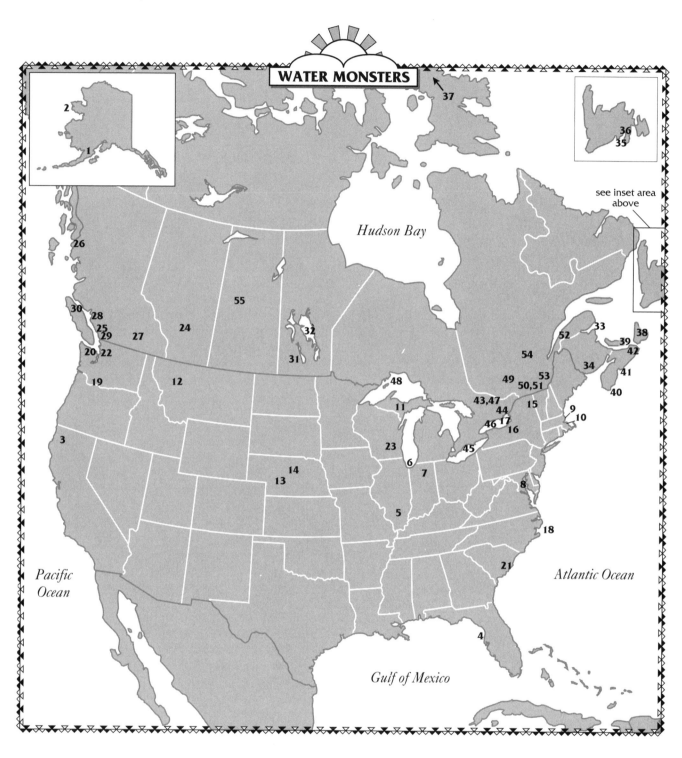

WATER MONSTERS

Hudson Bay

Pacific Ocean

Atlantic Ocean

Gulf of Mexico

see inset area above

Archetypal images (as discussed at great length by the great psychiatrist Carl Jung) transcend culture and are understood at a primitive level by all humans. It is believed that mass sightings of such images portend great cultural change.

The serpent is one of the human race's oldest archetypal symbols; in various cultures it represents evil, knowledge and healing. It was the first form to arise

spontaneously out of the primordial waters of chaos, according to the most common form of the creation myth. It also represents the emergence of consciousness from the unfathomed depths of the unconscious. The sea in all its mystery is also an archetypal symbol. So a serpent arising from the sea is certainly archetypal. Perhaps the sea monster encounter announces great spiritual change on the horizon, for the individual involved or for the human race in general. Keep in mind, however, that sea monsters have been photographed and filmed; if they are archetypal hallucinations, then are the witnesses capable of imprinting their hallucinations on film?

Through the Eyes of Science

Relatively little is known about this planet's marine environment; much of it is still unexplored. In 1939, a live specimen of coelacanth was found; prior to this discovery, the coelacanth was thought to be extinct for the last 70 million years.

Yet, because humans have not been able to capture a sea monster specimen—dead or alive—skeptics refuse to admit the possibility of these as-yet-unidentified sea creatures. They attribute all sightings to mistaken identification, overactive imagination and exaggeration. Faced with sightings that involve several people, skeptics claim mass hallucination. Faced with photographic evidence, they claim hoax. While some of these claims are undoubtedly the cause of many sightings, they don't explain them all.

But there are plenty of people—scientists among them—who are open to the possibility that sea monsters are no more mythical than the giant squid, which was thought to be mere legend until the 19th century. Legislatures in New York, Vermont and Canada have even gone so far as to legally recognize and protect the monsters in their lakes.

Cryptozoologists, who study "hidden" animals such as sea monsters, find that, indeed, many sightings of unidentified swimming objects can be explained. Sea monsters often do turn out to be floating logs, schools of fish, seals, oarfish and giant squid—or hoaxes. But there are still sightings that cannot be explained so easily.

Sightings that occur repeatedly over many years in a particular area, with similar descriptions from varied witnesses, are those that attract scientific investigation. While descriptions vary, they fall into the same few categories, based on types of appendages (or lack thereof), head and neck shape, skin and method of locomotion (whether it undulates vertically or horizontally). These categories can then be used tentatively to classify the creatures as mammals, reptiles or fish. Some

The "hafgufa," a reconstruction of a "typical" sea monster

In the late 19th century, scientist Antoon Cornellis Oudemans studied sea monsters and claimed that there was only one kind: a long-necked seal. Oudemans' work was flawed; he ignored reports that didn't match the description of his long-necked seal and therefore challenged his theory. However, his work instigated the first serious acceptance of the possible existence of sea monsters.

Around the same time, naturalist Reverend J. G. Wood collected reports of sea serpents and, from the descriptions, proposed that they were zeuglodons, primitive and supposedly extinct whales.

In the 20th century, Dr. Bernard Heuvelmans, founder of France's Center for Cryptozoology, classified nine types of sea monsters in his book *In the Wake of Sea-Serpents*. His classifications are as follows:

1. Merhorse: a pinniped-like mammal, 40 to 100 feet long, with large eyes, facial bristles and a mane, smooth skin and flippers; undulates vertically.
2. Multi-Humped: a whalelike mammal, 50 to 100 feet long, whalelike coloration with several small humps, and horizontal tail; undulates vertically; most often

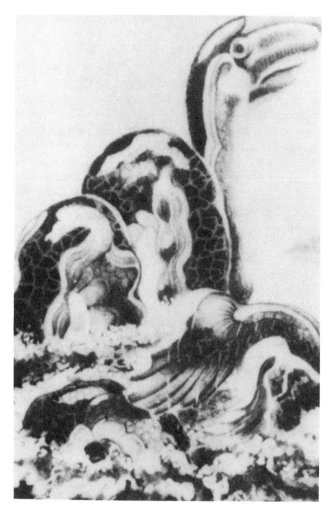

"King of the Deep," a Canadian sea monster who inspired a futile sea hunt   (Provincial Archives, Victoria)

researchers theorize that the creatures may be survivors from the age of dinosaurs.

The first researcher to suggest that not all sea serpents are truly serpents was naturalist Constantin Samuel Rafinesque-Schmaltz. In 1817, he wrote an article in *American Monthly Magazine* about a sea monster that was frequenting the coastal waters of Massachusetts, particularly Gloucester. Rafinesque named the creature Megophias. He also suggested that there were four different types of creatures, including what he calls a scarlet sea serpent (this was probably a giant squid, about which little was known at that time).

In 1833, English geologist Robert Bakewell suggested that a creature frequenting the waters of northeastern North America might be related to the ichthyosaur; however, Professor Benjamin Silliman later pointed out that the neck of the serpent was longer than that of an ichthyosaur, and that more likely, it was a plesiosaur. Several other scientists followed suit.

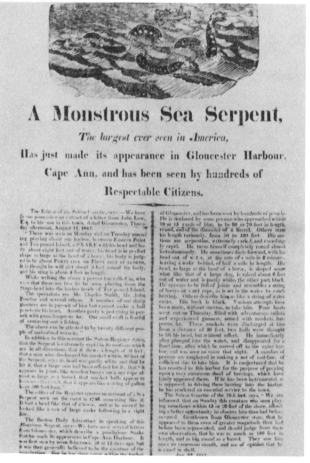

One of many articles publicizing the Gloucester sea serpent

Some "sea monsters" are large, known fish like this oarfish caught off Newport Beach, California, in 1901

seen off the east coast of the United States, particularly Massachusetts.

3. Long-Necked: a pinniped-like mammal, 30 to 70 feet long, with a small dog- or seal-like head on a long neck, four flippers and no tail; undulates vertically.

4. Multi-Finned: a whalelike mammal, 50 to 70 feet long, with many lateral fins, a segmented, armored body, and a dorsal fin or crest; spouts like a whale; undulates vertically.

5. Super-Otter: an otterlike animal with a slender neck, long tail and several vertical bends; coloring is uniformly light gray or beige.

6. Marine Saurian: an alligatorlike reptile, with a long head, many teeth, scales and a long muscular tail; undulates horizontally; possibly surviving mosasaurs from the Mesozoic Era.

7. Super Eel: an eel-like fish, 20 to 100 feet, with big eyes, eel-like coloration and no limbs; often leaps out of the water.

8. Father-of-All-the-Turtles: a huge turtle.

9. Yellow Belly: a tadpole-shaped creature, 60 to 100 feet long; coloring is yellow with a black stripe down its spine and black bands on its sides.

(*Note:* Regarding the humps often seen by witnesses, Heuvelmans points out that the fat on a seal's body, at

Merhorse sea monster swamping a ship by pumping water through its blowholes

Whalelike sea monster, by Olaus Magnus, 1555

high speeds, can look like humps in turbulent waves. However, this fact cannot explain the appearance of humps on an animal floating quietly on the surface.)

Contemporary investigators include cryptozoologist J. Richard Greenwell, who proposes that the creatures in Lake Champlain and Loch Ness are "extinct" marine reptiles called plesiosaurs. Greenwell believes that when the inland lakes were created during the last Ice Age, these animals were trapped in them. Zoologist Roy Mackal, who has also studied the Loch Ness and Lake Champlain creatures, subscribes to the theory that they are zeuglodons, and that they are not trapped in their lakes, but can reach the ocean via rivers. (In March 1994, investigators disclosed that a famous photo of the Loch Ness monster, taken in 1934, was a hoax. Despite the exposé, many researchers still believe the monster exists, and remains elusive.)

Recent research includes that of oceanographer Paul LeBlond and biologist John Sibert on coastal sightings in the American Northwest. LeBlond's manuscript on "Observations of Large Unidentified Marine Mammals in British Columbia and Adjacent Waters" examines sightings between Alaska and Oregon since 1812. In the reports of sightings that LeBlond has gathered, he finds patterns of three types of creatures: the serpentine shape, the horselike shape without a mane and the horse shape with tiny eyes and, sometimes, horns.

In December 1992, LeBlond along with zoologist Edward L. Bousfield presented a paper to the American and Canadian Societies of Zoology. The subject of this paper is the creature that frequents the waters off British Columbia. The study reports strong evidence for the recognition of the animal, which they describe as a "very large marine cryptid" and "distinct vertebrate species" embodying "major characteristics of both Reptilia and Mammalia," but "not clearly classifiable within existing subcategories of either."

What are these elusive beasts in our lakes and oceans? Are they flesh and blood or wishful thinking? Symbolic hallucination or primitive animals that have defied extinction? Perhaps reality is not as easily defined as we moderns usually suppose. If we can draw a line between what is real and what is not, it is a line drawn upon shifting sands that is constantly being obliterated and formed. There is a borderland, a twilight zone, which traditionally was the realm of the shaman—and perhaps the sea monster.

The following are major sightings of water monsters in North American lakes as well as coastal waters. Although they are arranged by state and province, many will overlap (e.g., Lake Champlain borders New York, Vermont and Quebec).

It is not known whether repeated sightings of a creature involve simply one or several different animals.

UNITED STATES

Alaska ✛

Iliamna Lake (1) The monsters in this 80-mile-long lake may be an unknown species of giant freshwater fish. Witnesses claim that these giant fish have broad heads, tapered, aluminum-colored bodies and vertical tail fins. While some have suggested that they might be whales, the fluke of whale is horizontal, not vertical. And the local Aleuts, who hunt whales and consider them harmless, are frightened by these monster fish and regard them as dangerous. They claim to have had a boat capsized by one of the fish, which proceeded to eat a crew member.

Bush pilots flying over the lake have reported seeing the huge fish just below the surface of the water, and some fishermen claim they have actually hooked the fish. Tom Slick, the wealthy Texas monster hunter of the 1950s, was involved in investigating these creatures of Lake Iliamna.

King Island (2) An unknown predatory sea creature exists here. The Inuit people call it Tizheruk or Pal Rai Yuk. The animal is seen sticking a seven-foot-long neck with a snakelike head out of the waters of the Arctic Ocean. It has a tail with a flipper on the end of it, and is aggressive enough to have snatched Inuit standing on piers at the shore. The animal inspires such fear that the Inuit are reluctant to talk about it. It may be a form of the carnivorous leopard seal, which has evolved a long neck.

California ✦

Trinity Alps (3) Fisherman have reported catching giant black salamanders up to nine feet in length. In January 1960, animal handler Vern Harden reported catching an eight-foot-long salamander in a lake in the Trinity Alps, using a shark hook on a line of piano wire. Giant salamanders up to six feet long are known to exist in Asia, in mountain streams in China and Japan. Stanford University biologist George Myers reported about a local fisherman who kept a three-foot salamander, taken from the Sacramento River, in a tub in his home. In the fall of 1960, a Dr. Rogers of Chico State University led an expedition into the Trinity Alps to search for the giant salamanders. These creatures also were searched for—unsuccessfully—in the 1950s by Tom Slick.

Florida ✦

Clearwater (4) What was described as an enormous penguin made a surprise appearance here in February 1948. It started with the discovery of huge footprints on the beach, prints that came out from the sea and then went back into it. Judging by the depth of the prints, which were 18 inches long, three-toed, and birdlike, the creature who made them weighed two to three tons. Following the discovery of the prints, several people reported a very large black creature waddling around the area. The bizarre footprints continued to appear through October of that year, and then appeared again on the beaches of Florida in 1966.

Illinois ✦

Du Quoin (5) Stump Pond has had its share of monster sightings. In 1880, two men spotted a dark green,

A common type of sea monster is the snakelike "super eel"

12-foot-long, serpentlike creature with a body the diameter of a telephone pole. Since then, one man claimed to have had his boat struck from underneath by something large and powerful; another man found a large, alligatorlike creature sleeping in a shallow area of the pond. In 1968, the pond was partially drained, but nothing resembling a monster was found.

Lake Michigan (6) In 1867 came the first report of something unusual living in Lake Michigan. This lake monster is between 40 and 50 feet long and has a human-sized neck. Witnesses have seen it near Evanston and Chicago.

Indiana ✤

Warsaw (7) In 1934, three people at Big Chapman's Lake watched a creature with a two-foot-wide head come to the surface. Its head was all that could be seen, and the witnesses said its eyes were cowlike.

Maryland ✤

Chesapeake Bay (8) Sightings of Chessie, the sea serpent of the bay, date to 1838. Like Lake Champlain's Champ, it may be another American answer to the Loch Ness monster. It has been described as a dragon, giant eel and giant snake; possibly different creatures have been given the same Chessie label. A flurry of sightings, including the finding of large reptilian footprints on a beach near Leonardtown, Maryland, launched Chessie into modern popularity.

In August 1840, a sea serpent spotted in the bay was pursued, killed and taken ashore. It was put on display at South Street wharf in Baltimore. It was described as being 12 feet long and nine feet from fin to fin, and having a seal-like head and a large shell. The creature may have been a large sea turtle. Another report of a captured sea turtle in the bay in July of the same year gives measurements of eight feet by nine feet.

Massachusetts and the Northeast ✤

Coastal Waters (especially Gloucester) (9) In the last two centuries, there have been numerous reported sightings of a multihumped creature in Northeastern waters, from Long Island Sound to Portland, Maine, usually in late summer. The summers of 1817 and 1818 were particularly busy ones for the monster, specifically in the Gloucester area (for this reason it was known as the Gloucester sea serpent). It was often seen by several people simultaneously; one sighting at Lynn, Massachusetts, involved about 200 people. The reports of these witnesses paint the portrait of a smooth-skinned beast

with at least 10 humps and a flattened head. Its body was dark brown with a white area under the jaw and no apparent blowhole or gills. Like most so-called sea monsters, it moved very fast, some said as much as 40 to 70 knots, and undulated vertically. Also like many of its brethren, it was able to descend vertically, or "sink like a rock."

In July of 1877, a 40- to 60-foot-long, shapeless creature was spotted by two men off Gloucester. It had dark brown, rough skin with many uneven bumps, and could rise and sink vertically. The witnesses could not see any eyes, mouth, fins or tail.

The Gloucester sea serpent received much scientific attention. It was written up in 1817 in *American Monthly Magazine* by naturalist Constantin Samuel Rafinesque-Schmaltz, who named it Megophias (Big Snake). Rafinesque was the first to suggest that not all such creatures were truly serpents, and that there were at least four types of sea monsters. Later, naturalist Reverend J. G. Wood suggested that the Gloucester creature was a zeuglodon, a theory that is still popular among cryptozoologists.

Swampscott (10) In July of 1875, several recreational boaters and fishermen spotted a creature whose head resembled that of a turtle or snake. It was black above and white underneath, and had a fin on the back of its neck. Witnesses saw a protrusion on its underside that may have been fins or flippers. Its head was about two and half feet in diameter. A ship's captain saw a similar creature in the area and estimated it to be about 100 feet long.

Michigan ✤

Paint River (11) In 1922, two women spotted a dark-colored, undulating creature with at least six humps showing above the water.

Montana ✤

Flathead Lake (12) The reported monsters in this lake have some type of protrusion—either horns or tentacles—on their heads. No one can seem to agree on their length, however; reports range from 5 to 60 feet long. The monsters resemble those reported in Lake Waterton, which straddles the Montana-Alberta border. The locals of Lake Waterton have dubbed their monsters Oogle-Boogles.

Nebraska ✤

Alkali Lake (13) In 1923, J. Johnson saw a 40-foot-long, alligatorlike creature here. Its skin was grayish-

Megophias ("Big Snake"), the Gloucester sea serpent

brown, and it had a hornlike protrusion between its eyes and nose. Like many lake monsters, it emitted a "very distinctive and somewhat unpleasant odor."

Walgren Lake   (14) A 40-foot-long, alligatorlike creature with an unpleasant odor was seen here on July 25, 1923, by J. Johnson, a duck hunter. However, the only unusual creatures to have been actually caught in this lake are some exceptionally large beavers. Zoologist Roy Mackal has suggested that the Walgren Lake monster was a sea-elephant that had wandered up the Mississippi River to Nebraska.

New York (with Vermont and Canada)   ✛

Lake Champlain   (15) Champ, the monster of Lake Champlain, is North America's answer to the Loch Ness monster. The 400-foot-deep lake is host to something that is usually described as snakelike with an earless, horselike head and small eyes; smooth, dark-green or gray skin; and a flattened tail. Some reports describe its head as snakelike and its skin as grainy. Descriptions of its length run between 10 and 90 feet.

Records of monsters in Lake Champlain extend back to the 17th century, and originated with the legends of local Indians. Although Samuel de Champlain did not mention a creature fitting the description of Champ, he did write of unusually large fish with shiny scales that the natives called chaousarou. Judging from his description, biologists have suggested that these were garfish, which are related to sturgeon.

In 1819, Champ was seen in Bulwagga Bay near Port Henry. Between 1870 and 1900, Champ was reported at least 20 times, and in almost all cases, it was witnessed by several people simultaneously. In 1915, several people saw the monster stranded in the shallows of Bulwagga Bay, struggling to get free; this report estimated Champ's length to be about 40 feet. There were several sightings in the 1930s and 1940s, including two off Rouse's Point, New York.

On July 5, 1977, Champ distinguished itself from most water monsters by getting captured on film. While picnicking with her family on the Vermont shore of the lake, amateur photographer Sandra Mansi saw Champ surface and twist its neck as if surveying the area. Its skin, she said, was slimy-looking and eel-like. Champ posed long enough for Mansi to get her camera and snap the photo. Mansi and her family kept the incident and the photo to themselves for three years. When Mansi heard of a group of scientists who were interested in the creature, she showed them the photo. It was examined by photography experts and found to be authentic.

In 1981, the *New York Times* and *Time* magazine published Mansi's photo, and Champ's popularity soared. It was seen by 21 people that year, and a conference was held in Shelburne, Vermont, to examine the mounting evidence of Champ's existence. In 1982, the Vermont House and the New York Senate passed a resolution protecting Champ "from any willful act resulting in death, injury or harassment."

Researchers of Champ include the Lake Champlain Phenomena Investigation team, organized by Joseph Zarzynski, a Saratoga Springs, New York, science teacher. Zarzynski, Champ's most ardent investigator, has documented many of the numerous sightings since the 1600s, and has published several books on the creature.

Other Champ researchers include cryptozoologist J. Richard Greenwell and zoologist Roy Mackal, who subscribe to the theory that sea monsters such as Champ are primitive creatures mistakenly thought to be long-extinct. Greenwell proposes that the Lake Champlain creature is an "extinct" marine reptile called a plesiosaur; he believes that when the inland lakes were created during the last Ice Age, creatures such as Champ were trapped in them. Mackal, who has also studied the Loch Ness creature, proposes that these animals are primitive whales called zeuglodons, and that they are not trapped in the lake, but can reach the oceans through rivers. (Many have wondered how the creature is able to survive in the winter, since the lake freezes solid.)

Lake Onondaga (16) The Tuscarora Indians believe that in this lake once lived a monster that they called Mosqueto. Unlike most lake monsters, which are generally shy and harmless, the reptilian Mosqueto is said to have killed several people.

Lake Ontario (17) According to Tuscarora Indian legend, Lake Ontario once hosted a horned serpent. One day, over 2,500 years ago, it rose out of the lake, and as legend has it, emitted an odor so tremendously bad that it killed a few witnesses.

North Carolina ✤

Coastal waters (18) The ocean liner *Santa Clara* apparently killed a sea serpent in December 1947. The eel-like creature was about three feet in diameter and 30 or 40 feet long, what could be seen of it. It was assumed that the ship cut the creature in two, so presumably it could have been even longer. Its skin was dark brown and smooth, with no visible fins or protrusions.

Oregon/Washington/Alaska ✤

Most creatures seen between Oregon and Alaska fall into two categories: One type is a serpentine, multihumped animal; the other is more seal-shaped. Some witnesses report seeing manes and horns. Some people claim that the animals have tiny eyes, while others see large eyes.

Columbia River, Oregon (19) Colossal Claude, as it is known in Oregon, was seen by a boat's captain feeding on halibut. The witness described it as having gray fur, with glassy eyes, a bent snout and a camel-like head. Claude was seen most frequently in the 1960s.

Dungeness Bay, Washington (20) In 1961, a family spotted a dark brown and orange, maned, tri-humped creature. They described it as looking like pictures of swamp-living dinosaurs.

South Carolina ✤

Charleston (21) In March of 1830, a controversial sighting took place in Simon's Bay. The captain of the schooner *Eagle* saw a 70-foot-long, gray, eel-shaped creature. It had scaly skin, humps and an alligatorlike head. The captain shot at the back of its head with his musket. When it was hit, the creature dived under the boat and smacked it hard with its tail, in what the captain seemed to think was a deliberate attack. The creature was later seen with a smaller animal of the same type, which had been spotted off in the distance during the original sighting.

The controversy over whether this incident was a hoax stems from the fact the animal apparently survived the shot, and that it attacked the boat. Cryptozoologist Bernard Heuvelmans points out that there are other large animals that can survive gunfire, and that the tail hitting the boat could have been accidental, not deliberate.

Washington ✢

Puget Sound (22) Kwakiutl Indians tell of the Pugwis, a race of mermen that inhabits Puget Sound.

Wisconsin ✢

Lake Mendota, Madison (23) In 1917, students from the University of Wisconsin claimed to have seen a long, snakelike head emerge from the lake. Mendota is one of the Madison Four Lakes, and monster sightings have also occurred in two of the other three lakes.

CANADA

Alberta ✢

Rocky Mountain House (24) In the early 1940s, a monster given the name Ogopogo (see LAKE OKANAGAN under British Columbia) appeared every summer in the North Saskatchewan River. The gray, loglike creature, about 15 feet long with huge, red-rimmed eyes, horns and a wide mouth, churned up water when boys threw rocks at it. On October 18, 1946, a fierce water monster similar to the one just described was seen snatching a calf from the bank of the Clearwater River. It was about 20 feet long, with horns, fiery red eyes, a scaly gray body and flashing, pointed teeth. The monster sank with the calf.

British Columbia ✢

Cadboro Bay (25) So many sea monster sightings have occurred in the waters near Vancouver Island that two scientists presented a paper on the subject to the American and Canadian Societies of Zoology in December 1992. Dr. Paul LeBlond (who has studied such sightings all along the Pacific Northwest) and Dr. Edward L. Bousfield report strong evidence for the recognition of a "very large marine cryptid" and "distinct vertebrate species" in these waters. Their description, based on 100 years of reported sightings and photos, is of a 40- to 50-foot-long-(10- to 15-foot juvenile)-flippered animal embodying "major characteristics of both Reptilia and Mammalia, but is not clearly classifiable within existing subcategories of either."

The apparently harmless creature has been described over the years as snakelike or whalelike, with a greenish-brown, serrated undulating body, and a camel-like head. The animal is known as Cadborosaurus or Caddy for short, because of its frequent appearance in this bay near Victoria.

Lake Kathryn (26) Located near the town of Smithers, Lake Kathryn is connected to the Pacific Ocean by the Skeena and Bulkley rivers. Indian descriptions of the creature inhabiting this lake match closely the appearance of a basilosaurus, a primitive form of whale thought to be extinct.

Lake Okanagan (27) Like most of the lakes where monsters are thought to reside, Lake Okanagan (meaning "snake in the lake") is large and deep, 79 miles long, two miles wide and 800 feet deep. Also it is cold and a rich source of Kokanee salmon.

The local native people named the lake's creature Naitaka. Today it is known as Ogopogo (which was coined by William Brimblecombe in a song he wrote in 1926 about the lake monster). A sighting in 1890 described Ogopogo as 15 feet long, with a ramlike head, and paper-thin fins. In July of 1974, Mrs. B. Clark jumped off a swimming raft and bumped right into Ogopogo. As it swam away, she noticed that it had a tail with flukes, rather like a whale. This detail lends credence to the theory that Ogopogo and many of its cousins in the lakes of North America might be a primitive form of whale.

Zoologist Dr. Edward Bousfield has studied the Cadboro Bay creature that frequents coastal waters in the Vancouver area. He believes that a juvenile Ogopogo may have come up the Columbia River from that area to feed on salmon, stayed, and could not get back after the hydroelectric dams were built. (See CADBORO BAY entry above for more information on Bousfield's study.)

Ogopogo seems less bashful than some of its cousins in other lakes around the world, having appeared nearly 200 times to the residents of the lakeside town of Kelowna in the last 300 years. The creature is also less camera-shy than most. An 8-mm film of Ogopogo was taken by Art Folden in August of 1968. The footage shows serpentine movement on the surface of the water. Boater Edward Fletcher, who photographed Ogopogo in August of 1976, estimated it to be about 70 feet long.

Ogopogo has been the subject of several films, some of which have been produced by companies coming over from Japan, where interest in monsters of all kinds is high. A Nippon TV crew apparently saw Ogopogo three times but was unable to capture anything more definite than a disturbance in the water. A guide later claimed he saw "something like flippers" on the animal.

The locals have expressed their appreciation of the sociable creature (and his saleability as a tourist attraction) by erecting a statue to Ogopogo. A sign put up by the Department of Recreation and Conservation claims that a cave at Squally Point is Ogopogo's home. Ogopogo is officially recognized by British Columbia law as "an animal in Okanagan Lake, other than a sturgeon, that is more than three meters in length, and the mates or offspring of that animal." The creature is also protected by law.

Strait of Georgia (28) Novelist Hubert Evan claimed to have seen a sea serpent off Roberts Creek on Vancouver Island in 1932. He and another witness watched a multihumped creature raise from the water its long, foot-thick neck supporting a horselike head and possibly a mane.

Two years later, off South Pender Island, several people observed a creature described as dark gray with a brown stripe on one side, about 40 feet long with a diameter of about two feet. The three-foot-long head was horselike but lacked ears and nostrils. Zoologist Roy Mackal suggests that, like the Loch Ness and Lake Champlain creatures, this animal might have been a zeuglodon, a primitive form of whale thought to be extinct. The creature was dubbed the Gulf Island Monster.

In 1951, three fishermen sighted a fast-moving creature in Heriot Bay that was described as about 40 feet long with gray-green skin and a foot-high, "codfish-style" fin down the length of its back.

Vancouver (29) In 1984, a man fishing in the Spanish Banks watched an animal of the following description surface: 18 to 20 feet long and two feet wide, with a whitish-tan throat, 12- to 15-inch horns, floppy ears and a black snout. It undulated vertically and moved very fast.

Also in the Vancouver area, two commercial fishermen in 1959 spotted a very fast-moving creature with red eyes and short ears. They judged it by its wake to be about 30 feet long. It was able to descend vertically. The witnesses claimed to be very familiar with marine animals, including sea elephants, seals and sea lions, and were sure that it was none of these.

Vancouver Island (30) In 1947, a man out fishing reported a creature raised its head out of the water and stared at him. Its head was a mottled gray and brown, about a foot and a half in diameter and had a manelike formation on the back. The mane, he said, looked more like a group of protrusions than like hair.

Manitoba ✤

Lake Manitoba (31) Manipogo, the creature of Lake Manitoba, has a reputation for being the noisiest of known lake monsters. Witnesses say the animal makes bellowing noises, not unlike that of a train whistle.

Many Manipogo sightings took place in the 1960s, often with numerous witnesses involved. On August 12,

The "Sea Hag" of the Strait of Georgia (Provincial Archives, Victoria)

1960, several beachgoers spotted a large serpentlike creature in the waters off Toutes Aides. (This beach is now known as Manipogo Beach.) On August 13, 1962, Richard Vincent and John Konefel were out fishing when they spotted Manipogo and managed to take a photo. The photo shows an eel-like creature about 12 feet long and about a foot wide. Two years later, again in August, several people in a motorboat spotted a 16-foot-long, dark green creature with two humps and a tail.

In July of 1960, University of Manitoba zoologist J. A. McLeod organized an expedition in search of Manipogo. While the McLeod expedition merely involved interviewing witnesses, it received much attention in the press.

Lake Winnipeg (32) The skrimski are serpents said to inhabit the depths of this lake. They are of enormous size and create thunderlike rumbles as they move through the water.

New Brunswick ✛

Chaleur Bay (33) In addition to its phantom ships, Chaleur Bay has also hosted a sea monster. The Gougou, according to Samuel de Champlain's reports of native legend, was a gargantuan, noisy, people-eating creature with the "form of a woman." It had a large pocket where it stored unfortunate humans for later consumption.

Lake Utopia (34) Back in 1872, an artist by the name of B. Kroup made a painting of the monster said to reside in Lake Utopia. The painting (now in the Webster collection in the New Brunswick Museum in St. John) shows an animal resembling a toothy whale with a serpentine body. The painting was based on a description by a Micmac medicine man, who claims his canoe was followed by the creature.

Over the years, local residents have described their lake creature as up to 100 feet long. However, in 1982, the monster was spotted by a man who described it as 10 feet long with a back like a whale's. Pilots of the Royal Canadian Air Force, on training missions over the lake, have taken photos of a long, dark shape under the water.

Newfoundland ✛

Grand Bank (35) In August of 1913, two crew members of the steamer *Corinthian* saw what they called a sea giraffe on the Grand Banks. It was described as having large blue eyes and it emitted a cry like that of a human baby. The witnesses said the creature watched the ship for a moment and then swam away.

St. John's Harbour (36) A "maremaid" was seen in 1610 by Captain Richard Whitbourne and several crew members, as well as observers on other ships in the harbor at the time. The creature, which had the upper body of a woman, attempted to climb aboard Whitbourne's ship but was thwarted.

Northwest Territories ✛

Baffin Island (37) A dead "sea unicorn" was found floating off the west coast of the island in 1577. It may have been a narwhal, a toothed whale with a single ivory tusk that projects through the lip. Various other sightings of sea unicorns were reported in Lancaster Sound, which lies between Baffin Island and Devon Island.

Nova Scotia ✛

Lake Ainslie (38) A serpent-type creature has been reported several times here. However, it has been suggested that the sightings are of "eel balls"—huge clumps of hundreds of eels.

Merigomish (39) In August of 1845, two witnesses saw in the shallows of Northumberland Strait near here a 100-foot-long, multi-humped creature with rough, black skin and a seal-like head. A similar creature had been seen all that summer off Prince Edward Island, and off Arisaig the year before.

Lake Utopia monster

Pollock's Shoal, Cape Sable Island (40) In July 1976, a huge toothy thing was spotted by several fishermen over a five-day period. According to their descriptions, it was about 70 to 80 feet long, with a long alligatorlike mouth, a large peak on its head, tusks, huge protruding eyes and a vertical tail like a fish. Its head cleared the water by at least 10 feet.

St. Margaret's Bay (41) In 1864, a dark gray creature, 70 to 100 feet long, with a mane, was seen here. It swam very fast and created a huge wake.

Strait of Canso (42) In 1656, the crew members of three fishing boats saw and attempted to capture a "merman." They described it as human looking, with hair and webbed hands. The men nearly roped the creature, but it dove under water and swam to freedom.

Ontario ✚

Kempenfelt Bay (43) Kempenfelt Kelly has been described as snakelike, with a small, horselike head, gaping eyes, fishlike tail and four fins with claws on their ends. It has also been described as a huge dolphin with flippers. A radar sounding made in 1983 showed Kelly to be a long-necked creature looking much like the one in Loch Ness.

Kempenfelt Bay is an extension of Lake Simcoe, which has its own lake monster—or perhaps the two creatures are one and the same.

Kingston (44) Various sea serpents have been spotted here, at the junction of the Great Lakes and the St. Lawrence River. Documented sightings go back to 1867, with varying descriptions. A modern nickname given them is Kingstie. Some reports tell of a snakelike creature 30 to 40 feet in length. Another account, from 1881, tells of a creature of "peculiar shape and great circumference, a head as big as a small house, numerous feet" and an incredibly powerful tail capable of boiling up the water. The creature also had horns. Yet another description, from 1931, included horns, a single eye like a Cyclops and a skin that changed color.

Lake Erie (45) The appropriately named Great Snake of Lake Erie has been reported intermittently since 1819. The animal is dark brown with a lighter underside, 35 to 50 feet long, and one to four feet in diameter. It has fins, a pointed tail and a large head, which has been described as doglike.

Lake Ontario (46) A mermaid or merman was seen in 1813. The creature, observed for several minutes, was described as about the size of a seven-year-old child, with a humanlike upper body clearly visible out of the water.

Lake Simcoe (47) The locals have named their lake creature Igopogo. Witnesses describe it as dark, 30 to 70 feet long, with dorsal fins and a doglike face.

Lake Superior (48) In 1782, Venant St. Germain and a companion saw an animal, about the size of a seven-year-old child, with a humanlike face and torso. St. Germain swore an affidavit of the account. The affidavit was later published by a magazine editor, who claimed it was proof of a mermaid.

Québec ✚

Gatineau River Region (49) There have been sightings of a horse-headed serpent in many of the lakes along this river. Blue-Sea Lake and Cedar Lake are home to what locals call Horse's Head, a serpent with a horse-shaped head and a mane. Both of these lakes share a feature common to "monster lakes": a very deep spot where divers reportedly become disoriented and frightened. Both lakes are also said to host very large and unusual fish.

Lake Brompton (50) There have been many sightings of the back of a green creature, looking in profile like an overturned boat. One woman saw a gray, trihumped creature, at least six feet long, with a horselike head, facial bristles and tail flukes.

At Indian Rock is a point where the lake floor suddenly drops into an abyss. The same area on the surface is associated with winds that come from every direction at once. The dark muddy lake is also rumored to possess huge, prehistoric fish that live near the murky bottom.

Lakes Memphremagog and Massawippi (51) A benign monster named Memphre has been spotted numerous times in Memphremagog. However, witnesses can't seem to agree on a description. Some have seen a fast-swimming, dark, serpentine figure with a long neck and horselike head. Another witness described it as a seal with a long neck. Another witness saw a creature 75 to 100 feet long with huge scales on its back and red eyes, and described an irridescence around the creature (this has also been said of the Loch Ness monster).

The creature is associated with a point called Owl's Head, which marks a 351-foot abyss in the lake, topped by a strong eddy at the surface. This is a feature common to "monster lakes."

Like its colleague in Lake Champlain, Memphre has inspired protective feelings and legislative action. The mayors of Magog, Québec and Newport, Vermont, signed an international agreement that Memphre should be a protected species. The legislative assembly of Vermont resolved in 1987 to recognize the "possible existence" of Memphre.

Local scuba diver Jacques Boisvert has also given Memphre much positive publicity through his International Dracontology Society, which promotes the creature as a friendly one. Boisvert has also studied the many similarities between Lake Memphremagog and Loch Ness. He has gone diving in Memphremagog many times, and has discovered something in the lake resembling cow feces. (Boisvert also discovered strange lights while diving in the lake.)

Nearby Lake Massawippi is believed to be linked to Lake Memphremagog by an underground passage. The lake, like several other "monster lakes," features an unfathomable abyss, at Black Point. It is greater than 1,200 feet deep, topped by a strong eddy, and is said to contain enormous fish, some described as fish with cows' heads.

Lake Pohenegamook (52) Pohenegamook, which means "place of hibernation," is an unusually cold lake near the Maine border, connected to the ocean by the St. John and St. Francis rivers. Only six miles long and no more than 300 feet deep, it is one of the smaller of the "monster lakes."

Pohenegamook hosts a creature, dubbed Ponik in 1974, that is 35 to 40 feet long, with a snakelike body and a dorsal ridge. It has two or three humps, flippers, a thick neck supporting a horselike head, and a large mouth. Like many other reported water monsters, it is capable of descending vertically, or sinking like a rock.

Investigators speculate that Ponik is either an abnormally large sturgeon or a plesiosaur, an "extinct" reptile. Dr. Vladim Vladykov of the Québec Department of Game and Fisheries investigated and concluded that some sort of large animal does indeed live in the lake.

Lake Saint-François region (including Lakes Aylmer, Moffat, Williams and Breeches) (53) There are very similar creature sightings in these neighboring lakes. Some attribute these to copycat rumors; others believe there are underground waterways connecting the lakes.

A few of the lakes share peculiar characteristics, such as an unfathomably deep point, marked on the surface by a strong eddy. Divers have been repeatedly frightened and disoriented while in these lakes, and it is said that the bodies of drowning victims never wash ashore. There are also reports of abnormally large fish, which some locals believe live at the bottom of the deepest parts of the lakes.

The sightings involve two types of creatures. One is about 20 feet long and brown, with a flat head, several fins on its huge back and scaly skin. The other is 30 to 40 feet in length with a long, tapering, dark, smooth-skinned body. It is often mistaken at first for a floating log, which, when approached, suddenly comes to life.

Some believe that the creature is a huge sturgeon, which has also been suggested regarding the Lake Pohenegamook animal. However, there have also been reports of a periscope-type object in the lake. One witness said it was definitely metallic, and spotted it at an eddy, which is associated with sighting of lake monsters. This has led to conjecture that there is a submarine in the lake with a periscope shaped like a horse's head, possibly built by one of the locals.

Lake Saint-Jean (54) This monster, which has also been seen in the connecting Ashuapmouchouan River, has been described as 50 to 60 feet long and muddy blue. Pointe Chambord, where the creature was seen by several people at once, marks a point where the lake floor drops into an abyss, and it is believed by some that underground rivers connect the lake to the sea.

Saskatchewan ✙

Turtle Lake (55) Reports have been made since the 1920s of a long-necked, tri-humped monster known as the Turtle Lake Terror. The creature, whose head has been described variously as piglike, doglike and horselike, has been accused of ripping fishing nets and frightening people.

MYSTERIOUS CREATURES

Animals that defy explanation are not the stuff of history, but continue to be reported in modern times around the world. North America has its share of weird creatures, most of whom seem to prefer the wild remote regions of the land, but some of whom invade our towns and cities. From cats with wings to giant ape men, all of these animals are rejected as impossible by conventional science. Do any of them actually exist? Sometimes evidence is found in the form of hair, droppings, tracks or photographs of varying degrees of quality. More often, the only proof of the sighting is the word of the witness. Frequently people report these sightings to their local police or sheriff's department. This behavior suggests they are telling the truth as they see it, for most people will not go out of their way to make false police reports, which is a crime.

When dealing with mysterious creatures, it is often hard to separate fact from folklore or legend. While some mysterious animals, like giant snakes, seem at least realistic, others, like Mothman, a giant humanoid with wings, seem too fantastic. Perhaps they are creatures from another dimension or plane of reality, who pass back and forth through a window between our world and theirs. Their existence perhaps is fed by folklore and legend, which reside deep in our collective unconscious. Occasionally, especially in remote places, the window between dimensions is flung open and seemingly fantastical creatures come into our own reality—or perhaps we intrude into theirs.

Perhaps some mysterious creatures are apparitions, thought forms or shape-shifted beings created by magic and sorcery, such as the American Indian skinwalkers (see below). One hypothesis holds that some of these bizarre animals are created by the minds or expectations of the witnesses, and that they are reflections of the fears and anxieties of modern people, most of whom are city dwellers with little familiarity with wildlife. Such psychological theories are interesting, but fail to account for tracks, hair samples or droppings left behind by the unknowns.

Some speculate that mystery animals may even be of extraterrestrial origin, and have been brought here by space travelers, much as humans introduced rabbits to Australia.

Some mysterious creatures may not be so mysterious at all. They may be animals long thought to be extinct, but which, in fact, are not. And, some may be the feral, or wild, form of a domestic animal that has gone back to living freely in the wilderness. Finally, some mysterious creatures seem to be real animals somehow geographically displaced. For example, there are numerous sightings of kangaroos throughout North America, especially in the United States.

Cryptozoologists, who are scientists who look for "hidden" animals, consider these and many other possible explanations for mystery animals. Unknown animals often match with animals in American Indian legends and myths, or with animals in written historical accounts of settlers or explorers of the 18th and 19th centuries.

As more people in the United States and Canada take up outdoor recreation, and as more wilderness areas are opened up for development and tourism, more mystery animals are being seen and reported—usually by people who have no knowledge about such animals, and who are not expecting to see anything out of the ordinary. Newspaper, radio and television accounts of sightings encourage other people to come forward with their own similar experiences. Ivan T. Sanderson, a zoologist with a keen interest in natural mysteries, noted that if one type of mystery animal is seen someplace, other mystery

Winged catlike monster

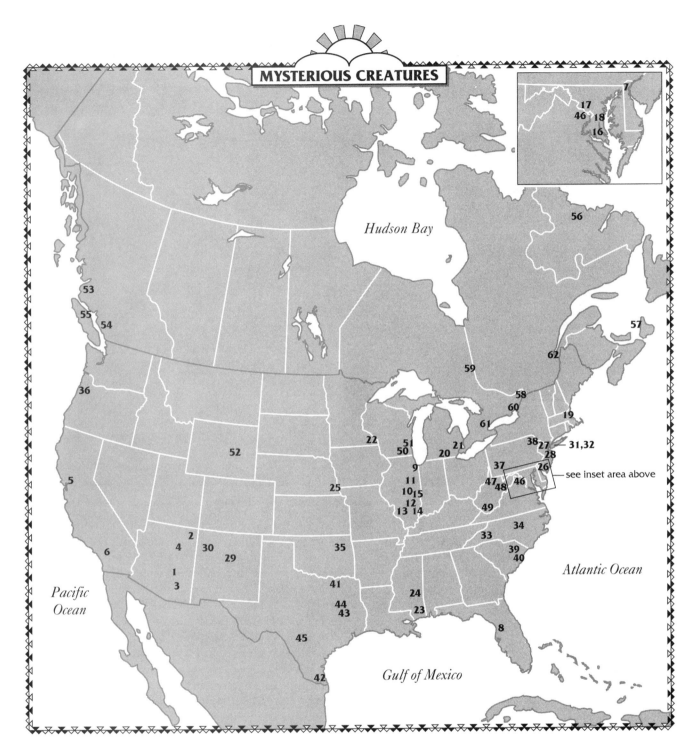

animals, even of different kinds, will soon be reported in the same area.

Unlike Europe and many other parts of the world, North America is still rich in vast tracks of wilderness area. In some parts of the United States and Canada, local people still live by hunting and fishing, and may rarely venture far afield. Even the densely populated eastern states still have many tracts of forest and swamp where few people ever go. There remains plenty of room in North America for at least some as-yet-unclassified animals to be roaming around.

All big cities are populated by numerous wild animals, not just mice or squirrels, but raccoons, opossums, rabbits, snapping turtles, bats, foxes and many others. Yet few people other than naturalists are aware of their presence, or see these animals going about their daily

What passed for the Devil centuries ago, shown with witches in this old woodcut, might be called a bat-man or lizard-man today

activities. If many animals, some of good size, like coyotes, can live in cities undetected, how much easier it is for animals to live in truly rural areas unknown to the people around them.

Some of the unknowns, such as Bigfoot, are seen frequently and over a wide geographic area. Yet, many zoologists refuse to accept the existence of such animals, or even the possibility. As time passes, however, old prejudices are breaking down, and more scientists are beginning to admit that unknown animals might be real.

Reports of mysterious creatures are in such great number that it would be impossible to catalog them all here. Many fall into general categories or types, such as swamp and lizard monsters, feline monsters, kangaroos or kangaroolike creatures, apelike monsters, dog or wolf monsters and more.

Dog and wolf monsters include werewolves. In folklore, werewolves are human beings who are cursed to turn into rapacious wolves every full moon, and ravage the countryside tearing up animals and humans alike. This curse can be caused by unfortunate birth circumstances (i.e., being born on unlucky days), or crimes,

sin or sorcery. Today we tend to think of werewolves as fantasy, but in earlier centuries in Europe, belief in them was strong. A number of werewolves or man-wolf creatures have been reported in the American Southwest, where Indian folklore beliefs about them are strong. So-called skinwalkers are human beings, such as sorcerers, who have the power to shape-shift into wolf form in order to carry out their evil intents. The Navajo term is Yee Naaldlooshii, which means "those who trot about with it." Presumably, the shape-shifting allows them to move about rapidly.

The following survey includes a sampling of bizarre encounters around the continent. The locations are given as precisely as possible. The section ends with a separate list of Bigfoot sightings.

UNITED STATES

Arizona ✛

Globe   (1) In 1955, a woman driving along the highway at night near Globe saw a creature three feet tall cross the road. It was covered with fur and had long arms, a round head like a pumpkin and glowing yellow-orange eyes. The description is comparable to that of Navajo skinwalkers or werewolves (see WINSLOW below).

Little Jadito Wash (2) In the fall of 1965, Roger Heath saw what appeared to be a werewolf crawling from a wash onto the road one night as he was driving north from Winslow. The area is near the 2nd Mesa of the Hopi village. For more on this incident see Winslow below.

Tombstone (3) A now-famous photograph, showing a huge, pterodactyl-like ThunderBird nailed to the side of a barn, was published in the *Tombstone Epitaph* newspaper in 1886. Some researchers recall seeing this photograph in a magazine sometime in the 1970s, but attempts to track it down have all failed. Like the Minnesota Ice-Man, this case of the missing photographs has become a classic among monster buffs.

Winslow (4) Navajos on the reservation near Winslow, Arizona, believe in the existence of werewolves, which they call skinwalkers, or Yee Naaldlooshi in the Navajo language. They say that certain sorcerers, both male and female, can wrap themselves in coyote skins and become werewolves. Curiously, this belief is very close to the werewolf legends of medieval Europe. The skinwalkers can move through the night at great speed, and they inspire tremendous fear. In the fall of 1965, Roger Heath saw one of these werewolves alongside the road at night as he was driving from Winslow to the nearby Hopi Village. He described it as being three feet tall, covered with black shiny fur and traveling with a hopping motion. Navajos and Hopis to whom he told his experience unhesitatingly identified what he had seen as a skinwalker. A scientific paper on these werewolves, "Human Wolves Among the Navajo," was published in the Yale University *Publications in Anthropology* in 1936—a rare instance when scientific recognition has been given to a mystery beast.

California ✤

Fairfield (5) Fairfield police fanned out in a search for a 150-pound, three-foot-long black panther that was sighted roaming the hills above Fairfield, a town some 35 miles north of San Francisco. The cat left tracks three inches in length, but was never captured.

Riverside (6) On November 8, 1958, Charles Wetzel was driving his car along North Main Street in Riverside, near the banks of the Santa Ana River. His car was attacked by a humanoid being that was covered with scales like leaves, with long claws and a protuberant mouth. Wetzel floored the accelerator, knocking the

creature down, and escaped. He reported the incident to the police, who found long scratch marks on the hood of the car. This story has become a classic to monster buffs. Curiously, at about the same time, another man named Charles Wetzel, in the Midwest, reported seeing a wild kangaroo. This is one of the odd synchronicities that seems to occur with such phenomena.

Delaware ✤

Concord (7) Police unsuccessfully pursued a dark-colored kangaroo that left tracks nine inches long.

Florida ✤

Elfers (8) Four teenagers parking at a local lover's lane were startled when an apelike animal resembling a green chimpanzee, with bright green glowing eyes, jumped up on the hood of their car. Police from nearby New Port Ritchie were impressed by the stress displayed by the teenagers and agreed to investigate. They found only some sticky green substance at the site.

Illinois ✤

Chicago (9) Chicago police officers Leonard Ciagi and Michael Byrne gave chase to a six-foot-tall kangaroo on Chicago's northwest side on October 18, 1974. When the officers attempted to capture the kangaroo, it fought back viciously and escaped. Shortly afterward, a South American tree-climbing mammal, a kinkajou, was captured in the area.

Decatur (10) A remarkable number of mystery cats, real and phantom, have shown up here. In 1917, a full-grown African lion was seen repeatedly, and was called

18th-century rendition of a werewolf

Nellie the Lion by local newspapers. On October 25, 1955, a black panther was spotted by a game warden, who fired his gun at it. On June 30, 1963, George W. Davidson, alerted by the sound of barking dogs, cornered a three-foot-long black jungle cat in a tree. The cat jumped out of the tree, scratching Davidson. On June 25, 1965, a woman saw a black panther in her car headlights as she pulled into her driveway. She reported the incident to the sheriff's department, which found tracks. The same, or a similar, black panther turned up in Decatur's Lincoln Park a few days later, where it frightened three children. In 1970, there was a "cat flap" in Decatur, with people reporting both cougars and black panthers in the area. In one instance, a black panther was seen accompanied by a cub.

But mystery cats are not the only unexplained fauna that appear in Decatur. Phantom kangaroos pop up too. On July 14, 1975, Rosemary Hopwood was driving along Route 128 just outside Decatur, when she spotted a five-and-a-half-foot-tall, beige-colored kangaroo walking along the road. When she stopped to watch, the kangaroo hopped off into a nearby cornfield. Kangaroos were also being seen at about the same time in Wisconsin.

Kangaroos and panthers are sometimes joined by crocodiles in Decatur. On August 30, 1937, one was captured in a bayou near Lake Decatur. Some small, 12-inch-long specimens turned up on October 24, 1966, and on June 26, 1967, a crocodile was seen taking a stroll on West Eldorado Street. Like Loveland, Ohio, Decatur, Illinois, is a place where "impossible" animals just keep appearing.

Delavan (11) On the road between Armington and Delavan, truck driver James Major saw two giant birds with eight-foot wingspreads attempting to carry off a pig. Major later compared the birds in appearance to the nearly extinct California condor. An expert at the University of Illinois declared the sighting to be impossible.

Mount Vernon (12) In 1941 and 1942, residents here complained that a baboon was roaming the countryside. Hunters with dogs chased the creature, but were never able to catch it. The Rev. Lepton Harpole reported that an ape jumped onto him from a tree, knocking away his hat and pipe.

Murphysboro (13) In 1974, this small southern Illinois town was terrorized by a Bigfoot-type creature that was recognized by its vile odor. Ponies at a local fair panicked when the creature was in the area. Police tracked it to a barn, but abandoned the hunt when their German Shepherd tracking dogs began to whimper with fear.

Olive Branch (14) While driving alone through the wild Shawnee National Forest on April 10, 1970, Mike

Busby stopped and got out of his car. He was immediately attacked by a black pantherlike animal that ran at him, standing erect on its hind legs. The animal slashed Busby with its claws, but ran away when a truck came by. The truck driver confirmed Busby's story. Black panthers are not native to Illinois, and they do not walk erect on two legs.

Tuscola (15) A professional outdoor writer named "Texas John" Huffer filmed two giant birds in a swamp. The birds had wingspans of at least 12 feet, according to Huffer. Skeptics insisted the birds in the film were just turkey vultures. There have been many reports over the years of such giant birds, resembling condors but larger, which are known to monster buffs as Thunderbirds. Many of these cases come from the Midwest, and some have involved attacks by the giant birds on children.

Maryland ✤

Hollywood (16) A gigantic man with huge wings was seen at St. John's Church on July 27, 1944, by J. M. Johnson, pastor. He went outside to watch an approaching storm, and saw the creature sailing down out of the sky toward the church. It landed in the church's cemetery and disappeared. It was described as having a massive body, enormous head, huge winged arms, extensive legs and enormous feet. The description is similar to the Mothman sightings of West Virginia in the 1960s (see MOUNDSVILLE in West Virginia below).

Also in the Hollywood area in the 1940s were sightings of hideous demons about the size of a three-year-old child. They were humanoid and jet black with horns.

Lanham (17) A legendary Boaman, a half-man, half-snake beast haunts the Lanham Severn Road.

Odenton (18) A swamp monster was reported in 1968 near a dirt road off Patuxent Road near here. The creature was described as 10 feet tall, three feet wide and covered with slimy green hair. During that year, about 25 similar sightings were reported to authorities.

Massachusetts ✤

Medford (19) Eels four feet long were found in the water pipes of an apartment building here in June 1972. The nearest body of water with eels in it is the Quabbin Reservoir, 100 miles away.

Michigan ✤

Clinton Township (20) A catlike animal was blamed for killing 197 chickens and 55 rabbits in August 1971.

Tracks were found showing extended claws, which is not normal for any of the big cats except the cheetah.

Monroe (21) In 1964, 17-year-old Christine Van Acker reported that a hairy, manlike monster reached into her car window on a lonely road and tried to grab her. She displayed a black eye from the encounter. A monster-hunting mania ensued in that part of Michigan for several months, but no creature was found.

Minnesota ✛

Rollingstone (22) One of the strangest of all monster stories concerns the Minnesota Ice Man, the corpse of an alleged humanoid being, covered with dark fur and with two bullet wounds. It was displayed frozen in a block of ice at country fairs and carnivals. Alerted to its existence by a Milwaukee herpetologist named Terry Cullen in 1968, the world's two foremost cryptozoologists, Ivan T. Sanderson and the Belgian zoologist Bernard Heuvelmans, journeyed to the remote hamlet of Rollingstone to visit the home of a carnival showman where the Ice Man was stored. Sanderson and Heuvelmans examined the frozen body under bad conditions of freezing cold and poor lighting, and concluded that the body was genuine. However, when federal authorities began to show some interest in the matter because of the possibility that a human corpse was being exhibited commercially, the owner declared that it was all a fraud, and that the Iceman was just a rubber model covered with animal hair. The controversy over the Ice Man has never died down among monster buffs, who insist that what Sanderson and Heuvelmans saw and examined was replaced later by an obvious fake. One theory is that the Ice Man was the body of a Tok, a Southeast Asian version of the Abominable Snowman, that was killed by a soldier in Vietnam and then shipped frozen to Hong Kong, where it was purchased by the carnival huckster. The Ice Man controversy inspired an article in a tabloid newspaper by a woman claiming that she had been sexually attacked by the animal in the forests of Wisconsin. The mystery of the Minnesota Ice Man remains unsolved.

Mississippi ✛

In the backwoods regions of Mississippi (23) live the Little Red Men of the Delta, small, manlike beings that steal laundry from clotheslines and wear fragments of the clothing. They stay out of gunshot range and talk a lot. Little Red Men also have been reported in Kentucky.

Jasper County (24) A doglike creature bigger than the biggest German Shepherd made a series of attacks

on penned hogs in the Nazarene Community in January 1977. The unknown animals bit off the ears of the hogs, severing them cleanly, as if with a knife. Charles Fort recorded a number of similar attacks by doglike creatures in Ireland in the 19th century.

Nebraska ✛

Falls City (25) A strange animal killed in October 1968 was identified as a coatimundi, a South American mammal related to the raccoon. The animal had been seen walking on its hind legs, abnormal behavior for almost any animal.

New Jersey ✛

Pine Barrens (26) Between New York City and Philadelphia, two of North America's largest cities, lie the Pine Barrens of New Jersey, several thousand acres of true wilderness, characterized by stunted pine trees, sandy soil and numerous bogs and swamps. Bog iron for cannons was mined here during the Revolutionary War, but the mining towns have long been abandoned. Some modern inhabitants are backwoods people who call themselves Pineys and avoid contact with outsiders. Strangely, many of the birds, mammals, amphibians and plants found in the Pine Barrens are native to the southern states, and are found nowhere else in the northeastern United States. Because of their isolation, the Pine Barrens are alleged to be a favorite spot for dumping dead bodies. They also are said to be roamed by packs of ferocious wild dogs.

Places where the Jersey Devil has been reported

The Pine Barrens are the haunt of the Jersey Devil, a semimythical monster that has been compared to a flying kangaroo or a pterodactyl. The Jersey Devil leaves huge, clawed tracks and utters unearthly screams. While New York City newspapers treat the Jersey Devil as a joke, local people take it seriously, and reports of its appearance have caused panic in the small towns of the region. Other odd things have happened in the Pine Barrens. The German dirigible *Hindenburg* exploded and burned at the Lakehurst Naval Air Station, which is located in the Barrens near Tom's River and Lakewood. The Georgian Court College has lakeside grounds so eerie that they were used as a location in the film *The Exorcist*.

Pompton Lakes (27) Schoolteacher Audrey Smith was amazed to see a two-foot-tall, gray baby kangaroo standing in the backyard of her home on Ringwood Avenue in Pompton Lakes on June 15, 1988. Police chief Albert Ekkers insisted that she must have seen a beaver. Other kangaroo sightings were reported from Ho-Ho-Kus, New Jersey, 10 miles away.

Wayne (28) In the 1970s, a motorist reported seeing a lizard man with a green, scaly body. The creature had bulging eyes and a lipless mouth.

New Mexico ✛

Albuquerque (29) A peculiar man-beast was seen about 20 times in the South Valley section of town during about a week-long period in October 1966. A family named McGuire reported to the sheriff's office that a monster about "five feet tall, hairy, and with a small blank face and crying like a baby" was seen roaming about their backyard. It left forklike footprints. Whenever it appeared, the McGuires' radio would stop playing, and their son felt pain in his chest. Subsequent to publicity, other sightings were reported.

Whitewater (30) Four Gallup youths reported a werewolf in January 1970. They were driving to Zuñi and were near Whitewater when a "kinda hairy thing with two legs" about five-feet-seven in height paced their car for awhile at 45 miles per hour. The terrified youths drove faster. One of them pulled out a gun and shot the creature. It fell but then got up and ran off.

New York ✛

Brooklyn (31) Anomalist Charles Fort recorded the sightings in September 1877 and September 1880 of a "winged man" seen flying over Coney Island in the

Werewolf attacking a man, in a 16th-century woodcut

direction of New Jersey. Newspaper accounts said the creature had "bat's wings" and "frog's legs."

New York City (32) The vast subterranean labyrinth of tunnels and pools that makes up New York City's sewer system is rumored to be infested with alligators. Supposedly, New York City tourists brought home pet baby alligators from southern vacations, then flushed them away when they tired of the little reptiles. The alligators survived and even flourished in the sewers, living on rats. There is some evidence that alligators have occasionally been found in the sewers, and small "out-of-place" alligators have been found in city reservoirs in Westchester County, just north of the city. A secret museum containing stuffed alligators and crocodiles from the sewers is supposedly maintained by the New York City Sanitation Department, but its existence has never been proved. (This case compares to a similar legend in London, England, that wild pigs live in the London sewers.)

North Carolina ✛

Biltmore (33) A motel clerk was startled on October 9, 1981, to see a kangaroo walking around outside the motel where he worked. Police attempted to capture the kangaroo, but it escaped.

Dunn (34) An eight-year-old boy saw a little man the size of a Coke bottle while the boy was playing in a cornfield near his home on October 12, 1976. The little man was wearing black boots and trousers, a blue top, and a "German-type" hat. The boy said the entity squeaked like a mouse and disappeared into the cornfield.

Oklahoma ✛

Tulsa (35) On April 30, 1981, a man walked into a Tulsa café and told a waitress that he had just run over a kangaroo on the road. When police officers responded, they found that the man did indeed have a dead kangaroo in the back of his truck. No one knows where the kangaroo came from.

Oregon ✛

Newport (36) A 16-year-old girl was terrified when she saw three brightly colored entities walking across a meadow. The only thing she could compare them to was walking tree stumps. Many other bizarre phenomena were witnessed in the same area at about the same time.

Pennsylvania ✛

Arnold (37) In February 1981, five young boys between the ages of 11 and 16 encountered a small, manlike creature while they were playing in a railroad yard. The creature was green in color, had no hair or fur, had "nipples" and a short tail. One of the boys grabbed it, but it wriggled away and escaped down a drainpipe.

Honeybrook Township (38) A mysterious "monkey" was killed here in October 1978. The monkey was two-and-a-half-feet long and weighed 50 pounds, which is big for a monkey of any kind. Veterinarians at the University of Pennsylvania who examined the body could not identify the species of the animal, which was reddish-brown in color and had canine teeth one inch long.

South Carolina ✛

Bishopville (39) One of the biggest creature flaps of all time occurred near here in the summer of 1988, with sightings of a lizard man from the Scape Ore Swamp nearby. The creature was described as a biped seven feet tall with green scales and red eyes. It chased a man in a car at 40 miles per hour, succeeding in grabbing the door handle and jumping on the roof. The driver saw that it had three-fingered hands with long black nails. Publicity created a sensation, spurring a rash of monster hunts and so many reports of sightings that the sheriff's office set up a lizard man hotline. Three-toed, clawed footprints were found. By August, the flap had died down. Some of the sightings were suspected or confirmed hoaxes.

Santee River (40) At Rice Hope Plantation in 1948, two men out hunting for poachers encountered a "lion" that stood up on its hind legs. The men jumped into their car and fled the scene.

Texas ✛

Farmersville (41) This incident was related in 1978 by a man who recalled the story from his childhood. In May 1913, a farmer's dogs tore apart a "little man" wearing a Mexican hat and a rubber suit. When he and his friends returned to the site the next day, there had been no trace of the bloody struggle.

Harlingen (42) On New Year's Day 1976, two children, ages 11 and 14, observed through binoculars a horrible birdlike creature with a face like a gorilla. It was five feet in height and had glowing red eyes. The parents of the children searched the field where the bird was seen, and found tracks eight inches wide with three toes.

Houston (43) On June 18, 1953, several persons sitting on the front porch of a home were disturbed by a black shadow passing over the lawn. They looked up and saw a tall manlike being with enormous bat wings perched on the branch of a pecan tree. A dim halo of light seemed to surround the being.

Richmondville (44) On January 14, 1976, a man was attacked by a birdlike creature with huge bat wings. The creature looked much like the one seen 14 days before by the children in Harlingen, Texas. The victim reported that the animal had a wingspread of 10 to 12 feet, a monkeylike face and red eyes.

San Antonio (45) Three schoolteachers driving to work on February 24, 1976, observed a huge birdlike creature flying along the road. It had a wingspread of 15 to 20 feet and a bony structure that was visible through the wings. The teachers later pointed to a picture of a pteranodon, an extinct giant flying reptile, as being most like what they had seen.

Virginia ✤

Arlington County (46) In 1974, an unknown animal went on a rampage here, killing dogs, rabbits and cats. The killings stopped when a palm civet, a tropical mammal native to West Africa, was captured.

West Virginia ✤

Moundsville (47) In 1966, this quiet, middle-class West Virginia community near the Ohio River was swarming with tales of encounters with an unearthly entity known as Mothman. This strange being stood six feet tall, had huge batlike wings and two glowing red eyes. It did not seem to have a head, however. The entity would take off straight up into the air without moving its wings, and would chase cars driving near the Chief Cornstalk Hunting Grounds, the location of an abandoned World War II ammunition dump. Mothman emitted a squeaking noise like a gigantic mouse. Local wildlife authorities asserted that people were seeing an owl or a sandhill crane, but people who had seen Mothman dismissed such explanations. Mothman eventually left Moundsville, but turned up again in Brownsville, Texas, in 1972. (See also MOUNDSVILLE, WEST VIRGINIA under "Haunted Places.")

Parsons (48) In 1960, a local man known as "Doc" Priestly was driving his car through the Monongahela National Forest, traveling behind a bus that contained friends of his. An apelike creature, walking erect on two legs, stepped from the forest to the edge of the road. The creature's hair stood up on end, and at that moment Priestly's car stopped. All attempts to restart the car failed. When the bus came back along the road looking for him, the car started again. Such electrical interference with car engines and radios has occasionally been reported in Bigfoot encounters, and also in UFO sightings.

Pineville (49) In 1959, a 15-year-old hunter captured a winged cat that his dog cornered in a tree. The cat appeared to be of the Persian variety, and had a furry tail. The cat was taken to New York City, where it was exhibited on the "Today" television program on June 8, 1959. It was later alleged that the cat's wings fell off when it shed its fur, but there was controversy as to whether the wingless cat that was displayed in a court battle over the animal's custody was the actual animal or a substitute.

Wisconsin ✤

Elkhorn (50) A werewolf was reported in the Elkhorn area between 1989 and 1992. Most of the sightings were along Bray Road. Various witnesses—men, women and children—reported seeing a huge, hairy wolflike man that could walk bipedally or quadrupedally, and used its front paws like hands (at least one witness described the paws and hands with claws). It was covered with silvery hair, had luminous yellow eyes, a wolf's head and a wide chest and left oversized wolf tracks. The front legs were wolflike and the back legs manlike. When upright, its height was estimated at about five feet to five-feet-seven. The creature chased terrified schoolchildren one afternoon but did not harm them. In the same time period, there were numerous animal mutilations (mostly pet dogs and cats), and reports of strange lights in the sky and men in black.

Waukesha (51) On April 24, 1978, two young men from Menominee Falls sighted a kangaroo in tall grass near the intersection of Highways SS and M. They snapped two pictures with a Polaroid SX-70 camera. One of the pictures clearly shows a kangaroolike animal, apparently the same one that had been spotted before in the area. These animals, known as phantom kangaroos, have often been reported, mainly in the Midwest. The usual official explanation given is that the animal escaped from a zoo or circus—but, invariably, no zoo has any missing kangaroos, and there is no circus around. While there are known to be several populations of wallabies (small kangaroolike animals) living wild in

Britain (they escaped from country estates), there are no such known groups of kangaroos living free in North America.

Wyoming ✣

Casper (52) In 1932, miners excavating a shaft in the Pedro Mountains found the perfectly preserved mummy of a human being only 14 inches tall. The mummy, named Pedro by newspapers, was taken to the American Museum of Natural History in New York City, where it was X-rayed and pronounced genuine. Shoshone and Crow Indians have a legend of a race of little people who once lived in Wyoming. Present whereabouts of the mummy are unknown, but photographs of it exist.

CANADA

British Columbia ✣

Bishop's Cove (53) A monkeylike wild man once haunted this fishing community north of Vancouver around the turn of the 20th century. It would appear on the beach at night, emitting chilling howls while it dug for clams. The creature was about five feet tall. The indigenous Indians were particularly fearful of it, saying they had attempted to shoot it several times, but failed.

Burke Channel (54) A dwarfish, hairy, manlike creature, the Boq, is known to the Bella Coola Indians. The Boqs live in the forested valleys along the coast of Burke Channel. They shriek and whistle when angered.

Campbell River (55) Indians long avoided certain areas along the river, in Vancouver Island, because they were haunted by "monkey men." These men were covered with reddish-brown hair; one was observed washing roots.

Labrador ✣

Inuit people of Labrador (56) and other regions of arctic Canada talk in whispers about the Tornit or Toonijuk. These are subhominid giants, very aggressive and bloodthirsty, that preyed on the Inuit until fairly late in the 20th century, when they were supposedly killed off. Belief in such giant ape men is common among Indian tribes in northern Canada. Names for these creatures include Brush Men, Mountain Men, Weetigo and Nakani.

Nova Scotia ✣

Inverness (57) A small, haystack-shaped hill near this community on the west coast of Cape Breton Island is inhabited by the Shean, or fairies. The term derives from Sithean, Gaelic for "The House of Fairies." According to lore, the little folk can be seen at night by the thousands. But, if humans approach too close, they vanish.

Ontario ✣

Alfred (58) A bizarre black cat with furry wings and long, pointed teeth was shot here in 1966 as it was chasing a pet cat and making long leaps into the air. The cat had glassy green eyes. Other instances of winged cats have been reported, and purported photographs of them exist.

Cobalt (59) A hairy, apelike creature with a light-colored head of hair has been seen lurking about mines near here since 1906. It also has been described as bearlike, though it walks on two legs with a stoop. The creature is called Old Yellow Top and the Precambrian Shield Man.

Kingston (60) At Bon Echo Provincial Park, north of Kingston, are old Algonkian rock paintings of a rabbit man, a legendary humanoid who either had wings or antennae or both.

Toronto (61) In May 1979, a Toronto police officer reported seeing a kangaroo hopping along Markham Road–Finch Avenue in Toronto. The Toronto Metro Zoo reported that all its kangaroos were accounted for.

Québec ✣

Kamouraska (62) A "ware-wolf" reportedly roamed about for several years in the mid-1700s, doing "great destruction." Various attempts were made to kill it, but an item in the *Quebec Gazette*, dated December 10, 1764, said the attempts had been unsuccessful. The eventual fate of the creature is not known.

BIGFOOT

Thousands of sightings have been reported all over North America of large apelike humanoids living in remote forested areas. These creatures are lumped into a common category of Bigfoot, or Sasquatch, an American Indian term. Sightings occur throughout the continent, but many are clustered in certain areas, such as the west coast of both the United States and Canada, and the eastern woodlands. Bigfoot has been sighted in most of the Canadian provinces and every state but Rhode Island and Hawaii.

Bigfoot does have very big feet, ranging in length from 14 to 22 inches and five to seven inches across, with three to five toes. He has long arms, a short neck

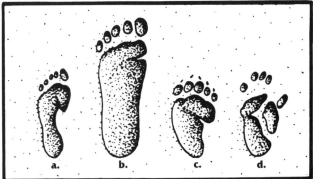

a. Human
b. Sasquatch
c. Grizzly Bear
d. Gorilla

(Drawn by Robert Michael Place. Used with permission)

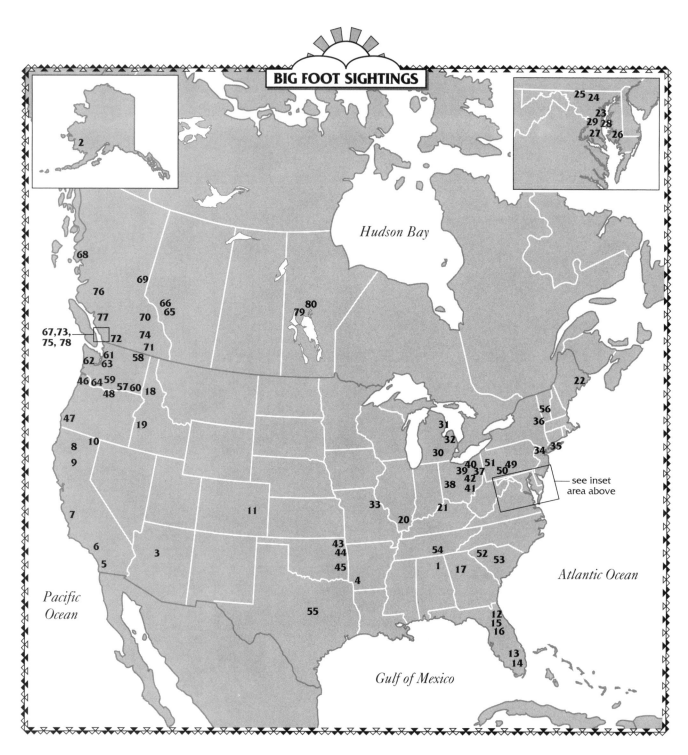

BIG FOOT SIGHTINGS

Hudson Bay

Pacific
Ocean

Atlantic Ocean

Gulf of Mexico

see inset
area above

(or no neck at all), a body covered entirely in fur, apelike features and usually an overpoweringly fetid, sulphurous body odor. Some of the creatures are predominantly gray-brown, while others sport reddish fur. Bigfoot has a large forehead and brow. He walks upright, unlike an ape or bear, and can run swiftly across rough terrain. His stride can reach from 40 to as much as 72 inches. He usually grows to about seven or eight feet in

height, but can be 10 feet. He's a hefty creature, weighing anywhere from 300 to 1,000 pounds, and can be either a vegetarian or an omnivore.

Bigfoot is mostly a nocturnal creature, extremely shy, and prefers to live in dense, wooded areas, perhaps in caves. He has been spotted alone most often, but occasionally accompanied by an apparent female or young one. His eyes are usually described as red and reflect light in the same way a cat's eyes do. Some who have encountered Bigfoot say the creature makes a fearful screaming noise; others say he mumbles what sounds like "boom, boom." He has faithful followers, who long for verifiable proof of his existence, and detractors who doubt the sanity of his fans.

The creature, generally lumped in the category of Big Hairy Monsters or BHMs, goes by many names. In the Pacific Northwest, where Bigfoot feels most at home, he answers to Sasquatch, from the Salish Indian word for "wild man" or "hairy man." A cousin of the Abominable Snowman ("abominable" is the English translation for the Tibetan word for stench), he is known as Alma or Almasty in Russia, Yeti in the Himalayas, Kangmi in Tibet and Kaptar in the Caucasus. In the South Pacific, Australians call him Yowie and New Zealanders know him as the Great Hairy Moehau. To Nicaraguans, he is the monkey man Xipe, and Guatemalans call him El Sisemite. He resembles the Big Grey Man of Ben Mac-Dhui in Scotland, although "Benny" is 20 feet tall.

The term "Bigfoot" was coined in August 1958, when Jerry Crew, an employee of contractor Ray Wallace, allegedly found mysterious large, humanoid footprints near Bluff Creek, in northern California. The story was carried by media around the country.

Stories about such wild and hairy creatures appear in Indian lore long before the coming of the white man. Algonquin Indians in eastern Canada told of a *windigo*, or a spectral man with no clothes, with cannibalistic habits. One of the earliest European accounts comes from Spanish naturalist José Mariano Mozino as he accompanied Juan Francisco de la Bodega y Quadra on his exploration of the British Columbian coast in 1792. Mozino wrote about a monstrous Matlox, covered in black animal hair with a human head, long sharp teeth and huge arms that struck terror in the local inhabitants.

Some believe Bigfoot is a leftover from Giganto pithecus, one of modern man's forebears. Numerous historical accounts tell of such wild men with excessive body hair all over the world, although western science does not recognize their existence. Mark Chorvinsky, editor and publisher of *Strange* magazine, makes a case for real wild men, who have contributed to the Bigfoot legend.

The study of hidden animals—creatures believed to exist but not yet proven conclusively—is called cryptozoology. One of America's leading cryptozoologists is Dr. Grover Krantz, an anthropologist at Washington State University in Pullman and active "Sasquatchologist." Dr. Krantz firmly believes that no one in the scientific community will accept Bigfoot until a carcass can be brought in for examination and autopsy. Many of his colleagues agree.

Unfortunately, Bigfoot's nature and penchant for surprise appearances make tracking the creature with nothing but a camcorder highly difficult. The most conclusive film footage to date was shot by Roger Patterson and Bob Gimlin, two hunters who captured what they called Bigfoot near Bluff Creek in Del Norte County, California, on October 20, 1967, in the same area as the Wallace Footprints of 1958. Other video evidence since has been judged a hoax. Researchers have been left to glean what proof they can from plaster casts of footprints and handprints, a few dried droppings and the earnest accounts of witnesses.

Since 1958, Wallace has claimed to have seen numerous Bigfoot creatures, and to have filmed them on many occasions. He also has acknowledged to Chorvinsky that he told Patterson where to go to try to capture Bigfoot on film. The Patterson creature closely resembles a Bigfoot photographed by Wallace.

Bigfoot Sightings

Encounters with Bigfoot, and creatures resembling Bigfoot, number in the thousands. The following are some of the more notable ones recorded:

UNITED STATES

Alabama ✤

Arab (1) Barbara Demers spotted Bigfoot near the side of Ruth Road in October 1989. First she saw the creature's red eyes, then she noticed it crouching in the underbrush. When it stood up, it was taller than her van and weighed 300 to 400 pounds. It crossed the road in front of the van with one step and disappeared.

Alaska ✤

Manokotak (2) Passengers on a MarkAir flight from Togiak to Manokotak reported seeing the Hairy Man, a large, hairy, apelike creature, west of here in November 1992. Pilot Randy Quinto circled to allow the passengers to get another look. Riders confirmed the sighting, but Quinto never saw the creature.

Arizona ✤

Paulden (3) Lyle Vann, director of the Arizona Bigfoot Center here claims to see Bigfoot often while hiking in the rugged parts of northern and central Arizona. He claims the beasts are nocturnal and live in caves, whose sulphurous emissions give the creatures their miserable smell. He also believes aliens control the gentle giants in order to mine gold and silver.

Arkansas ✚

Miller County (4) The home of the legendary Fouke Monster has been the site of Bigfoot encounters since the 1940s. The most recent was by Oklahoman Jim Walls in October 1990. Walls and his friend Charles Humbert were heading north along U.S. Highway 71 when they saw a large, furry, smelly creature run along a riverbank and then jump down the 30-foot embankment and disappear. Walls also heard the creature's piercing scream.

In 1979, Tracy Wilson, then a small child, saw Bigfoot while she was outside playing. The monster was only 30 yards away from her, and she remembers getting up slowly and walking back inside the house, where she hid under an afghan until her mother returned home.

The most famous incident at Fouke occurred in May 1971, when Bobby Ford reported that a large, hairy creature attacked him. A large paw came through Ford's house window, and later pulled him to the ground when he went outside. The encounter became the plot for the movie *The Legend of Boggy Creek* a year later.

California ✚

Alpine (5) Although Bigfoot has not been seen here, many residents report hearing weird screams and cries attributable to the monster.

Antelope Valley (6) Residents of the valley reported seeing Bigfoot seven times in 1973. On March 14, three Marines said the creature jumped in front of their car. Ten days later, a 19-year-old woman saw a seven-foot-tall beast rise up out of the grass near her trailer home and run away. An ex-Marine later in the year reported seeing Bigfoot near a telephone booth, where the foul-smelling creature sneezed like a human. Bigfoot has appeared occasionally in the valley both before and since 1973.

Big Sur (7) Virginia Swanson, a female miner after World War II, encountered Bigfoot while working her ore claims in the 1950s. Awakened by a powerful stench, she found herself and her cot being lifted off the ground. When she screamed, the beast put her down. She reported that she did not get a good look at him because her flashlight didn't work.

Bluff Creek/Willow Creek (8) Construction workers found hundreds of footprints at a work site here in 1958, accompanied by 55-gallon drums thrown about like toys. One worker was awakened by one of the creatures, who supposedly accepted a chocolate bar and left. Bigfoot researcher and author John Green of British Columbia traveled to Bluff Creek and did indeed find many tracks over 16 inches long and nearly one inch deep into the soil. His own prints barely scuffed the dirt.

At Bluff Creek, a now-famous film of Bigfoot was taken by Roger Patterson and Bob Gimlin, two amateur monster hunters who had been searching for several years to find and photograph a Bigfoot. On October 20, 1967, at the dry creek bed of Bluff Creek, Patterson's horse began to rear and snort, and the two men saw a black, fur-covered humanoid being walking across the creek bed on two legs, swinging its arms widely. Patterson was able to shoot a few hundred feet of film of what appeared to be a female creature with large, pendulous breasts. This film has been extensively studied, and most scientists who have seen it admit that it would be almost impossible to duplicate the anatomy and stride of the being in the film by using a man in a monkey suit. Patterson insisted on his deathbed that the film was genuine, and such a sophisticated hoax would indeed have been beyond his resources at the time. The Patterson-Gimlin film remains the strongest evidence to date.

More than four dozen Willow Creek residents claim to have seen Bigfoot, making the tiny northern California community the "Bigfoot Capital of the World." Locals have capitalized on the phenomenon, naming their stores and services after Bigfoot.

Butte County (9) Residents claimed to see Bigfoot seven times in 1969, mostly near the town of Oroville. Sightings continued into 1971, then ceased until 1991, when some residents of the Magalia-Stirling City area saw Bigfoot run across the road.

Fort Bidwell Paiute Indian Reservation (10) Kenneth Sam, a resident of the reservation, reported seeing a giant, hairy, manlike creature in June 1989. His cousin, Neasha Comanche, saw what she believes are baby Bigfoot prints, also on the reservation.

Colorado ✚

Green Mountain Falls (11) Residents of this small town west of Colorado Springs on Ute Pass Highway have reported long-armed, hairy creatures since 1944, when Bob White saw what he believes was Bigfoot on a Boy Scout camping trip.

In 1980, Dan Masias found strange footprints in the snow outside his home here. Then on March 28, 1987, Masias and his son Jeff saw two creatures running down a road that passes their house. In the summer of 1988, hairy, blond creatures crashed into the door of a nearby cabin, leaving long, light-brown hairs and overturning garbage cans. Prints found at the scene appeared more like a hoof with a clawlike spur on the side, much different than more traditional Bigfoot tracks. Masias's sighting has been recreated by NBC-TV's "Unsolved Mysteries" and investigated by former Omaha, Nebraska, English teacher and dedicated Bigfooter Bob Brienzo.

Florida ✛

Bardin (12) The Bardin Booger, legendary since the 1960s, appeared to a crowd hanging around the local church in 1981. The immense, apelike creature approached and scattered the frightened group. In 1987, Randy Medlock and his brother-in-law Ronny Cone encountered a huge creature with long, swinging arms while they were hunting at night. The beast's footprints were much larger than Medlock's size 13 tracks.

Broward County (13) The Skunk Ape is Florida's version of Bigfoot. The creature gets its name from its bad smell, which is like the odor of rotting vegetation. At the Manor Estates Trailer Park in Broward County, rabies control officers tracked two Skunk Apes, one of which appeared to be covered with sores. Skunk Apes often leave three-toed footprints, different from the five-toed tracks made by Bigfoot in the Northwestern states and in western Canada.

Also in Broward County, a rancher reported unusually large, humanlike tracks near the mutilated bodies of a calf and horse in 1973. An investigating highway patrolman said the footprints looked like an ape.

Dade County (14) A driver in 1974 claimed to hit a beast seven or eight feet tall covered in dark-colored hair.

Gainesville (15) A man claimed he fired four shots at an ape man who jumped at him in 1974.

Ocala Forest (16) Large footprints, complete with toes, were discovered in the forest in 1980. Given the print size and impression, sheriff's investigators estimated the beast weighed close to 1,000 pounds and stood 10 to 12 feet tall.

Georgia ✛

Dog River (17) Residents of this Atlanta suburb heard strange growls in early 1992 accompanied by the slaughter or disappearance of family cats and dogs. Not called Bigfoot in these parts, the creature—sometimes described as being a humanoid with seal skin and clawed feet—goes by the name Skunk Ape, so called because he smells awful.

Idaho ✛

Lapwai (18) Eight witnesses reported seeing a large, hairy creature descending a hillside in the Nez Perce National Historical Park near Spalding. Three or four lines of tracks with a long stride were found on the hill, although the prints were smaller than usual Bigfoot tracks.

Payette National Forest (19) A man driving along U.S. Highway 95 in 1980 reported seeing two creatures walk by the road then jump over the embankment in one step.

Illinois ✛

Murphysboro (20) Residents and campers near the wooded community reported seeing a smelly creature several times during 1973, as well as hearing it scream.

Kentucky ✛

Trimble County (21) Reports of a gorillalike creature that walked on its hind legs surfaced in 1962, witnessed by farmers Owen Powell and Byrd Varble. In 1972, Steve Jackson was hiking near a cave when he discovered hog blood running over a cliff. He and a friend threw a rock up to the cave area and saw a Bigfoot run off after emitting a low growl.

In 1977 or 1978, Teresa Wise and Elaine McCutchen saw a creature about six feet tall with green eyes standing at night in some cattails. Also in the mid-seventies, two boys were parked along a gravel road when an inquisitive gray paw reached in their car window and searched for the dashboard lights.

In 1980, Steve Jackson again heard about a gorillalike beast that was shaking trailer homes so hard that dishes were breaking. Residents were terrified.

Maine ✛

Ellsworth (22) Artist Jay Adams claims to have seen Bigfoot several times near his home here, in the Acadia National Park and also in New Jersey. His primitive paintings often include two red eyes secretly watching the other figures in the scene.

Maryland ✛

Anne Arundel County (23) In August 1978, Tracy's Landing resident Ronald L. Jones spotted an eight-foot-tall creature at the intersection of Brooks Woods Road and Route 258. Jones reportedly hit the beast with a tire iron, then drove away as the Bigfoot chased his truck. Bigfoot researcher Mark Opsasnick of Greenbelt reports at least nine encounters with Bigfoot in the county.

Baltimore County (24) Opsasnick reports at least 49 sightings in Baltimore County, most of them in the

1970s. In 1975, police officer Gordon Clark investigated a man who claimed to find Bigfoot in his backyard. The man squirted the creature with the garden hose. About 2:00 A.M. a few nights later, Officer Clark saw what he described as "two hairy tree stumps" running across the road. He and a canine patrol tracked the scent for about three miles but lost it on another highway.

Carroll County (25) During May and June 1973, the Sykesville Monster appeared 20 times to area residents. Anthony Dorsey of Sykesville heard his dogs barking on May 29 and followed them into the woods. His flashlight found two red eyes about seven feet above ground. Five nights later Bessie and Elston Gassaway and Diane Coleman discovered an eight-foot-tall creature walking through their backyards, also in Sykesville. Carroll County residents have spotted Bigfoot 48 times.

Dorchester County (26) Bigfoot was seen several times around the Blackwater National Wildlife Refuge in 1967. During the 1950s and 1960s, county residents reported unearthly screams from Green Briar Swamp. The swamp is the legendary home of Big Liz, the ghost of a slave killed while guarding her master's gold from invading Union troops.

Prince George's County (27) County police responded to a call reporting a gorilla-type animal running into a cornfield near the Beltsville Agricultural Research Center in August 1982. In March 1977, a NASA engineer sighted a Bigfoot tossing a large dog across Interstate 95 where it runs under Powder Mill Road, also in Beltsville.

On a rainy morning in the fall of 1976, Francine Abell saw a gorillalike beast walk in front of her car on Route 198. The creature was tall, round-shouldered and covered with grayish-brown fur. Its eyes reflected red in the headlights. After seeing her car, the creature stepped over the guard rail and disappeared.

Scaggsville (28) A 30-year-old man who wished to remain anonymous reported seeing a nine-foot-tall creature in his backyard on January 15, 1988. This was the first reported sighting of a Bigfoot creature in Maryland in six years, according to researcher Opsasnick.

Spencerville (29) Martha Kelley reported that her son saw a large, hairy creature with long arms and no neck along the banks of the Patuxent River in September 1978. The creature also was seen by landfill workers as it rummaged through garbage. After her son saw the beast a second time, he made a cast of the 13-inch by 5-inch footprints. The prints had four toes. Landfill workers spotted the creature again in October, and one worker, Willard McIntire, found prints with three toes.

Altogether, Opsasnick has collected over 200 modern sightings in Maryland, with 49 in Baltimore County; 48 in Carroll; 47 in Harford; 32 in Prince George's; 22 in

Frederick; nine in Anne Arundel; six each in Montgomery and Somerset; five each in Calvert and Howard; four in Garrett; three in Dorchester; two each in Charles, Worcester and Cecil; and one each in Washington and Wicomico. Since the 1600s, when Piscataway and Susquehanna Indians worshiped giant, hairy half-men and painted the creatures on their breastplates, Opsasnick has collected 339 reported sightings.

Michigan ✤

Lost Nations State Game Area (30) Squirrel hunters spotted huge footprints alongside a wooded path in Hillsdale County in February 1989.

Oscoda County (31) Two teenagers reported seeing a dark, upright, hairy creature in Foley Swamp Huron National Forest on September 28, 1990. Hunters report seeing Bigfoot-like monsters nearly every autumn.

Tuscola County (32) Two drivers near Mayville spotted a pair of beasts on Pattison Road in January 1992. Both creatures—ranging in size from seven to eight feet and 500 to 600 pounds, to five feet and 300 to 400 pounds—seemed unperturbed by the auto headlights and began walking toward the stopped car when the men jumped back in and drove off. According to Mayville researcher Wayne King, there have been 38 sightings of the beast in Tuscola County since 1977.

Missouri ✤

Elsberry (33) Harley Rutledge of Cape Girardeau was on a campout with friends in July 1978. At about 2:00 A.M., they found a mutilated calf, and then they remember smelling a terrible, sulphurous odor. He never saw Bigfoot, but believes the creature was responsible for the calf.

Cliff LaBrecque of Raytown also believes Bigfoot mutilated cattle in Webster County and scared cattle in Ozark County during April 1992. He claims to have shot at Bigfoot in 1977, but was grabbed by the creature. LaBrecque says Bigfoot talked to him telepathically, asking, "What in the hell are you doing?" LaBrecque also notes that mid-April is the migrating season for the creatures, known in Missouri as MoMo (the Missouri Monster).

New Jersey ✤

Sussex County (34) In May 1977, a farmer in Wantage, in rural upstate New Jersey, claimed a Bigfoot creature broke down an inch-thick oak door and killed his rabbits. Some had their heads missing, some were twisted and crushed, and there was no blood. That night the family saw a big, hairy, brown creature standing in the yard lights; the beast appeared quite human, with an apparent beard and mustache. It had no neck and red, glowing eyes. The next night (Friday the 13th!), four adults waited with loaded guns for the creature to reappear, and it obliged the shooters at dusk. The farmer shot at the beast three or four times, claiming to hit it, but the animal merely growled and ran off. It reappeared days later apparently injured, but no body was found.

New York ✤

Hampton (35) A teenager walking down Route 22A South spotted a dark figure by the roadside on August 18, 1989. On August 24th, the young man and a friend camped near the site of the first incident and sensed something watching them. The boys saw oblong red eyes about six feet off the ground. Footprints measuring 10.5 inches by 4.5 inches with a stride of 56 inches were found. The boys' encounter fell on the 13th anniversary of a similar sighting in 1976, when nine witnesses saw a large, hairy, red-eyed creature walking upright into the woods. On August 28th, following the boys' sighting, area residents heard high-pitched screams.

Whitehall (36) Sheriff's deputies chased and tracked a Bigfoot creature in 1976. Most of the upstate sightings have occurred near Whitehall or Kinderhook, south of Albany. Whitehall is several miles from Hampton.

Ohio ✤

Alliance (37) In this farming community just 50 miles from Cleveland, Ron Brunner saw a nine-foot-tall creature in a field across from his house in December 1991. The sighting was investigated by researcher Robert W. Morgan of Montana, who claims to have seen Bigfoot while hunting in Washington State in 1957. Morgan believes there are 18 of the beasts living in Ohio and about 2,500 in North America.

Champaign County (38) A large, light-brown, furry and smelly creature, walking upright, was sighted several times in 1989.

Coshocton County (39) Several sightings occurred here in late December 1988 and early 1989. Footprints were discovered.

Euclid Creek Reservation (40) Hikers in 1982 spotted what they believed were bears until the animals stood up. Following that encounter, more sightings occurred in nearby Magadore, Solon and Brecksville.

Salt Fork Wildlife Area (41) A Bigfoot lifted the back of a pickup truck with a ranger asleep inside in late 1988.

Tuscarawas County (42) Researcher Don Keating says that there were 36 Bigfoot sightings in the county during 1989. Keating pleaded with hunters not to shoot the creature but instead to report any encounters to him.

Oklahoma ✤

Adair County (43) Residents spotted what they described as Bigfoot several times in the early 1970s. Cherokee legends dating back to the last century talk about tall, hairy beasts in various parts of the state.

Cherokee County (44) Bigfoot was sighted outside the Doss mobile home here near Tahlequah, close to the Arkansas border, in August 1990. Briefly seen on August 1 by Jeanie Moore, Bigfoot was discovered a few days later by eight-year-old Janet Doss after she stormed outside during an argument with her mother. Janet found the animal rummaging in the garbage, and when she hushed so quickly, her mother came outside and saw the creature as well. He was covered in black fur except for the face, which was white, and he smelled like rotten eggs and a wet dog. The creature continued to eat the Dosses' table scraps for three weeks or more, emitting the same foul odor. It also gave off high-pitched screams that unnerved the family.

McCurtain County (45) Hunter Joe Atwood reported seeing two creatures he believed were Bigfoot in 1989. He said they made such unearthly screams that his dogs wouldn't go into the woods.

Oregon ✤

Mt. Jefferson (46) Two fisherman saw a pair of monsters on the shores of the Columbia River in 1972. The creatures, described as graceful and not at all fierce, disappeared after staring intently at the anglers.

Rogue River National Forest (47) Following a sighting of 18-inch tracks in Perry Lovell's garden near the Applegate River in 1974, rangers built a Sasquatch trap. The 10-foot-square wooden box is reinforced with steel bolts and plates and attached to poles. The door is a metal grate in a steel frame. The rangers baited the trap with rabbits, enticing Bigfoot to grab for a rabbit and pull down the door. The trap remains in the forest but is no longer baited.

The Dalles (48) There have been sightings of Bigfoot in this area of the Columbia River Gorge since 1810. All of the more recent sightings occurred around Crate's Point: three in 1969, two in 1972 and two in August 1989.

Pennsylvania ✤

Chestnut Ridge (49) Bob France, an outdoorsman from Latrobe, encountered Bigfoot on December 12, 1988, while deer hunting. The tall, dark, hairy creature got France's attention by throwing something at him, but France also smelled the beast's rancid odor. France started to shoot at the creature, but found it too human-like for him to kill.

Somerset County   (50) A homeowner in Scullton was awakened in June 1992 by his barking dogs, and when he arose to investigate, he saw a humanlike creature looking in his living room window. The beast was almost nine feet tall and over three feet wide and completely covered with hair. When the homeowner turned on the front light, the creature disappeared. About a year earlier, the man's young son reported seeing Bigfoot, and in May of 1988, the man's 21-year-old daughter saw Bigfoot standing in the woods not far from the house's driveway.

Another witness in Rockwood reported discovering a tall, hairy creature standing in the road one morning as she drove four teenagers to school. Reported sightings in the county date back to 1981.

Wheatland   (51) Chris Baroni and his wife, Diana, became believers in March 1989 when they followed their barking dogs into the woods the night of the 13th. They both heard crunching noises in the brush and the footsteps of a two-footed animal. Large footprints, measuring 11.5 inches long and 7.5 inches wide, were found in the dirt spaced about 72 inches apart. The one-inch impressions indicated that the creature weighed 600 to 700 pounds.

Pennsylvania researcher Stan Gordon reports that Chestnut Ridge, the Monongahela River Valley and western parts of the state are the most common Bigfoot sites, with over 130 incidents in the last 20 years.

South Carolina   ✥

Laurens   (52) Martha Tollison reported seeing a tall creature beside the road while she was driving near Cold Point in May 1989. Not long thereafter, Arlene McCall reported that something tall, dark and with long arms stood in her path while she was driving home from work; when her car headlights hit the animal, its red eyes glowed. Cold Point residents Ken and Pam Treadway, along with some of their neighbors, rode out on horseback with dogs to track the creature, but found nothing.

Richland County   (53) In September 1992, Sylvester Arnold and his wife encountered a huge, black-furred creature walking toward them swinging its arms while they were walking along railroad tracks near the Wateree River. When Arnold fired a .22-caliber shot into the air, the creature ran off. Footprints were found later near the tracks.

Tennessee   ✥

Flintville   (54) Ever since the spring of 1976, some residents of this farming town in the Appalachian foothills say they have been bothered by a Bigfoot creature that attacks cars and leaves behind 16-inch footprints and a terrible odor. Several have seen Bigfoot from their cars and homes, and one small boy was nearly kidnapped in April 1976. His mother, Jennie Robertson, ran outside when her four-year-old son, Gary, screamed. She saw the black furry beast round the corner of the house and come up to the child. Just before Bigfoot could grab the boy, his mother snatched him up and ran back into the house.

Neighbors armed with shotguns roamed the woods looking for the boy's attacker. Several rounds were fired into the bushes, followed by screams and thrown rocks. Although no one ever saw the creature, deep 16-inch footprints, blood and mucus were found. Hair samples were analyzed but could not be identified.

Texas   ✥

Hamilton   (55) Someone using the name Daniel Fisker wrote the *Hamilton Herald-News* to report seeing a huge, hairy creature on the riverbank outside Stephenville. No one in this small town knew a Daniel Fisker, but all the interest sparked resident Hilda Lunsford to tell of her Bigfoot encounter in 1985 while driving between Olin and Cranfills Gap. Prior to the closing of the Texas Bigfoot Research Society in 1978, 30 sightings had been reported in the state.

Vermont   ✥

Rutland   (56) Locals reported several Bigfoot sightings about the same time each year during the 1970s in this town near New York State, leading researchers to speculate that the creatures migrated through the area.

Washington   ✥

Blue Mountains   (57) This area about 35 miles east of Walla Walla has yielded several reported sightings of Bigfoot, some to former Forest Service official Paul Freeman. Freeman first encountered Bigfoot in June 1982, when he saw the reddish-brown, eight-foot giant while patrolling a watershed area. In January 1991, tracks appeared near Mill Creek that Freeman identified as those of Bigfoot, and a year later, tracks appeared at almost the same place. The 1992 discovery yielded footprints and a handprint the size of a baseball mitt.

In April 1992, Freeman saw Bigfoot again, something he'd yearned for since the first sighting. This time he captured the black-furred creature on videotape, but unfortunately Freeman forgot to use the camera's zoom feature, thus details are not visible.

Freeman encountered two creatures at Deduct Spring, near Mill Creek, on August 20, 1992, an event that nearly made him quit looking for the giants. He again videotaped the incident, but this time the tape was good enough to interest the producers of television's "Hard Copy." When the crew arrived in September to film Freeman and the area, they were rewarded with the discovery of more fresh tracks.

One of Freeman's neighbors and another veteran Bigfoot researcher, Wes Sumerlin, claims to have seen the creature three times in the Blues, the first in 1962. At that time, Sumerlin says the monster was shot by some elk hunters but escaped, only to be observed two days later near a stream stuffing leaves and pine needles into a large, bleeding wound in its abdomen.

Bossburg   (58) One thousand eighty-nine footprints were found at a garbage dump here in 1969. Some of the prints showed a club foot, with a raised or missing middle toe.

Carson   (59) Farmer Datus Perry says he has seen and heard Bigfoot so often near his property that he doesn't pay any attention to the creature any more. He has an audiotape of Bigfoot's angry, muffled roar, described as worse than any punk rock record.

Couse Creek   (60) A cattle rancher who had been running his herd in the Touchet Valley in eastern Washington for 40 years encountered a Bigfoot in the summer of 1992. The creature frightened his horse, who reared and ran off. Another Touchet Valley resident said a Bigfoot tried to scratch his way into her cabin in 1947 and again in 1953.

Duvall   (61) Cliff Crook of Bothell has been looking for Bigfoot ever since he encountered the creature on a camping trip in 1956. Crook and three teenage friends heard something in the woods and took a piece of burning log with them to investigate. The creature reared up on its hind legs, cried something like "Agar Lar-gar" (which Crook understood to mean "get out of here"), and threw the German Shepherd that had accompanied the boys back into the firelight.

Grays Harbor County   (62) Several sightings of Bigfoot have been reported in this oceanside area since 1982. Deep footprints, more than nine feet apart, indicate the creature stood more than seven feet tall and weighed more than 600 pounds. Hairs found at the Porter Creek site were sent to the Arizona State Museum's Human Identification Laboratory, but were not found to resemble any known primate.

Mount Rainier   (63) Two separate groups of mushroom pickers on Mount Rainier south of Seattle reported hearing noises in the bush and smelling an awful odor in early September 1990. When they investigated, they found huge footprints spaced two and a half times the normal stride of a man.

Yacolt   (64) Brenda Goldammer and her teenage stepson, Nickolas, were inside their home on a Sunday night in June 1989 when they heard screeching outside. Their dogs were barking crazily, and the two went outside to investigate. They discovered a big, hairy, gorillalike creature standing six or seven feet tall and weighing 300 to 400 pounds. Nickolas chased the beast, who turned and disappeared.

CANADA

Alberta ✤

Big Horn   (65) A "silent watcher" lurks about the Big Horn Dam. Observed in 1969 by five construction workers, it was estimated to be between 12 and 15 feet tall.

Jasper   (66) Supposedly the first white man to find evidence of the Sasquatch here was fur trader David Thompson, who discovered huge footprints in the ice while crossing the Canadian Rockies in January 1811.

British Columbia ✤

Chehalis Indian Reserve   (67) The name Sasquatch originated here, where numerous sightings of the creature have been reported. The reserve is located along the Harrison River near Chilliwack.

Cougar Lake   (68) In 1915, three prospectors saw an eight-foot-tall Sasquatch eating berries. It was light brown, standing upright and bearish-looking. It disappeared when it heard the men.

Dawson Creek   (69) Four members of a gas drilling operation southwest of the creek witnessed a Sasquatch moving through the trees on several occasions in March 1987. Many footprints were later found.

Mica Mountain   (70) Mica Mountain is located in the Monashee range near the Alberta border. In 1955, a climber in search of a deserted mine came upon a female Sasquatch dining on leaves. The creature was about six feet tall, nearly three feet wide, and weighed an estimated 300 pounds. It had breasts, and was covered with dark brown, silver-tipped hair. It walked rapidly away when it noticed the man watching it from about 20 feet away.

Nelson (71) A berry picker encountered competition from a Sasquatch also wanting a sweet treat in October 1960. The witness described the creature as covered in bluish-gray hair and standing seven to nine feet tall.

Ruby Creek (72) A mother and two young children fled from a Sasquatch they believed was chasing them in October 1941. One account states that the creature followed them to a river and drank after overturning a barrel of salted fish. Sixteen-inch footprints were later found circling the farmhouse and a nearby shed. Witnesses reported Sasquatch sightings in the Ruby Creek area for the next 50 years.

Sechelt (73) In June 1973, a huge, hairy creature was seen on an extension of a logging road near Mile Nine of Chapman Creek. The creature, which had a goatee, jumped up and down and did a somersault. Footprints were later found in the mud.

Silver Creek (74) In either 1939 or 1940, a prospector came upon four or five Sasquatch wrestling each other near the headwaters of Silver Creek, near Harrison Hot Springs. The creatures were about seven feet tall and weighed an estimated 400 pounds each. Their play lasted for about half an hour, and then they disappeared into the woods.

Squamish (75) While working on a ski development north of here in April 1969, builders found several miles of 14-inch footprints in the snow. Researchers speculated that the creature was stripping spruce buds off trees and eating them. Eight months later, a driver in the same vicinity reported seeing a large, hairy humanlike animal run across the road carrying a fish in its hands.

Stuart River (76) Walter Patrick found large footprints in the clay riverbank in September 1989. The prints, about 17 inches long, left impressions two inches deep. They had five toes and a strange, spurlike bump on the heel.

Toba Inlet (77) In the summer of 1924, Albert Ostman was camping in the mountains behind the inlet. One night, as he lay dozing, his sleeping bag was picked up and carried off through the forest. He traveled for about three hours, feeling very uncomfortable and unable to move. When he was finally put down and able to get some air, he discovered he was among four Sasquatch creatures, two big and two small: a family. He believed he had been kidnapped as a mate for the daughter.

Ostman described his captors as covered in hair and standing about seven feet tall. The young male, ostensibly the son, weighed about 300 pounds, had wide jaws, a narrow forehead and a chest about 55 inches around. The older female, or mother, weighed about 500 to 600 pounds and had very wide hips. The older male stood about eight feet tall and had a big barrel chest and powerful back and arm muscles. He had wide hands and fingernails like chisels. The only places they had no hair were on their palms, the soles of their feet and the upper part of the nose and eyelids. The soles of the creatures' feet were padded, and the big toe was quite strong and longer than the rest, enabling the animals to climb rocks with ease. Ostman couldn't see the animals' ears, as they were covered with hair.

Ostman, although he had ammunition for his rifle, decided to stay with the Sasquatches until he could make a safe escape.

After several days, he was able to leave when the older male stole all of Ostman's snuff and swallowed it. The Sasquatch was soon in distress and ran for water. While the others watched in confusion, Ostman escaped, eventually making his way back to a logging camp and eventually to Vancouver.

Thirty years later, Ostman signed a legal document verifying his account of life with the Sasquatches, maintaining the truth of his story and the creatures' presence in the Canadian woods.

Yale (78) On July 3, 1884, a young specimen of Bigfoot allegedly was captured by a train crew that found the animal sleeping by the railroad tracks outside of Yale. The creature was named Jacko, and was said to be four feet, seven inches tall, and covered with glossy black hair. The incident was reported in detail in the local newspaper, leading some researchers to conclude that the story was just a newspaper hoax. However, in 1959, an elderly resident of Yale was found who remembered the capture of Jacko, and who said that the young apeman was sent off to London. This is another classic monster tale that has been reproduced in virtually every book dealing with Bigfoot. It has been suggested that Jacko might have been an escaped chimpanzee.

Manitoba ✚

Cedar Lake (79) Sightings of Bigfoot began south of here in 1968, shortly after a new road was opened through the bush country. One observed creature was about nine feet tall and covered with short hair.

Landry Lake (80) In 1974, three huge footprints, 21 inches long and seven inches wide, were discovered in fresh mud. Photographs of the so-called Uchtmann Tracks, named after their discoverer, R. H. Uchtmann, were sent to the Manitoba Museum of Man.

ORGANIZATIONS AND PUBLICATIONS

There are numerous organizations and publications, many of them small, devoted to researching and reporting on the subjects in this book. Most of the organizations publish newsletters, magazines or journals. Also, most of them operate on limited budgets. Please help them by enclosing a self-addressed, stamped envelope when you write to inquire about membership and subscriptions.

State folklore societies may have additional information on other local and regional organizations.

The following is a list of some of the organizations, researchers and publications related to the subjects in the atlas.

Organizations and Researchers

Lyle Vann
Arizona Bigfoot Center
P.O. Box 412
Paulden, AZ 86334

International Society of Cryptozoology
P.O. Box 43070
Tucson, AZ 85733
(602) 884-8369

Borderland Sciences Research Foundation
P.O. Box 429
Garberville, CA 95440

Ghost Research Society
Dale Kaczmarek, president
P.O. Box 205
Oaklawn, IL 60454-0205

Mark Opsasnick
Bigfoot Information Project
(affiliate of Strange Research)
114 Rosewood Drive
Greenbelt, MD 20770
(301) 985-5408

Mark Chorvinsky
Strange Research
P.O. Box 2246
Rockville, MD 20852
(301) 881-3530

Wayne W. King
Michigan/Canadian Bigfoot Information Center
Caro, MI 48723
(616) 673-2715

Art Kapa
Bigfoot Investigation Center
4180 Cat Lake Road
Mayville, MI 48744
(517) 843-6302

American Society for Psychical Research
5 West 73rd Street
New York, NY 10023
(212) 799-5050

New York Fortean Society
John Keel, president
Box 22024
New York, NY 10025

International Society for the Study of Ghosts and Apparitions
Jeanne D. Youngson, president
29 Washington Square West PHN
New York, NY 10011
(212) 533-5018

Lake Champlain Phenomena Investigation
P.O. Box 2134
Wilton, NY 12866

North American Bigfoot Information Network
1923 Glenwood Drive
Twinsburg, OH 44087

Stan Gordon
Pennsylvania Association for Study of the Unexplained
6 Oak Hill Avenue
Greensburg, PA 15601
(412) 838-7768

International Fortean Organization
P.O. Box 367
Arlington, VA 22210

John Andrews
Camano Island, WA 98292
(206) 387-9692

Cliff Crook
Bigfoot Central
P.O. Box 147
Bothell, WA 98041
(206) 483-4007

Publications

FATE Magazine
170 Future Way
Box 1940
Marion, OH 43306-2040
(800) THE-MOON

Fortean Times
Box 2409
London NW5 4NP
United Kingdom

Ghost Tracker's Newsletter
(see Ghost Research Society above)

INFO Journal
(see International Fortean Organization above)

Pebbles
RDM Publications
P.O. Box 469
Arlington, VA 22210-0469

Strange Magazine
P.O. Box 2246
Rockville, MD 20847
(301) 460-4789 phone
(301) 460-1959 fax

BIBLIOGRAPHY AND SUGGESTED READING

General

A number of books provided information for several sections in this book. Among them are:

Brandon, Jim. *Weird America*. New York: Dutton, 1978.

Coleman, Loren. *Mysterious America*. London & Boston: Faber & Faber, 1983.

Colombo, John Robert. *Mysterious Canada*. Toronto: Doubleday Canada Ltd., 1988.

Guiley, Rosemary Ellen. *The Encyclopedia of Ghosts and Spirits*. New York: Facts On File, 1992.

Power Points and Sacred Places

Dane, Christopher. *The American Indian and the Occult*. New York: Popular Library, 1973.

Davidson, Alison, and Tom Brown. "Chaco Canyon: One of the Great Wonders of the World." *Journal of Borderland Research*. November–December 1992, pp. 1–8.

Devereux, Paul. *Places of Power*. London: Blandford, 1990.

————. *Secrets of Ancient and Sacred Places*. London: Blandford, 1992.

Folsom, Franklin, and Mary Etling Folsom. *America's Ancient Treasures*. 3rd ed. Albuquerque: University of New Mexico Press, 1983.

Furneaux, Robert. *Ancient Mysteries*. New York: McGraw Hill, 1977.

Greenberg, Ronald M., and Sarah A. Marusin, eds. *The National Register of Historic Places, 1976*. Washington: National Park Service, 1976.

Holzer, Hans. *America's Mysterious Places*. Stamford, Conn.: Longmeadow Press, 1992.

Joseph, Frank, ed. *Sacred Sites: A Guidebook to Sacred Centers and Mysterious Places in the United States*. St. Paul, Minn.: Llewellyn Publications, 1992.

Kirby, Doug; Ken Smith; and Mike Wilkins. *The New Roadside America*. New York: Simon and Schuster, 1992.

Mann, Nicholas R. *Ancient Lore, Modern Myths: A Guide to the Red Rock Country*. Prescott, Ariz.: Zivah, 1989.

Mavor, James W., and Byron Dix. *Manitou: The Sacred Landscape of New England's Native Civilization*. Rochester, Vt.: Inner Traditions International, 1989.

Mysterious Lands and Peoples. Alexandria, Va.: Time-Life Books, 1991.

Peterson, Natasha. *Sacred Sites: A Traveler's Guide to North America's Most Powerful, Mystical Landmarks*. Chicago: Contemporary Books, 1988.

Stern, Jane and Michael. *Amazing America*. New York: Random House, 1978.

Swan, James A., ed. *The Power of Place*. Wheaton, Ill.: Quest Books, 1991.

Terrell, John Upton. *American Indian Almanac*. New York and Cleveland: World Publishing Co., 1971.

Versluis, Arthur. *Sacred Earth: The Spiritual Landscape of Native America*. Rochester, Vt.: Inner Traditions International, 1992.

Earthworks and Mounds

(Many of the titles listed above were used for this section as well.)

Bridges, Marilyn. *Markings: Aerial Views of Sacred Landscapes*. New York: Aperture, 1986.

Capes, Katherine H. *The W. B. Nickerson Survey and Excavations, 1912–1950, of the Southern Manitoba Mounds Region*. National Museum of Canada Anthropology Papers. Ottawa: Department of Northern Affairs and Natural Resources, 1963.

Coe, Michael; Dean Snow; and Elizabeth Benson. *Atlas of Ancient America*. New York: Facts On File, 1986.

Kenyon, W. A. *Mounds of Sacred Earth: Burial Mounds of Ontario*. Royal Ontario Museum, 1986.

Korp, Maureen. *The Sacred Geography of the American Mound Builders*. Lewiston, England: Edwin Mellen Press, 1990.

Lewis, T. H. "Effigy Mounds in Northern Illinois." *Science*, September 7, 1988, pp. 1–3.

MacCord, Howard A. *The Lewis Creek Mound Culture in Virginia*. Richmond, Va.: Privately printed, 1986.

Mainfort, Robert C. *Pinson Mounds*. Tennessee Department of Conservation, Division of Archeology, Research Series, No. 7, 1986.

McDonald, Jerry N., and Susan L. Woodward. *Indian Mounds of the Atlantic Coast*. Newark, Ohio: McDonald and Woodward Publishing Co., 1987.

Radin, Paul. *The Winnebago Tribe*. Lincoln: University of Nebraska Press, 1970.

Ritchie, William A. "Certain Recently Explored New York Mounds and their Probable Relation to the Hopewell Culture." *Research Records of the Rochester Museum of Arts and Sciences No. 4*. Rochester, N. Y. 1938.

Waldman, Carl. *Atlas of the North American Indian*. New York: Facts On File, 1985.

Westwood, Jennifer, ed. *The Atlas of Mysterious Places*. New York: Weidenfeld and Nicolson, 1987.

Woodward, Susan L., and Jerry N. McDonald. *Indian Mounds of the Middle Ohio Valley*. Newark, Ohio: McDonald and Woodward Publishing Co., 1986.

Stoneworks

General

Fell, Barry. *America B. C.* New York: Simon and Schuster, 1976.

———. *Saga America*. New York: Times Books, 1980.

Fergusen, James. *Rude Stone Monuments*. London: Murray, 1872.

Hitching, Francis. *Earth Magic*. New York: William Morrow, 1977.

Trento, Salvatore Michael. *The Search for Lost America*. Chicago: Contemporary Books, 1978.

Medicine Wheels

Brumley, John H. *Medicine Wheels on the Northern Plains: A Summary and Appraisal*. Archaeological Survey of Alberta Manuscript Series No. 12. Alberta Culture and Multiculturalism Historical Resources Division, 1988.

Hall, Robert L. "Medicine Wheels, Sun Circles, and the Magic of World Center Shrines." *Plains Anthropologist*, 1985, vol. 30, pp. 181–193.

Kehoe, Thomas F., and Alice B. Kehoe. "Stones, Solstices and Sun Dance Structures." *Plains Anthropologist*, 1977, vol. 22, pp. 85–95.

Williamson, Ray A., ed. *Archaeoastronomy in the Americas*. Center for Archaeoastronomy Technical Report No. 1. Santa Fe, 1979.

Williamson, Ray A. *Living the Sky: The Cosmos of the American Indian*. Boston: Houghton Mifflin Co., 1984.

Wilson, Michael. "Sun Dances, Thirst Dances, and Medicine Wheels: A Search for Alternative Hypotheses." *Megaliths to Medicine Wheels*. Edited by Michael Wilson, Kathie L. Road, and Kenneth J. Hardy. Proceedings of the 11th Annual Chacmool Conference. Calgary, Alberta: Archaeological Association of the University of Calgary.

Petroglyphs and Pictographs

Delabarre, Edmund Burke. *Dighton Rock: A Study of the Written Rocks of New England*. New York: Walter Neal, 1928.

Grant, Campbell. *The Rock Art of the North American Indians*. Cambridge, England: Cambridge University Press, 1983.

———. *The Rock Paintings of the Chumash*. Berkeley and Los Angeles: University of California Press, 1965.

"Guardian Spirit of Nazca Lines." Auckland: *New Zealand Herald*, November 4, 1991.

Jauregui, Emily. "Protecting Ancient Art." *The El Paso Times*, November 15, 1992, pp. A1–2.

———. "Hueco Tanks Pictographs Victims of Gang Graffiti Wars, Ranger Says." *The El Paso Times*, November 15, 1992, p. A2.

Keyser, James D. *Indian Rock Art of the Columbia Plateau*. Seattle: University of Washington Press, 1992.

Lundy, Doris, ed. *CRARA '77: Papers from the Fourth Biennial Conference of the Canadian Rock Art Research Associates*. British Columbia Provincial Museum Heritage Record No. 8. Vancouver, B.C.: Ministry of the Provincial Secretary and Government Services, Province of British Columbia, 1979.

Patterson, Alex. *A Field Guide to Rock Art Symbols of the Greater Southwest*. Boulder, Colo.: Johnson Books, 1992.

Preston, Robert A., and Ann L. Preston. "Evidence for Calendric Function of 19 Prehistoric Petroglyph Sites in Arizona." Astronomy and Ceremony in the Prehistoric Southwest. John B. Carlson and W. James Judge, eds. Papers of the Maxwell Museum of Anthropology No. 2, 1987.

Spanne, Laurence W. "Rock Art Sites as Solar Observatories: Two Possible Examples from Vandenberg Air Force Base, Santa Barbara County, California." *In Earth and Sky*. Edited by Arlene Benson and Tom Hoskinson. Thousand Oaks, Calif. Slo'w Press, 1985.

Steward, Julian H. "Petroglyphs of the United States." *Annual Report of the Smithsonian Institution, 1936*. Washington: Government Printing Office, 1937.

Whitley, David S. "Shamanism and Rock Art in Far Western North America." *Cambridge Archaeological Journal*, 1992, vol. 2, pp. 89–113.

Haunted Places

Allen, Robert Joseph. *The Story of Superstitious Mountain and the Lost Dutchman Gold Mine*. New York: Pocket Books, 1971.

Alexander, John. *Ghosts: Washington's Most Famous Ghost Stories*. Arlington, Va.: Washington Book Trading Co., 1988.

Anderson, Jean. *The Haunting of America*. Boston: Houghton Mifflin, 1973.

Canning, John, ed. *50 Great Ghost Stories*. New York: Bonanza Books, 1988. First published 1971.

Decatur House. Washington, D.C.: National Trust for Historic Preservation, 1967.

Gallagher, Trish. *Ghosts & Haunted Houses of Maryland*. Centreville, Md.: Tidewater Publishers, 1988.

Jarvis, Sharon, ed. and comp. *Dark Zones*. New York: Warner Books, 1992.

————. *Dead Zones*. New York: Warner Books, 1992.

McNeil, W. K., comp. and ed. *Ghost Stories from the American South*. New York: Dell, 1985.

Munn, Debra D. *Ghosts on the Range: Eerie True Tales of Wyoming*. Boulder, Colo.: Pruett Publishing Co., 1989.

Myers, Arthur. *Ghosts of the Rich and Famous*. Chicago: Contemporary Books, 1988.

————. *The Ghostly Register: Haunted Dwellings—Active Spirits, A Journey to America's Strangest Landmarks*. Chicago: Contemporary Books, 1986.

Riccio, Dolores, and Joan Bingham. *Haunted Houses USA*. New York: Pocket Books, 1989.

————. *More Haunted Houses USA*. New York: Pocket Books, 1991.

Scott, Beth, and Michael Norman. *Haunted Heartland*. New York: Warner Books, 1985.

Taylor, L. B., Jr. *The Ghosts of Williamsburg*. Williamsburg, Va.: L. B. Taylor, Jr., 1983.

————. *The Ghosts of Fredericksburg . . . and Nearby Environs*. Williamsburg, Va.: L. B. Taylor, Jr., 1991.

Winer, Richard, and Nancy Osborn. *Haunted Houses*. New York: Bantam Books, 1979.

Ghost Lights

"America's First Crop Circle." Marfa, Tex.: *Desert Candle*, May–June 1992.

Bentley, Chris. "Odd Cattle Deaths Intrigue Webster County Residents." Springfield, Mo.: *News-Leader*, April 8, 1992.

Brueske, Judith M. "Those Mysterious Marfa Lights." *Big Bend Area Travel Guide 1992*, p. 10.

Chorvinsky, Mark. "1989 Ten Strangest List." *Strange*, October 1989.

Devereux, Paul. *Earth Lights Revelation: UFOs and Mystery Lightform Phenomena—the Earth's Secret Energy Force*. London: Blandford Press, 1989.

Etter, Jim. "Legends Illuminate Eerie Spook Lights." Oklahoma City: *Sunday Oklahoman*, October 28, 1990.

Hadley, Diana. "The Mysterious Marfa Lights." *Star Date*, June 1987, pp. 4–5.

Hannah, Mike. "Mystery Light Show." Boone, N.C.: *Watauga Democrat*, August 31, 1988.

Henderson, Jeff W. "How We Wonder What You Are." *Towns West*, October 1982, pp. 31–32.

Hughes, Clyde. "Film Crew Looks for Bragg Road Lights." Beaumont, Tex.: *Enterprise*, March 23, 1989.

Miles, Elton. *Tales of the Big Bend*. College Station, Tex.: Texas A&M University Press, 1976.

Munn, Debra D. *Ghosts on the Range: Eerie True Tales of Wyoming*. Boulder: Pruett Publishing, 1989.

"Powerful Tremors Baffle Dutch Scientists." Little Rock: *Arkansas Democrat-Gazette*, August 21, 1992.

Strauss, Neil. "Hydrogen Jukebox." *LA Weekly*, May 22–28, 1992.

Phantom and Mystery Ships

Botkin, B. A., ed. *A Treasury of New England Folklore*. Rev. ed. New York: American Legacy Press, 1989.

Colombo, John Robert. *Mysterious Canada*. Toronto: Doubleday Canada Ltd., 1988.

Gaddis, Vincent. *Invisible Horizons*. New York: Ace Books, 1965.

Seibold, David J., and Charles J. Adams III. *Ghost Stories of the Delaware Coast*. Reading, Pa.: Exeter House Books, 1990.

Whedbee, Charles Harry. *Legends of the Outer Banks and Tar Heel Tidewater*. Winston-Salem, N.C.: John F. Blair, 1966.

Water Monsters

Benedict, W. Ritchie. "The Unknown Lake Monsters of Alberta." *Strange*, No. 5, n.d., pp. 47–49.

Farnsworth, Clyde. "Nessie's Canadian Cousin: Scientists Are Believers." *New York Times*, December 2, 1992, p. A4.

Gordon, David G. "What Is That?" *Oceans*, August 1987, pp. 44–49.

Graham, J. McEwan. *Sea Serpents, Sailors and Sceptics*. London: Routledge & Kegan Paul, 1978.

Heuvelmans, Bernard. *In the Wake of the Sea-Serpents*. New York: Hill and Wang, 1968.

Meurger, Michel, with Claude Gagnon. *Lake Monster Traditions: A Cross-Cultural Analysis*. London: Fortean Times, 1988.

"The Day They Caught Chessie." *Strange*, No. 3, n.d., pp. 30–31.

Mysterious Creatures

"The Abominable Werewolves of the Southwest." *Strange*, No. 7, n.d., pp. 40–41.

Baumann, Elwood D. *Monsters of North America*. New York & London: Franklin Watts, 1978.

Bord, Janet & Colin. *Alien Animals*. Harrisburg, Pa.: Stackpole Books, 1981.

Chorvinsky, Mark. "New Bigfoot Photo Investigation." *Strange*, No. 13, n.d., pp. 10+.

Chorvinsky, Mark, and Mark Opsasnick. "A Field Guide to the Monsters and Mystery Animals of Maryland." *Strange*, No. 5, n.d., pp. 41–46.

Coleman, Loren. *Curious Encounters*. London & Boston: Faber & Faber, 1989.

Keel, John A. *Strange Creatures from Time and Space*. Greenwich, Conn.: Fawcett, 1970.

————. *The Mothman Prophecies*. New York: E. P. Dutton, 1975.

Mackal, Roy P. *Searching for Hidden Animals.* Garden City, N.Y.: Doubleday, 1980.

Opsasnick, Mark, and Mark Chorvinsky. "Lizard Man." *Strange,* No. 5, n.d. pp. 32–33.

Bigfoot

Backman, Peter J. "Morrisette Outlines Sightings Here." Aberdeen, Wash.: *Daily World,* June 26, 1992.

Bangert, Dave. "Believers Search for Bigfoot." Lafayette, Ind.: *Journal and Courier,* March 19, 1990.

Bartholomew, Paul. "Bigfoot Sighting Reported by Startled Teen in Hampton." Whitehall, N.Y.: *Times,* September 7, 1989.

Bentley, Chris. "Bigfoot, the Latest Explanation for Cattle Scare." Springfield, Mo.: *News-Leader,* May 6, 1992.

Berry, Rick. *Bigfoot on the East Coast.* Stuarts Draft, Va.: Rick Berry, 1993.

"Bigfoot a Passion of Canadian Investigator." Gastonia, N.C.: *Gaston Gazette,* June 28, 1991.

"Bigfoot Reportedly Making Tracks Through Oscoda County Boonies." Saginaw: *News,* October 25, 1990.

———. "Bigfoot Trackers Get Big Hand." Waitsburg, Wash.: *Times,* February 6, 1992.

Bord, Janet and Colin. *Alien Animals.* London: Granada Books, 1985.

Bowden, Bill. "Neighbors Say Bigfoot on Prowl." Little Rock: *Arkansas Democrat,* August 30, 1990.

Bozman, Nedra. "Bigfoot Is Real." Elyria, Ohio: *Chronicle-Telegram,* January 12, 1989.

Brandon, Craig. "Bigfoot!" Albany, N.Y.: *Times Union,* February 16, 1992.

Chorvinsky, Mark. "The Monster Is a Man: Hairy People, Wild People, and the Bigfoot Legend." *Strange,* No. 5, n.d., pp. 24–29.

Cockle, Dick. "Finding New Tracks of Bigfoot Gives Hunter Fresh Hope." Portland: *Oregonian,* February 11, 1991.

Coleman, Loren. *Tom Slick and the Search for the Yeti.* London & Boston: Faber & Faber, 1989.

Cox, Billy. "Bardin Bigfoot." Melbourne, Fla.: *Florida Today,* September 8, 1989.

Drier, Mary. "Bigfoot Returns, Area Men Maintain." Bay City, Mich.: *Times,* March 24, 1992.

Fletcher, Shelby R. "Is a Bigfoot Roaming the Hills?" Somerset, Pa.: *American,* June 29, 1992.

Floyd, E. Randall. "Bigfoot Makes Enormous Impression." Birmingham: *News,* June 6, 1992.

Foster, David. "Big Foot Tracker." Jackson, Mich.: *Citizen Patriot,* March 9, 1989.

Foster, Randy E. "Bigfoot in Magalia? Professor Wants Solid Evidence." Chico, Calif.: *Enterprise-Record,* September 20, 1991.

"Giant Beast Seen." Vancouver, B.C.: *Province,* June 25, 1989.

Gordon, David George. *International Society of Cryptozoology Field Guide to the Sasquatch.* Seattle: Sasquatch Books, 1992.

Hayes, Merry. "Researcher Says He's Convinced Sasquatch Exists." Spokane: *Spokesman-Review,* April 2, 1992.

Hitching, Francis. *The Mysterious World: An Atlas of the Unexplained.* New York: Holt, Rinehart & Winston, 1978.

Horne, Elizabeth. "Bigfoot Tracked in Area." Monesson, Pa.: *Valley Independent,* January 24, 1989.

Hutchinson, Julie. "Tiny Colorado Town Believes in Bigfoot." Boulder: *Sunday Camera,* February 26, 1989.

Jackson, Becky. "Strange Beast Tales Abounded Here." Bedford, Ky.: *Banner,* February 2, 1989.

Jackson, Kathy. "Sasquatch Watch." *The Dallas Morning News,* February 27, 1992.

Johnston, Steve. "Let Your Bigfoot Do the Walking . . ." *The Seattle Times,* July 3, 1991.

Joyner, Jim. "Does Bigfoot Roam Tri-County Area?" Burtonsville, Md.: *Tri-County Free Press,* October 20, 1988.

Kelly, Tom. "Reports of Bigfoot Vanish in Sands of Time." Washington, D.C.: *Times,* October 18, 1988.

Kimball, Richard W. "Paulden Man Says Bigfoot Creatures Roam in Arizona." Chino Valley, Ariz.: *Review,* December 1990.

Martin, Claire. "Is Bigfoot on Pike's Peak?" *The Denver Post,* June 3, 1989.

Milbank, Dana. "A Bigfoot Tracker Is Hot on the Trail in the Buckeye State." *Wall Street Journal,* February 25, 1992.

Monk, John. "Lizard Man is Quiet . . . Really Quiet." Charlotte: *Observer,* July 23, 1989.

Morello, Carol. "Unbelievable: Strange Sights Are Common Along Chestnut Ridge." Philadelphia: *Inquirer,* February 12, 1989.

———. "Mythic Legend of 'The Thing' Noted in National Books." Bedford, Ky.: *Banner,* January 26, 1989.

Neufeld, Matt. "Boo! That Thing Could Be Bigfoot." Washington, D.C.: *Times,* October 31, 1989.

Olson, Scott. "Bigfoot: Seven Report Sightings in The Dalles." The Dalles, Ore.: *Weekly Reminder,* August 17, 1989.

Orchard, Vance. "Caught Bigfoot on Movie Film, Man Says." Waitsburg, Wash.: *Times,* April 16, 1992.

Paris, Stuart Wavell. "Expedition Goes Hunting Russia's Elusive Ape Man." London: *The Sunday Times,* March 29, 1992.

Pynn, Larry. "Sasquatch Sage Suggests Man-Beast May Make Last Stand in B.C." Vancouver, B.C.: *Sun*, June 4, 1992.

Sands, Shannon. "They're on the Trail of Something Big." *The Los Angeles Times*, July 2, 1991.

Sanderson, Ivan T. *Abominable Snowmen-Legend Come to Life*. Philadelphia & New York: Chilton Book Co., 1961.

Schofield, Matthew. "Bigfoot, Big Bear or Big Fake?" *The Kansas City Star*, August 19, 1990.

Seubert, Greg. "Family Says Bigfoot Lives." Marshfield, Wisc.: *News-Herald*, August 1, 1991.

————. "Sightings of Strange Creatures Abound in Florida." Melbourne, Fla.: *Florida Today*, September 8, 1989.

Shoemaker, Michael T. "Searching for the Historical Bigfoot." *Strange*, No. 5, n.d., pp. 18–24.

Sisson, Bob. "Yacolt Family Tells Tale of Bigfoot." Vancouver, Wash.: *The Columbian*, June 7, 1989.

Soergel, Matthew. "Twenty Years on the Trail of Elusive Bigfoot." Denver: *Rocky Mountain News*, December 18, 1989.

Swogger, Judi. "Mystery Left Imprint on Man's Beliefs." Sharon, Pa.: *Herald*, April 5, 1992.

————. *The Evidence for Bigfoot and Other Man-Beasts*. Wellingborough, Northamptonshire, England: The Aquarian Press, 1984.

Torpy, Bill. "Strange Creatures Prowling Douglas Woods." *The Atlanta Journal-Constitution*, February 1, 1992.

————. "Touchet Valley Ramblings." Waitsburg, Wash.: *Times*, October 29, August 12 and April 23, 1992.

Tuten, Jan. "Lizard Man Tale Is Real Sob Story." Columbia S.C.: *State*, January 2, 1989.

Wiley, Walt. "Bigfoot Remains Real to Ex-Big Sur Woman." Monterey, Calif.: *Herald*, May 25, 1989.

Wood, Mark. "Monster '89: Creature Sightings Increase." Spartanburg, S.C.: *Herald-Journal*, August 1, 1989.

Yount, Sheila. "Boggy Creek 'Monster' Still Stalks Fouke Folks." Little Rock: *Arkansas Democrat*, May 22, 1989.

Index

Page numbers followed by *"m"* indicate map.
Page numbers followed by *"t"* indicate table.
Italic page numbers indicate illustrations